“...(i) imagined they probably smelled amazing, too”

— **LINDA ZHENGOVÁ,** 10 × 10 interview, *page 147*

Sex and Design: A Perspective On Artistic Publications

Lars Harmsen

"Every generation has to make its own discoveries, even if they are old discoveries," remarked Milton Glaser. This idea has stayed with me since I first immersed myself in the world of design. While Glaser was speaking about design in general, I find his insight particularly relevant to this subject. Few themes are as universal yet as deeply shaped by their era as the representation of sexuality. Sex is an analog experience, rooted in the physical, the emotional, and the personal. While the digital realm has carved out a space for pornography, the analog world remains an essential site for intimacy and cultural discourse. At the same time, many traditional print formats—atlases, phone books, and even magazines—have lost prominence in the digital age. Yet, rather than diminishing the relevance of print media, this shift only intensifies its allure. Sex is dead. Long live porn? Or rather: Long live print!

BRAVO: A GATEWAY TO GERMAN YOUTH CULTURE

Born and raised in Geneva, I moved to Germany at twelve and attended an international school. Initially, my exposure to German culture was limited—until I stumbled upon the *Bravo* magazine during a school trip. Some of the girls in my class had smuggled in a copy, and we found ourselves in fits of laughter over the magazine's photostories—those overly staged narrative love tales—and, of course, the iconic Dr. Sommer column. Despite its playful tone, *Bravo* addressed sexuality openly, using language accessible to teenagers. Its design—garish, loud, and chaotic—was not to my taste, but it perfectly suited the content. I once heard a rumor that the entire magazine was designed in Photoshop. Whether true or not, BRAVO left a lasting cultural imprint.

TEMPO AND THE FACE: A LEAP INTO SUBCULTURE

My first visit to London in 1986 introduced me to *The Face*. Designed by Neville Brody, the magazine was revolutionary: experimental typography, bold layouts, and a distinct aesthetic that was unlike anything I had seen before. It was at that moment that I realized I wanted to become a graphic designer. That same year, Germany saw the launch of *Tempo*, a lifestyle magazine that immediately attracted attention with provocative covers—one boldly headlined "Generation Sex." While *Bravo* played an educational role, *Tempo* and *The Face* were different: they engaged with aesthetics and subculture, presenting sexuality as a cultural statement. These magazines did not merely inform; they seduced, provoked, and redefined the intersection of design and content.

PLAYBOY: AESTHETIC EROTICISM OR VANITY?

Although *Playboy* was always present on newsstands, I cannot recall exactly when I first held a copy. As a photo assistant at the Burda Studio in Offenburg in the late 1980s, I once met a photographer who proudly claimed responsibility for lighting that particular area—the pubic region. Given *Playboy's* strong emphasis on aesthetic refinement, I found his boasting more vulgar than impressive. Founded by Hugh Hefner (1926-2017), *Playboy* peaked in 1975 with 5.6 million copies in U.S. circulation, in the early 1970s, it expanded into Europe. As of 2024, Playboy Germany still cirulates 105,000 copies. With online nudity reducing its appeal, Playboy adopted a non-explicit, artistic approach in 2016 but reversed the decision a year later. In December 2019, Florian Boitin and Myriam Karsch acquired Playboy Deutschland through a management buyout, preserving it under Kouneli Media GmbH. *(We conducted an interview with Florian, which can be found in the 10 × 10 section, starting on page 145).*

TWEN: A HISTORIC SHIFT

During my design studies in the early 1990s, I discovered *Twen,* the groundbreaking 1960s magazine designed by Willy Fleckhaus. It brought a fresh, minimalist aesthetic to post-war Germany while tackling then-revolutionary topics like premarital sex and homosexuality. Its collaboration with photographer Will McBride stood out, capturing intimate moments with unprecedented honesty. Twen fused visual innovation with cultural relevance, proving that design could challenge conventions and spark dialogue.

ROBERT BROWNJOHN: SEX AND TYPOGRAPHY

Remember the mesmerizing title sequence of *From Russia with Love?* The iconic typographic projections onto naked bodies were the work of Robert Brownjohn, a visionary designer who masterfully merged sensuality with graphic design. He also authored *Sex and Typography* (Laurence King, 2005), a book regrettably absent from this volume as it's not part of the AAP collection. Despite its title, the book focuses less on sex itself and more on the inherent sexiness of Brownjohn's design—his ability to infuse typography with movement, elegance, and cinematic allure.

SLANTED: TYPE PORN

In 2005, we published the first issue of *Slanted Magazine.* Inspired by trailblazing magazines like *Ray Gun* and *Emigre,* we sought to carve out our own space in the world of typography. The early issues were devoted entirely to type—we called it *Das Gefühl Typographie* ("The Feeling of Typography"). Some even labeled it "Type Porn," and perhaps they weren't far off. *Slanted* became our creative playground, a space to experiment, disrupt, and reinvent with every issue. Now, 20 years and 45 editions later, we find ourselves looking back at an archive of printed matter, reflecting on the role of publications in exploring gender and sexuality.

THE AAP ARCHIVE. THE ENDURING POWER OF ARTISTIC PUBLICATIONS

Despite the dominance of digital media and social networks, printed matter—particularly artist publications—remains a vital medium for creative expression. Rejecting digital oversaturation becomes an artistic statement, especially in artist books and zines, where content and process are inseparable. Here, creation holds as much significance as the final work. As digital culture expands, the physicality of printed design gains importance, reminding us that tangible objects can convey meaning, intimacy, and resistance in ways the digital world can only aspire to replicate.

As Glaser noted, every generation must create something unique to its time. The works in the AAP archive stand as living proof of this pursuit. Now, it's your turn—dive in and explore.

4 cover/typography.

Typographic covers in zines and artist publications can be analyzed through two primary lenses: formal design and conceptual intention. From a formal perspective, a defining characteristic is their minimalist approach. Many zines within the AAP archive adopt a restrained aesthetic, often employing default system fonts and minimal design choices devoid of ornamentation or well thought typeface decisions. This reductionist style emphasizes clarity and immediacy, directing focus to the publication's core message.

Despite this formal simplicity, these typographic covers frequently conceal content of significant visual intensity, as demonstrated in publications like VARIOUS SMALL DICKS. The choice to avoid imagery on covers, even when addressing photography, reflects deeper conceptual considerations.

Conceptually, this design strategy aligns with principles of conceptual art, which prioritize the idea over aesthetic representation. Typographic titles can act as provocations, challenging conventional modes of viewing and interpreting photography. They engage readers by stimulating mental imagery and encouraging them to consider photography beyond its function as a visual medium. The absence of visual elements on the cover prompts a critical examination of the medium's conceptual framework.

In some cases, the typographic design elevates the book to an art object, where the formal qualities of the cover—its typography, layout, and materiality—take precedence over its content. This approach can for example be seen in works like LIEBE IST DA, where the design becomes integral to the artistic statement.

Minimalism in typographic design often hinges on a stark, reductionist approach. This strategy not only ensures clarity but also transforms the cover into a gateway for engaging with the publication's deeper themes. Examples include the eighth volume of **001 → BOYS! BOYS! BOYS! THE MAGAZINE – VOLUME 8, Ghislain Pascal (ed.), The Little Black Gallery, 2024, 160 pp., 20 × 27 cm** **(↦ see № 160)**, which spotlights queer and gay fine art photography with contributions from ten photographers across the globe, presenting works that span various photographic styles, including portraiture, studio imagery, fashion, and documentary photography. The magazine's carefully crafted visual presentation, enhances the impact of the imagery while maintaining a cohesive design. The written content complements the visuals with

001 002 003 004 005

additional insights. Published by The Little Black Gallery, known for its dedication to promoting queer art through exhibitions and auctions in cities like London, Amsterdam, and Cologne, this edition reflects the diversity and richness of global queer artistic expression. By blending compelling visual storytelling with thoughtful commentary, **BOYS! BOYS! BOYS!** offers a comprehensive and nuanced look at contemporary male-focused photography.[1, 2, 3] Building on this theme of minimalism, **002 → I WANT A PRESIDENT, Zoe Leonard & Gato Negro Ediciones, 2017, 32 pp., 8.5 × 10.5 cm, riso print (↦ see № 218)** demonstrates a different implementation of simplicity, emphasizing text as the core visual element. The poem *I Want a President* was written by Zoe Leonard in 1992 and was inspired by the presidential candidacy of Eileen Myles, a poet and activist who ran as an "openly female" candidate in the U.S. presidential election. Myles ran as an independent against George H. W. Bush, Bill Clinton, and Ross Perot, and their identity as a lesbian woman created a stark contrast to the male, wealthy opponents. Myles came from a community directly affected by poverty and AIDS. The poem opens with the line "I want a dyke for president" and consists of a series of "I want ..." statements in which Leonard describes the kinds of people she wishes to see as president. Originally, the poem was meant to be published in an LGBT magazine, but the publication ceased production. Instead, it was photocopied and distributed. Vice later described it as "a kind of pre-Internet meme"—something shared, copied, and reinterpreted before most people had access to the Internet.[4, 5] Continuing in this vein, **003 → TEXTE ZUR REPRODUKTIVEN FREIHEIT 1981–2024, Hannah Stöwe, 56 pp., 14 × 20 cm** takes a more understated approach to typographic design, reinforcing its academic tone. This booklet is a collection of perspectives on reproductive rights from 1981 to 2024, highlighting the relations between gender, race, class, and bodily autonomy. The booklet functions as part of an installation that provides a space for the long and diverse history of feminist fights for reproductive rights. Expanding the exploration of minimalism, **004 → LIEBESLEXIKON, Fons Hickmann, Martin Conrads & Franziska Morlok, Verlag Hermann Schmidt Mainz, 2016, 84 pp., 10.7 × 15 cm (↦ see № 203)** softens the starkness of minimalism through color and tactile design elements. 33 young creatives gathered in a secluded manor house deep in the forests of Brandenburg to explore the essence of love. In this quiet, atmospheric setting, they drew, talked, danced, drank, and smoked—putting onto paper everything they had always wanted to express about love but had never dared to draw before. This unique collaboration resulted in **LIEBESLEXIKON**, a collection of 141 terms that are both illustrated and defined. From the French kiss to the cigarette after, from wedding vows to jealousy, and from cybersex to a change of position, the book captures the multifaceted nature of love with bold creativity. The design by Marie Scheffzük and cover design by Marc Damm, combined with the Softy Frutta cover, enhances the tactile and visual experience of the book, adding another layer to its exploration of love.[6, 7] From love to identity, **005 → QUEER IDENTITIES: EIN A–Z AUS QUEEREN BEGRIFFEN**

DID
YOU
READ
NAKE[D]
?

trans*_homo
differenzen,
allianzen,
widersprüche.
differences,
alliances,
contradictions.

LIEBE
IST
DA
FEICHTER

Legacy Russell
Glitch Feminismus
Merve Verlag

006 007 008 009

015 016 017 018

Endre Tót

DIRTY RAINS

Edition Sellem

VARIOUS SMALL DICKS

TOY

J.M

I * 1 * I

010 011 012 013 014

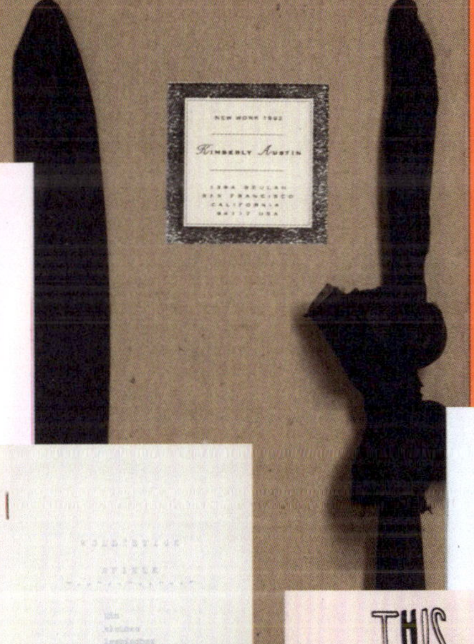

Love letters from Grindr

THIS IS NOT ABOUT SEX!

TO SEE

TO SEE

DER zungenkuss

MARTIN DISLER

KUSS/STADTKUNST

019 020 021 022 023 024

UND PERSÖNLICHEN GESCHICHTEN, Katharina Heigl, 2015, 132 pp., 13 × 19 cm presents a starkly minimalist aesthetic while incorporating a visual symbol to enhance its conceptual depth. Katharina Heigl's bachelor thesis in Communication Design at the Münchberg Campus of Hof University invites readers to explore the diverse stories of the LGBTQIA+ community. Before taking readers on a journey through queer terminology and personal experiences, the book offers an intimate glimpse into the lives and identities within the queer community. **006 → READ NAKED, Erik Kessels Skinnerboox, 2019, 148 pp., 16 × 24 cm (↦ see № 186)** takes a more playful turn, using bold color and oversized typography to command attention. It explores the entertaining idea of reading while completely naked. Collected and edited by Erik Kessels and designed by Erik Kessels and Geraldine MacDonald, the book presents black and white images printed on pink paper in a hardcover with hotfoil print. The collection of "found" photographs sparks curiosity: Who are these men and women? Why were these photos taken, and what are they reading? The images evoke a sense of a bygone era, when people would spend carefree days in bed, unashamed of their bodies and unbothered by the concept of wasted time. The book invites readers to embrace this idea, encouraging submissions of their own "reading nude" photographs to *readnaked.org,* and to experience the simple liberation found between the pages. The bold playfulness of **READ NAKED** gives way to the typographic clarity and subtle contrasts of **007 → TRANS*_HOMO, Jannik Franzen & Justin Time (eds.), NoNo Verlag, 2012, 288 pp., 14.8 × 21 cm.** Published on the occasion of the exhibition *Trans_Homo—Of Lesbian Trans* Gays and Other Normalities** at the Schwules Museum Berlin, the focus is placed on the "gap" or underscore (_) between these categories, inviting critical reflection on inclusion and exclusion within these spaces. **TRANS_HOMO** discusses lived realities across language, law, and medicine, highlighting the complexities of identity and experience within these fields. The artistic works and supplementary texts contribute a trans* perspective, offering reflections on both the scientific and social dimensions of gender, sexuality, and identity. The anthology also looks back at the history of gay and lesbian spaces and examines the question of whether, and how, trans* identities should be situated within these spaces.[8, 9, 10] Moving from **TRANS_HOMO'S** precise design, **008 → LIEBE IST DA, Fabian Feichter, icon Verlag Hubert Kretschmer, 2024, 21 × 29.7 cm** surprises with its tactile cover—a bold and unconventional design choice. The sturdy cardboard cover with an applied cast of Feichter's navel makes each copy a one-of-a-kind piece. Designed by Carina Müller, this book offers a comprehensive look into Fabian Feichter's works from the past years, presents stories, personal texts, and Feichter's artistic world, which he describes with the words: "Liebe ist da." Feichter emphasizes the importance of moments of feeling, creating experiences filled with a wide range of emotions and giving great significance to small moments.[11] From this tactile innovation we shift to the cutting-edge typography of **009 → LEGACY RUSSELL: GLITCH FEMINISMUS, Merve Verlag, 2021, 168 pp., 17 × 12.1 cm.** Legacy Russel rethinks cyberfeminism from an intersectional perspective, offering a deeply personal investigation of Blackness, queerness, and technology. The glitch, defined as a technical malfunction, a break in the interface, and discomfort with the machine, becomes a starting point to transform singular identities into collective networks. Russel examines how ethnicity, class, gender, and sexuality affect identity formation and sees the glitch as an opportunity to escape categories and liberate the body. The book intertwines reflections on contemporary artistic practices, personal narratives, and critical theory.[12, 13, 14, 15] Continuing with explorations of conceptual and visual intensity, **010 → ENDRE TÓT – DIRTY RAINS – FROM RAINPROOF IDEAS, Edition Sellem, 1979, 20 pp., 14.4 × 21 cm** bridges textural and typographic elements. This catalog was issued on the occasion of Endre Tót's exhibition *Dirty Rains,* held at Galerie S:t Petri in Lund, Sweden in 1979. The publication features a series of appropriated nude graphic adult images overlaid with Tót's signature typewriter slashes and texts. Endre Tót (1937 in Sümeg, Hungary) is one of the most significant artists of the Hungarian Neo-Avantgarde. He holds a singular position within both the Fluxus movement and Conceptual Art. His extensive body of work spans various media, including works on paper, photography, video, and painting, integrating visual, performative, and conceptual elements.[16, 17] Shifting from conceptual art to provocative critique, **011 → SO-VIELE.DE HEFT 21 VARIOUS SMALL DICKS, Hubert Kretschmer, icon Verlag Hubert Kretschmer, 2013, 16pp., 10.5 × 14.5 cm (↦ see № 183)** juxtaposes refined typography with bold thematic contrasts. The publication references the publication *Various Small Books* by Ed Ruscha. **VARIOUS SMALL DICKS** combines cropped images from Internet pornographic sites with images of Michelangelo. Women mock the small penis, and sometimes it only appears that way. The gesture made with thumb and index finger, often used to indicate something very small, is referenced by various speakers.[18] To be explicit or not to be explicit? That's what Jurgen Maelfeyt questions in his new book **012 → TOY Jurgen Maelfeyt, Art Paper Editions, 2024, 48 pp., 23 × 30 cm (↦ see № 172).** Inspired by his personal collection of vintage erotica, the Belgium-based photographer's latest page-turner features a series of reproduced photographs taken from '70s and '80s porn magazines. "There's actually no toys in this book, they're just alluded to throughout," Maelfeyt says. "In fact, I wanted to hide a lot more in **TOY**." From images of bodies strewn across sun loungers to close-ups of hands clasping glasses of red wine and stiletto-clad feet tucked under legs on sofas, **TOY** examines how images in erotic magazines aren't always about explicit, hardcore sex. They also showcase intimacy in all of its glorious, sexy manifestations.[19] Adding a layer of inclusivity and linguistic exploration, **013 → GENDER + ZEICHEN – VORSCHLÄGE AUS DER TYPOGRAFIE, Viktoria Hager, 2020, 14.8 × 21 cm** challenges existing norms in writing and type design. In her bachelor thesis, Hager explores the typography of gender symbols, questions their use, and proposes three new designs based on typographic and gender theories. Hager emphasizes that language, as a tool for thought, constantly evolves within society. Typography, as a tool of language, must evolve with it. Hager's work bridges the gap between type design and the need for linguistic inclusion of all genders.[20] Concluding this exploration of minimalist design,

014 → RESHAPING THE SKY, Simon Emond & Michel Lemelin, 2020, 96 pp., 30 × 40 cm (↦ see № 179), presents an understated but dense typographic approach. This publication is a photo-literary project that explores the realities of queer communities living far from large urban centers through grainy, blurred, and almost abstract images. Edited by Sophie Gagnon-Bergeron and designed by Criterium, the book features texts in French, Atikamekw, and Nehlueun, blending language, photography, and narrative into a singular work of art. The book draws a parallel to the 16th-century discovery of heliocentrism, which challenged the belief that earth was the center of the universe. In much the same way, **RESHAPING THE SKY** calls for a transformation in how human identities, genders, and desires are understood. The book resists easy classification, combining documentary and artistic invention.[21, 22]

In contrast to minimalist design, some publications employ sophisticated typography and deliberate compositional strategies to enhance both conceptual and visual impact. One of them is **015 → LUST OPFER, Volker Derlath, Buchendorfer Verlag, 2002, 78 pp., 30.5 × 24.5 cm** (↦ see № 175). Volker Derlath juxtaposes his *Oktoberfest* photo series with the erotic stories of Fabienne Pakleppa, responding to the frequent redundancy between images and texts that he finds tiresome. Both works share the perspective that desire does not necessarily lead to a climax but can just as easily descend into the abyss. This exploration of desire, a timeless theme in literary history, is reflected in the choice of the title.[23, 24] **016 → B.L.A.D. HEROES II NO.11, Fett Burger, Sex Tags & Blank Blank, 2013, 52 pp., 9.5 × 13.5 cm** (↦ see № 201 & 204) takes a more compact and playful approach, embracing simplicity while maintaining a dynamic visual rhythm. The pocket-sized zine series explores visual and conceptual practices. **HEROES II** features new and previously unreleased drawings from the deep vaults of the Sex Tags drawing archive and presents "lost and found heroes" from across the universe, most of whom remain unknown to this day.[25] Moving from playful zine aesthetics to visual subtlety, **017 → FOTOGRAFÍA ERÓTICA ANÓNIMA DE OPORTO, Doza Enrique, TD Papeles, 2018, 40 pp., 21 × 29.7 cm** employs gradients and muted tones to create a more evocative and introspective design. The zine, created by Doza Enrique, who is known for his striking black-and-white zines and posters, is a compilation of images extracted from newspaper sex ads and dating contacts from the city of Porto, Portugal.[26] In contrast to this subdued elegance, **018 → SHIT TITS FUCK CUNT, Klára Zápotocká, Deset Deka Dekadence & Deset Deka Design, 2019, 296 pp., 12 × 21 cm,** adopts a brash and unapologetic design to demand attention. A thematically organized English-Czech handbook for those who want to communicate with some extra "oomph" and love the linguistic scraps and debris. Featuring guidelines on how to call your junk and all the stuff you can do with it, a brief historical exposé about the terminological development of various bodily orifices, and ample visual aids. Printed in batches of 100 copies, This deep dive into the linguistic junkyard, authored by Klára Doudlová Vozábová, offers a thematically arranged and illustrated exploration of unjustly neglected linguistic marginalia. Graphic design and book concept by Klára Zápotocká. Returning to softer tones and layered meaning, **019 → LOVE LETTERS FROM GRINDR, Maurits De Baets, 2022, 24 pp., 18 × 29 cm, riso print** employs a more nuanced interplay of typography and color. With concept and design by Maurits De Baets and body pink images by Andre Vautour, it offers a glimpse into Grindr's duality. Love or lust? The design uses pink riso ink to capture the lustful aspect while a red layer symbolizes love. The scrollbars pair explicit imagery collected over years with romantic love poems from *Gay Love Letters Through the Centuries* by Rictor Norton. **020 → WOLLÜSTIGE SPIELE: EIN KLEINES LESBISCHES GETÄNDEL VOLL SINNLICHER LUST, Bernhard Cella, One Night Production & Edition Ostblick, 2003, 40 pp., 12 × 18,1 cm** opts for a raw and typewriter-like aesthetic to emphasize authenticity and intimacy. This short erotic story by Bernhard Cella is illustrated with small tipped-in black-and-white photographs. The cover design features typewriter-style lettering reminiscent of classic mechanical typewriters, complemented by decorative elements such as a series of dots and dashes.[27, 28, 29] **021 → KIMBERLY AUSTIN 1992 Kimberly Austin, 1992, 16 pp., 15.5 × 29 cm** combines material craftsmanship with elegant typography. This artist publication, designed by Paul Weingartner, consists of a folder made from two cardboard pieces tied together with a black ribbon. Inside, 16 loose pages—also held together by a black fabric ribbon—feature text and images printed on transparent paper. Kimberly Austin photographs men and women inspired by Renaissance paintings and sculptures to reconstruct nudity and sexuality free from gender stereotypes.[30] **022 → THIS IS NOT ABOUT SEX Heidi Fuchs, Katharsis und Tumult, ca. 2015, 16 pp., 10 x 10,5 cm** employs hand-drawn typography to underscore its casual and humorous tone. This small publication features jokes about queer topics, presented with a playful yet provocative tone. The cover is hand-drawn with irregular black letters, set against delicate light pink paper. Its design captures a blend of statement and provocation, inviting readers to engage with its bold and humorous content. Stepping into tactile and artisanal territory, **023 → HEFT 27, TO SEE AND NOT TO SEE, Hubert Kretschmer, icon Verlag Hubert Kretschmer, 2014, 16 pp., 10.5 × 14.5 cm** returns to conceptual minimalism, using restrained typography to convey its themes of perception and visibility. This zine is a homage to Lawrence Weiner's work *To See and Be Seen* (1969) and adopts Weiner's minimalist aesthetic with reduced text, few graphic elements, and the use of contrasting colors like red and blue. Inside, the zine features images from Gerhard Theewen's pin-up collection, where colorful geometric shapes are used. **024 → DER ZUNGENKUSS, Martin Disler, Edition Galerie Seevorstadt, 1980, 48 pp., 8,3 × 12,4 cm** closes this sequence with a raw and expressive typographic style. This small-format artist book, stapled and printed entirely in red, combines handwritten poetry with drawings. It serves as a facsimile of holograph and drawn variations on the themes of kiss and tongue. The publication, allegedly an unauthorized print with a limited run of 50 copies, features texts and illustrations by Disler and Silvia Steiner.[31, 32, 33, 34, 35]

cover/illus tration.

Illustration abstracts reality, stripping it down to essential or stylized elements. This opens up a duality: content can become less explicit or, alternatively, far more overt and provocative. This flexibility draws us into an imaginative engagement with the work, as illustrations are not bound by the exacting realism of photography. By shifting away from depictions of real people or specific situations, abstraction makes topics like sex and eroticism more approachable and less taboo.

The AAP Archive houses a vast array of publications featuring illustrated covers, encompassing styles from minimalist linework to expressionistic or cartoon-inspired imagery. Zines, intrinsically tied to subcultural movements, embrace a raw DIY aesthetic. Illustration is a natural fit for this ethos: it feels personal and unfiltered, created with simple tools, and often delivers a bold, immediate impact.

025 → **PARADISE OF EYES, Keiichi Tanaami, United Dead Artists, 2017, 40 pp., 30 × 40 cm** expresses this with its obsessional patterns. **PARADISE OF EYES** showcases the kaleidoscopic visions of Keiichi Tanaami, intertwining his signature intensivee patterns—eyes, eroticized flesh, a military aircraft, and pop culture icons—into a grotesque yet colorful tapestry.[36, 37] 026 → **LA TRANCHÉE RACINE #08, United Dead Artists, 2016, 12 pp., 47.5 × 66 cm,** United Dead Artists' graphic periodical, features a bold layout and marks a special milestone as the first in full color, showcasing a diverse selection of images, strips, photographs, and texts.[38] Returning to black and white, 027 → **LA TRANCHÉE RACINE #14, United Dead Artists, 2019, 12 pp., 47.5 × 66 cm** continues the bold creativity with its raw aesthetic. The 14th issue of the tabloid showcases United Dead Artists' distinctive raw aesthetic and—like in every issue—represents the works of more than 40 authors, reflecting the publishing house's bold and unfiltered creative vision.[39] Following this vibrant showcase, 028 → **LE MUSCLE CARABINE – TROISIÈME GORGÉE, United Dead Artists, 2011, 40 pp., 30 × 40 cm** layers visuals with avant-garde audio elements. Known for its eclectic and provocative content, this issue includes a vinyl record with a vocal performance by William S. Burroughs on the A-Side and an interview titled *Burroughs Called the Law* on the B-Side.[40] 029 → **EROTIC REVIEW ISSUE 2, Lucy Roeber & Saskia Vogel, (eds.), 2024, 168 pp., 17 × 24 cm, litho print** (↦ see № 190, 193 & 218) transitions into a softer, colorful aesthetic. **EROTIC REVIEW** was relaunched in spring 2024 as a biannual art and literary journal exploring desire through essays, poetry, stories, and visual art. Originally founded in London in 1995 as a photocopied newsletter about erotic art, **EROTIC REVIEW** evolved into a humorous bimonthly magazine with a wide readership. The publication redefines the cultural discussion of desire, focusing on shared human experiences rather than specific genders or practices. Publishing essays,

PARADISE OF EYES
眼の楽園
KEIICHI
TANAAMI
PARADISE OF EYES
WHRAAM!!

EROTICISM
ON THE LINE
BAC

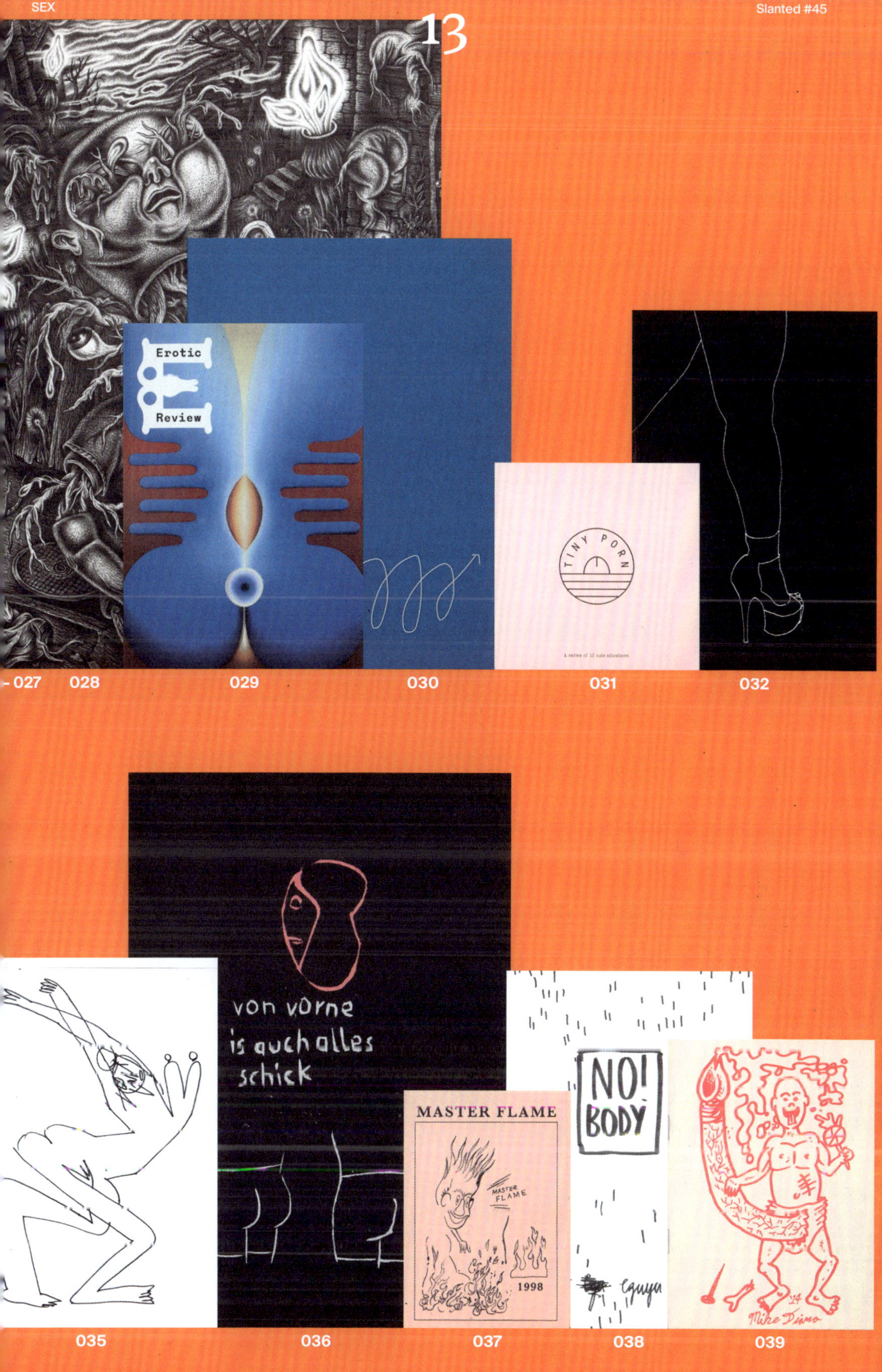

– 027 028 029 030 031 032

035 036 037 038 039

poetry, and stories for a contemporary audience, it is a collaboration between editors Lucy Roeber and Saskia Vogel, designers Studio Frith, and a guest art curator.[41, 42] In contrast to the preceding detailed and vibrantly illustrated covers, line art emphasizes simplicity and elegance through clean, often monochromatic drawings. This can be seen, for exmple, in 030 → **ALLES GLÜCK DIESER ERDE, Romina Abate, 2023, 264 pp., 19.6 × 25.5 cm,** where intricate compositions and minimalist drawings examine relationships and movement across diverse contexts. The artist book delves into the loose relationships between different entities and their multiplicity of meanings in diverse contexts, exploring what it means to relate to other bodies, including the practice of riding horses and the sexual behavior of sea animals.[45] The exploration deepens in 031 → **TINY PORN, Funs Kurstjens, 000Z Club, 2018, 10 pp., 12 × 12 cm,** which explores the perception of forms through abstract representations of sexual situations. The imagery retains its sensual essence by distilling it into simplified shapes, offering a unique and playful take on eroticism. The concept of **TINY PORN** draws inspiration from a passage in Ovid's Metamorphoses, which reflects on the transformative nature of existence: "Nothing keeps its own form, and Nature, the renewer of things, refreshes one shape from another."[43, 44] 032 → **100FOR10 – STUDIES OF ECSTASY – EDITION NO. 016, Myla Dalbesio, Melville Brand Design, 2017, 106 pp., 14.8 × 21 cm** continues with clear linework to connect femininity with the natural world in a striking yet delicate visual narrative. Published as part of the *100for10* series by Melville Brand Design, **STUDIES OF ECSTASY** explores the relationship between femininity and the natural world. Myla DalBesio, an American artist, examines identity and the intersection of sexuality and mysticism in her work. The cover features a minimalist design: the lower part of a leg in a platform high heel, sketched with white lines on a black background. Inside, the book continues with clear and simple line drawings on white paper.[46] Transitioning into bold contrasts, 033 → **MOAN ZINE ISSUE 5, Moan, 2024, 98 pp., 13 × 18 cm, riso print by Dizzy Ink** (↦ see № 164 & 196) uses a vibrant combination of risograph printing and dynamic design to juxtapose its linework with rich textures and provocative themes. **MOAN ZINE ISSUE 5** is a bold exploration of sexual liberation, featuring 98 pages filled with honest and unique submissions from around the globe. Each piece delves into fantasies, fetishes, and desires, showcasing new voices and experiences while sparking essential conversations about safe sex, consent, and positivity. As a radical and political statement, **MOAN** continues to challenge societal norms that shame and limit sexual freedom.[47] Rounding off this series, 034 → **100FOR10 EROTICISM ON THE LINE EDITION NO. 086, Fabio Bacchini, Melville Brand Design, 2017, 106 pp., 14.8 × 21 cm** distills desire into its most essential forms, using single-line drawings to create an intimate and elegant exploration of sensuality. **EROTICISM ON THE LINE** features a captivating collection of erotic illustrations in a minimalist single-line style. Each piece is a delicate exploration of sensuality, with the reduced forms evoking passion and intimacy. This book uniquely combines art and desire, drawing viewers into a world of subtle yet powerful eroticism.[48]

Rough, sketch-like drawings that exude raw energy—doodles that feel unpolished and spontaneous, aligning with the irreverent, anti-establishment attitude of many zines. 035 → **100FOR10 – HI – EDITION NO. 104, Guillaume Kashima, Melville Brand Design, 2019, 106 pp., 14.8 × 21 cm** reflects Kashima's versatile approach to visual aesthetics, rooted in boldness and humor. The idea for this publication stemmed from life-drawing sessions in Berlin bars, where Kashima began experimenting with markers. He accumulated drawings weekly, eventually creating a fanzine to pause, review, and select the best.[49, 50, 51] Shifting from this minimalism, 036 → **VON VORNE IS AUCH ALLES SCHICK, Franziska Schaum, Re:Surgo!, 2011, 20 pp., 12 × 23 cm, screen print** (↦ see № 212) incorporates vibrant silkscreen techniques to create a sense of layered depth and playful irreverence. This publication captures a mosaic of observations and experiences, blending personal anecdotes with a broader social commentary. 037 → **MASTER FLAME, Patrick Rieve, Bone Response Publications, 2015, 8 pp., 7.7 × 10 cm** (↦ see № 206) takes a more intimate approach to illustration with its compact and highly personal format. The original seven ink drawings of **MASTER FLAME** were created "in one night's pour" in 1998. The pages feature juicy and occasionally violent ink drawings, exploring themes of Eros and Thanatos. Due to its sexual content and eight-page format, the work bears a resemblance to a Tijuana Bible. This reprint from 2015 consists of a folded A4 sheet, printed on one side on pink paper.[52, 53] 038 → **100FOR10 – NO!BODY! – EDITION NO. 012, Esther Czaya, Melville Brand Design, 2015, 106 pp., 14.8 × 21 cm** shifts to bold, graphic pencil drawings that reject refinement in favor of raw expression. This monography features 100 pages of bold and uninhibited pencil drawings by Hamburg-based illustrator and graphic designer Esther Czaya. Her work reflects a balance between introspective creativity and thoughtful social engagement.[54, 55] Building on this boldness, 039 → **NEEDLER, Mike Diana, Re:Surgo!, 2014, 16 pp., 10.8 × 14.8 cm, screen print** intensifies the energy with chaotic and provocative imagery. **NEEDLER** is a mini zine featuring perverse doodles by Mike Diana, an iconoclastic and provocative underground cartoonist. Known for his crass humor and controversial themes, Diana's work often explores sexuality, violence, and religion. He is the first person in the United States to receive a criminal conviction for artistic obscenity, stemming from his comic *Boiled Angel*.[56, 57, 58] Moving toward a more figurative yet abstract style, 040 → **SHVANTZ: AXIS, Baumann E. Walther (ed.), 1982, 21 × 29.7 cm, Xerox print** employs expressive red line-work to blur the boundaries between illustration and emotion. "**SHVANTZ** is not an art magazine—it is the artwork itself." **SHVANTZ** is a series of handmade and limited-edition publications, primarily produced using Xerox with added collage and other manual techniques. Each issue was limited to 50 copies. The cover illustration features an intimate scene depicted with expressive linework, blending abstraction and figurative elements. Many of the lines resemble doodles or notations, introducing a sense of unease and movement to the composition. Dominated by the color red, the provocative title "Shvantz" is derived from the Yiddish word meaning "penis."[59] 041 → **GRIECHISCHE MYTHEN 03 – ZEUS, Frank Klaus-Peter & Hans von Rimscha, icon Verlag Hubert Kretschmer, 2017, 48 pp., 14.8 × 21 cm** builds on the abstraction of **SHVANTZ: AXIS** by incorporating vibrant, painterly strokes that evoke mythological themes. The booklet features a short and bold text in Cypriot dialect and colorful, unconventional drawings and paintings, designed by Johannes Bissinger with philological input from Theodora Hadjimichael.[60, 61] From bold strokes to refined linework, 042 → **DAS TYPISCHE DING, Tabea Blumenschein, Dagmar Dimitroff, Wolfgang Müller & Nikolaus Utermöhlen, Die Tödliche Doris, 1981, 7 × 11 cm** simplifies its composition to convey a conceptual narrative. **DAS TYPISCHE DING** was released as an audiotape in 1981, reissued in 1986, and later as a vinyl edition in 2004. The cover design was created by Nikolaus Utermöhlen and Wolfgang Müller (© Archiv der Tödlichen Doris). 043 → **TABEA UND DORIS DÜRFEN DOCH WOHL NOCH APACHE TANZEN, Tabea Blumenschein, Dagmar Dimitroff, Wolfgang Müller & Nikolaus Utermöhlen, Die Tödliche Doris, 1981, 7 × 11 cm** concludes this series with playful and provocative cartoon-like illustrations. **TABEA UND DORIS DÜRFEN DOCH WOHL NOCH APACHE TANZEN** was first released as an audiotape in 1981, with a reissue in 1986 and a vinyl edition the same year. The cover design, by Wolfgang Müller and Nikolaus Utermöhlen, features a drawing by Tabea Blumenschein. The music, composed by Die Tödliche Doris, includes contributions from Tabea Blumenschein, Nikolaus Utermöhlen, and Wolfgang Müller (© Archiv der Tödlichen Doris).

Illustrations that employ satire, irony, or exaggerated forms approach sensitive themes like sex and eroticism with humor and accessibility. This section explores how zines use playful and bold graphic language to reframe provocative ideas into entertaining, thought-provoking narratives. 044 → **¡QUE SUERTE! 22 – CANIBAL, Olaf Ladousse (ed.), 2013, 124 pp., 15.6 × 21 cm, screen print** features black-and-white comics by various international artists. Contributions come from both professionals and amateurs, offering a diverse and eclectic collection. The cover is always a multicolored screen print, and each zine includes unique, handmade details added post-production.[62, 63] 045 → **DAS MAGAZIN HEFT 06/1982, Manfred Gebhardt (ed.), Berliner Verlag, 1982, 80 pp., 16.2 × 23 cm** shifts to a softer, illustrative aesthetic with refined linework. **DAS MAGAZIN HEFT**, a cultural and entertainment magazine founded in 1924, remains one of the few East German publications to continue after reunification. The magazine became known for its unique blend of provocative themes, including erotic photography, intelligent puzzles, and literary contributions. The cover for this issue features artwork by Werner Klemke.[64, 65, 66, 67] With a sharper edge, 046 → **MINI ZINE – SMOKING TAL-R'S STASH Frodo Mikkelsen, Re:Surgo!, 2017, 16 pp., 10.8 × 14.9 cm, screen print** introduces caricature and stylized exaggeration, contrasting the subtlety of its predecessor. This mini zine, printed by Johnathan Lawes, showcases Frodo Mikkelsen's unique approach to visual art. The cover features a stylized illustration of a nude female figure, blending sketch-like elements with printmaking techniques. The caricatured stylization, unusual details, and ironic exaggeration reflect Mikkelsen's distinct artistic voice.[68] The abstraction and vibrant color schemes of 047 → **HOLOGRAMA, Llucia Font & Grip Face (ed.), Rua Ediciones, 2014, 32 pp., 8 × 14.8 cm** further push the boundaries of visual expression, moving away from stark minimalism. **HOLOGRAMA** is a provocative zine featuring pornographic and sexual illustrations by various artists, with a focus on women, the female body, and their sexuality. This graphic book-zine delves into themes of shamanism and fetishism, interpreted through the lens of nine international illustrators.[69, 70] Building on abstraction, 048 → **SPRING #16 – SEX, Mairisch Verlag, 2019, 256 pp., 20 × 24 cm, neon print (↦ see № 209)** explores identity through collaborative and dynamic visual storytelling. The 16th issue, **SEX**, tackles the deeply private and culturally shaped topic of sex. Thirteen illustrators explore themes such as the evolutionary history of sexuality, personal experiences from puberty, everyday sexism, the absence of physicality, and female identity across generations. The issue is brought to life with the cover design by Nina Pagalies.[71] Shifting to an introspective tone, 049 → **SPRING #12 – PRIVÉE, Mairisch Verlag, 2015, 200 pp., 24 × 20 cm (↦ see № 208 & 210)** delves into the private sphere with a subdued color palette. Life is divided into two boxes: one labeled public and the other private. While the public box sometimes resembles a bargain bin in a department store—anyone can rummage through it as they please—the twelfth issue of **SPRING** focuses primarily on the private box: that side of us we only share with chosen people, a side filled with secrets. This intimate exploration is framed by the cover design of Line Hoven. In contrast, 050 → **MINI ZINE – FRANCIS BACON ON MUSHROOMS, Fuzz Ohriss, Re:Surgo!, 2019, 16 pp., 10.8 × 14.8 cm, screen print (↦ see № 207)** embraces bold symbolism and satirical humor through exaggerated visuals. This mini zine combines spirit and satire in a unique exploration of themes through a bold, graphic style. The cover features a stylized illustration with strong symbolic and humorous elements, blending spiritual and sexual motifs. The imagery employs exaggerated, ironic symbols that reflect the zine's playful yet thought-provoking tone.[72] With playful reinterpretation, 051 → **NOT SO NUDE – NUS VESTIDOS, Neo Nuvens, Serrote, 2016, 32 pp., 16 × 16 cm,** humorously reframes classical art through a contemporary lens. **NOT SO NUDE** is a tribute to Daniele da Volterra, nicknamed "the breeches maker," the infamous Mannerist Italian painter tasked with covering the genitals of Michelangelo's *The Last Judgment* in the Sistine Chapel with loincloths and fig leaves under the recommendations of the Council of Trent, which condemned nudity in religious painting. The author of this book humorously went beyond these historic prescriptions, using a ballpoint pen to draw underwear on thirteen reclining nudes from secular paintings. Odalisques, goddesses, nymphs, lovers, prostitutes, and wives—displayed on the walls of famous museums—were reimagined, dressed in bodysuits, nightgowns, bras, panties, and socks.[73] The exaggerated comic style of 052 → **SEXACIONAL DE COLEGIALAS Y ESTUDIANTES NO 24, Guillermo Dominguez Muñoz, Editorial Ejea, 1997, 80 pp., 12.5 × 14 cm** adopts a humorous, vibrant approach to provocative themes. The cover features a sexualized and humorous illustration in an exaggerated comic style. Below the title "Colegiala" ("Schoolgirl"), the text "¿Qué Nalgotras Clasca No Nos Vimos?" appears a playful pun referencing the female figure. Translated, it humorously asks, "What (other) butt classes did we miss?"[74, 75, 76] Turning reflective, 053 → **ALMANAC JOURNAL OF TRANSPOETICS ISSUE #2 SEXUALITIES, Almanac Press, 112 pp., 21 × 13 cm,** combines poetic expression with graphic experimentation. This second issue focuses on transsexuality, featuring a mix of text, photographs, and poetry. It examines transsexuality in its many forms and expressions—vague, exposing, perverted, asexual, relatable, messy, horny, and fantastical. Inspired by anonymous queer sex parties, darkrooms, and graphic design from porn films and magazines, the visual elements feature slick, inky colors reminiscent of dimmed lights, condensation, and reflections on steel and glass.[77] The bold monochrome visuals in 054 → **KINKIES NO. 1, ... LITERATURA QUE ENSUCIA, Karla Guerrero & Raul Lara (eds.), Kinkies, Mexico City, 2015, 42 pp., 14 × 21.5 cm, laser copies** offer a raw, unapologetic exploration of sexuality and artistic provocation. **KINKIES** is a publication dedicated to pornographic literature, paraphilias, and manic contradictions. This zine merges provocative literature with visually striking black-and-white illustrations, creating a unique exploration of sexuality and artistic expression.[78, 79] Simpler yet surreal, 055 → **MINI ZINE – HOCKNEY ON STELLA, Too Bob, Re:Surgo!, 2015, 16 pp., 10.9 × 14.7 cm, screen print** (↦ see № 205) incorporates minimalist lines and dotted shading to amplify its abstract narrative. This mini zine, published by Re:Surgo!, features a provocative and surreal cover with a humorous, minimalist illustration. Rendered in a single pink tone using screen printing, it emphasizes the raw and bold graphic aesthetic. With vibrant colors and fluid forms, 056 → **QUIEREME MONSTRUO, Math de Andrés Abad, Juliana Gómez Tolosa, Lauredal, 2020, 12 pp., 13.4 × 18.9 cm** celebrates individuality and inclusion through bold visuals. It is an illustrated zine reflecting dissident-affective experiences in the first person. Its pages boldly declare, "I am more than what you see ... I am more than what you think." With bright colors and diverse forms, it expresses a wide range of bodies, realities, and possibilities, offering a powerful celebration of individuality and inclusion.[80, 81] The vibrant, fluid forms and bold colors of **QUIEREME MONSTRUO** lead seamlessly into the playful yet structured aesthetic of **HOMEMADE SEXMACHINES**. While **QUIEREME MONSTRUO** celebrates individuality with expressive illustrations, 057 → **HOMEMADE SEXMACHINES, Antonia Rib, 2023, 6 pp., 10.5 × 14.8 cm, riso print by Studio Sowieso** uses clean, minimalistic Riso printing to spotlight the eccentric ingenuity of DIY creativity. This limited edition zine, with only 30 copies produced, explores the eccentric and unexpectedly wholesome subculture of American DIY sex machine builders. **HOMEMADE SEXMACHINES** captures a curious intersection of craft, creativity, and unconventional hobbies within a subculture that challenges traditional perspectives (based on Sex Machines: Photographs and Interviews by Timothy Archibald).[82] From these bright yellows and modernist forms we move to the raw, intricate black-and-white drawings of 058 → **100FOR10 – 101 MAGICAL MOVEMENTS EDITION – NO. 052, Monoperro, Melville Brand Design, 2017, 106 pp., 14.8 × 21 cm** (↦ see № 211). The shift in tone—from contemporary craft to spiritual symbolism—underscores a transition from lighthearted exploration to introspective depth, with the stark monochrome design creating a meditative and mystical atmosphere. **101 MAGICAL MOVEMENTS** is a symbolic embodiment of the spiritual movements of the "ultra-human" in friction with the matter of the world. The book consists of drawings that delve into dark, disturbing, sexual, religious, ancestral, and magical themes.[83, 84] Collaborative and experimental, 059 → **OUTSIDE THE BOX – HAAR, Silke Jaspers & Ludmilla Bartscht (eds.), ILLU Freiburg e.V., 2024, 24 pp., 15 × 21 cm, riso print** (↦ see № 188) reflects queer-feminist creativity with handcrafted neon Risoprints. We all have hair, whether we like it or not. Depending on the context, a hairstyle can be anything from fashion to a reason for an execution. This zine reflects the perspectives and thoughts of eleven participants, exploring themes such as body perception, societal roles, clichés, political power, and capitalism. The concept, developed by Silke Jaspers and Ludmilla Bartscht, was realized during a two-day workshop at Literaturhaus Freiburg as part of the queer-feminist series Outside the Box.[85] Finally, 060 → **[KON] NO. 1 SEX, Julia Hell & Pia Lobodzinski (eds.), [kon] Paper e.V., 2015, 24 pp., 31.3 × 46.5 cm** blends cultural critique with striking visual experimentation to close this thematic journey. Founded and published by the Fachschaft AVL at LMU Munich, **[KON]** takes a single word and reinterprets it through the lens of professors, poets, and artists from various disciplines. The first issue focuses on the theme of sex. The texts delve into fundamental questions about the relationship between nature and culture, erotics and literature, human and animal desire, and the writeability of the discourse on sex.[86]

Painterly illustrations bring the depth and texture of traditional art into zines, using vivid colors and intricate shading to explore themes of eroticism and intimacy. Their lush, emotive style captivates, making provocative themes both visually and emotionally compelling. Starting with 061 → **NIGHT TRAIN, Stu Mead, published by Re:Surgo!, 2015, 28 pp., 23.4 × 31 cm, screen print**, which features reproductions of acrylic paintings by Stu Mead, an American artist based in Berlin. Mead's work occupies a space on the fringe of the art world, blending elements of underground culture with a formal artistic background. **NIGHT TRAIN** showcases Mead's provocative and direct approach, with vibrant, fluorescent screen-printed reproductions that highlight his distinct aesthetic.[87] 062 → **EXTRA EXTRA MAGAZINE ISSUE NO 23 URBAN EROTIC ENCOUNTERS, Samira Benlaloua (ed.), Extra Extra, 2024, 210 pp., 17 × 24 cm** (↦ see № 200 & 220) shifts to a textured and emotive depiction, blending raw sensuality with a refined urban aesthetic. **EXTRA EXTRA MAGAZINE** is a multidisciplinary platform that delves into the intersections of eroticism and culture. With its biannual print magazine, online platform, temporary projects, and live events, **EXTRA EXTRA** celebrates the sensual and vibrant life of the city. Issue No. 23 immerses readers in a sensual journey of desire and artistry.[88] Moving on from surrealism, 063 → **REIGEN BLÄTTER FÜR GALANTE KUNST HEFT 1, Wilhelm Borngräber, 1925, 24 pp., 24 × 32 cm** celebrates the exuberance of 1920s risqué art through dancing couples and vibrant sketches. The magazine **REIGEN** draws its name from a term associated with art history and depictions of dancing couples, a prominent theme in the 1920s. True to its name, the magazine showcases risqué sketches, paintings, and artworks, accompanied by texts and poems that explore similarly provocative themes.[89, 90] In contrast, 064 → **DER JUNGGESELLE NR. 28, Max Schievelkamp (ed.), Verlag der Junggeselle, 1922, 22 pp., 24.5 × 32 cm** reflects the Art Deco elegance and societal attitudes of the Weimar Republic through refined, yet provocative illustrations. The men's magazine **DER JUNGGESELLE** was a weekly publication released in Berlin from 1919 to 1929. Likely the first German mass publication exclusively targeting male readers, it featured overtly sexual content alongside a focus on refined aesthetics. While visually elegant, the magazine's tone was distinctly misogynistic, portraying women as needing to conform to rigid male ideals.[91, 92] **065 → BODIES THAT SHED TEARS 3, Sayo Senoo, 20 pp., 20 × 13.3 cm** presents photocopied images transformed to evoke the emotional depth of paintings. This third installment in Sayo Senoo's series reflects her personal experiences working in the Japanese sex industry to fund her art studies. The demanding nature of these jobs often leads to mental and physical strain, with high pay preventing workers from quitting before their health deteriorates. The photographs, sourced from sex industry websites, undergo several transformative processes using inkjet printers. Printed on incompatible paper, the resulting images are fragile and ephemeral, symbolizing the hidden pain, fatigue, and damage behind the seductive poses and smiles of the individuals portrayed.[93, 94, 95] In **066 → X1 DON'T WAKE DADDY, Brendan Danielsson, Cross One, 2012, 36 pp., 14.7 × 20.8 cm (↦ see № 186)**, the first in the **X1** Editions series, **DON'T WAKE DADDY** features over 30 illustrations by Brendan Danielsson. The publication, designed by Heiko Kiendl-Müller, presents Danielsson's playful and surreal pencil drawings, which embody the quirky and subversive essence of Lowbrow art.[96] Finally, **067 → SOUS TA BARBE MON ÂME EST MORTE, Aurélie William-Levaux, United Dead Artists, 2011, 78 pp., 17 × 26 cm** offers a dreamlike fusion of embroidery and feminist themes. Aurélie William-Levaux's work combines colorful embroidery and poetic visuals, immersing the reader in a tenderly erotic, dreamlike world. Her creations intertwine powerful feminist themes with a sense of lightness and delicacy.[97]

040 041 042 043

044  045  046  047

051 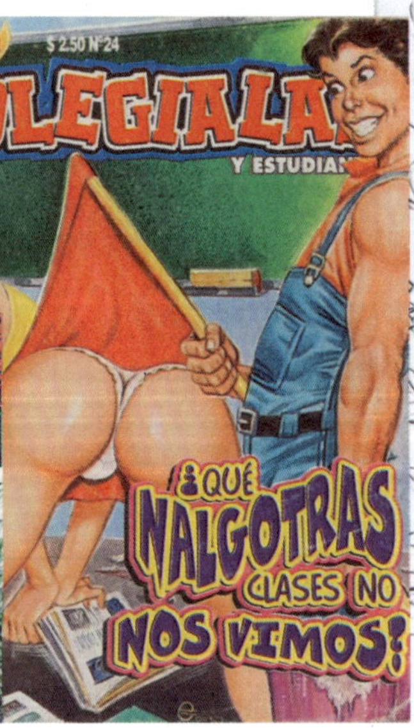 052  053 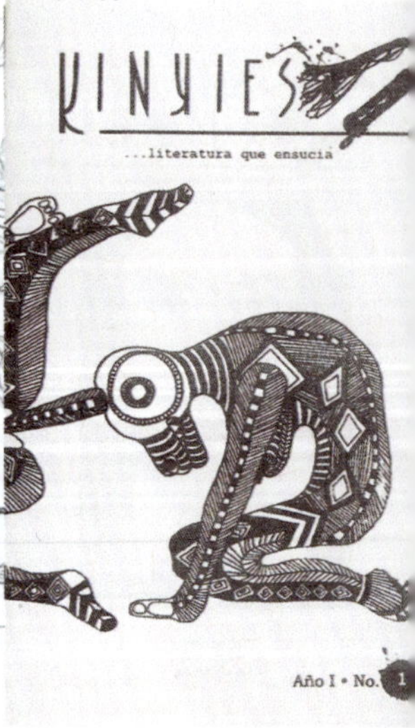 054

048

049

050

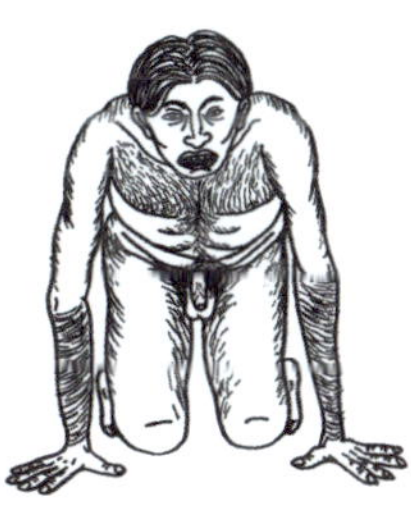

055

056

057

058

PREIS: 1 EURO

QUEER-FEMINISTISCHE PERSPEKTIVEN IM COMIC

Outside the Box

HAAR

AVL

kɔr

059 060 ↓ 061

NO. 1
S E X
FRÜHJAHR /
SOMMER
2015

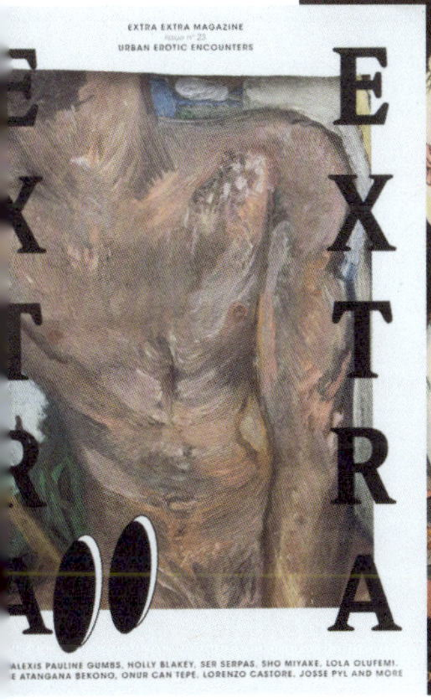

062

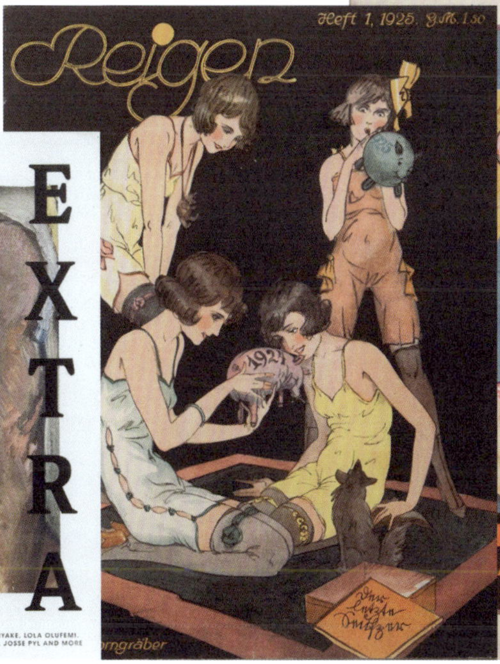

063

064

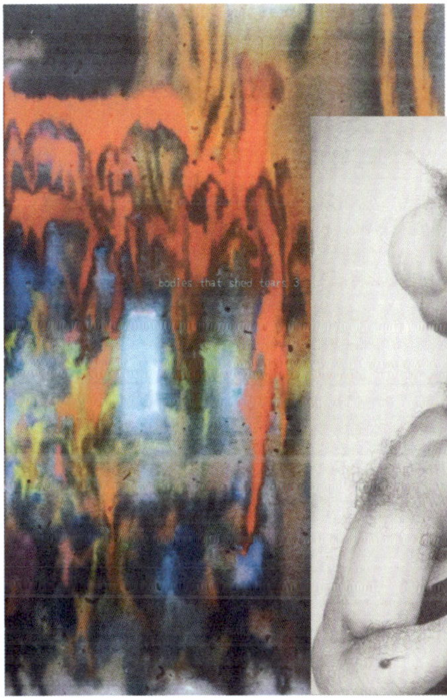

065

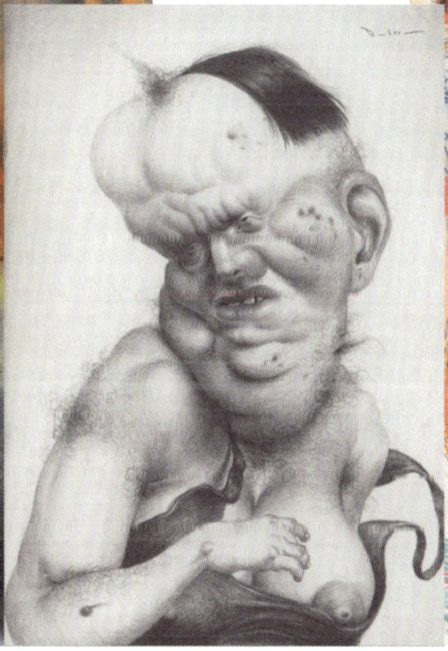

066

067

cover / photog raphy.

Unlike illustrations, photography on covers is often perceived as more commercial or "polished." Some titles in the archive do indeed exude a classic appeal, yet a notable sense of humor emerges. This humor can stem from inherently comical subjects or the way a specific crop highlights the situational comedy.

It's all about the crop! Nude photography, when framed just right, often transforms into graphic art.

068 → **VENUS INTERNATIONAL. EINE DOKUMENTATION DER FOTOKUNST, Horst Mössler (ed.), EHAPA-Verlag, 1970, 281 pp., 21.5 × 30 cm**, gives a sense of timeless elegance, where the warm lighting and intimate framing elevate the nude photograph on its cover into a refined work of art. This publication is a comprehensive documentation of photographic art, featuring both black-and-white and color photography. The refined sensuality of **VENUS INTERNATIONAL** transitions seamlessly into 069 → **ULALUME, Evren Tekinoktay, Lubok Verlag, 2015, 4 pp., 17 × 24.5 cm**, where Evren Tekinoktay's pastel-toned collages reinterpret elegance with a surreal and poetic edge. This artist book, printed in a limited run of 500 editions and designed by Jacob Birch, features 44 full-page color illustrations. Evren Tekinoktay's artistic practice centers around the exploration of media images of women. She describes her approach as "gender science fiction—where gender collapses or disintegrates."[98, 99] From the dreamy collages of **ULALUME**, the black-and-white photograph on the cover of 070 → **THE COMPLETE COLLECTION OF NUDISTS, Gerhard Theewen, Salon Verlag im Verlag Kretschmer & Großmann, 1982, 160 pp., 14.8 × 21 cm** (↦ see № 180 & 182) captures a playful yet timeless elegance, blending simplicity with natural beauty. Nudist photography can be divided into different categories, and Gerhard Theewen focuses on its humorous aspects. His work emphasizes the lighthearted and genuine comfort found in nudist camps, showcasing why nudism thrives: it is both amusing and provides people with a sense of well-being. To lose sight of this core perspective is to misunderstand the essence of nudist photography. Moving from **THE COMPLETE COLLECTION OF NUDISTS'S** candid charm, 071 → **DER SPRENGREITER NO. 2 – EMPIRIE UND ORNAMENTIK, Der Kern Verlag, 1984, 12 pp., 30 × 42 cm, linocut** combines linocut ornamentation with nostalgic photography, adding a layer of irony to its aesthetic. This photo issue of **EMPIRIE UND ORNAMENTIK** was printed in an edition of 300 copies on pink paper, combining black-and-white photographs with ornamental linocuts. 072 → **TEMPO 07, Markus Peichl (ed.), Jahreszeiten-Verlag, 1986, 21 × 29.7 cm** captures the bold and dynamic energy of late 20th-century culture, combining sleek design with provocative themes. **TEMPO** was a German monthly magazine that captured the zeitgeist of the late 1980s and early 1990s, blending themes of lifestyle, rebellion, consumerism, AIDS, pop culture, and high culture. It served as a vibrant cultural barometer, establishing itself as a cult favorite before succumbing to increasing competition from other zeitgeist magazines like *Wiener* and *Max*.[100, 101, 102] From the refined compositions and timeless aesthetics, the focus shifts to works that embrace humor and satire, blending playful irreverence with sharp social commentary. Describing itself as, "a literary magazine for queers and their friends," 073 → **THE BITTERSWEET REVIEW NO. 02 – I STARTED A JOKE, Fulmine Kole, Benoît Loiseau & Louis Shankar (eds.), The BitterSweet Review, 2023, 200 pp., 13 × 19 cm** is a

enus
ernational
Eine Doku- mentation der Fotokunst

ULALUME
EVREN TEKINOKTAY

Salon

068 069 070

071 072 073

BUTT

BUTT magazine 34
Spring 2024

Yes, please.

alien
planet
erde

FLASH
The Garden and The Cave

PINUPS

Nº16

074 075 076 077

081 082 083

bert Heinecken Food, Sex and TV
DINNER
SHRIMP
t, easy and fun Edition Fotoforum Ein Bermuda Dreieck für Fotografie

078

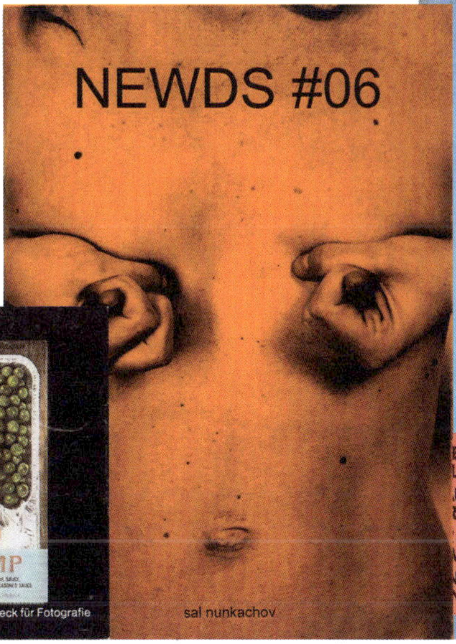

NEWDS #06
sal nunkachov

079

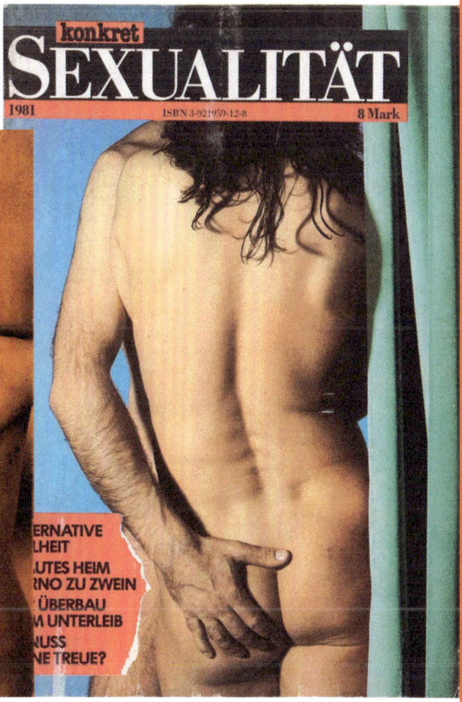

konkret
SEXUALITÄT
1981 ISBN 3-921959-12-8 8 Mark
ERNATIVE
LHEIT
UTES HEIM
RNO ZU ZWEIN
ÜBERBAU
M UNTERLEIB
NUSS
NE TREUE?

080

SPRENGEL MUSEUM HANNOVER
SEX&
CRIME
Von den Verhältnissen der Mensche

084

VILE
CHRISTMAS SPECIA

085

NOTHING
TASTES
QUITE
LIKE IT

086

publishing platform dedicated to the advancement of queer literature and visual culture. This second issue is themed **I STARTED A JOKE**, exploring the intersections of queer culture and humor. The cover image from the series *Amor Entre Cucas* (2019) is by Bárbara Sánchez-Kane in collaboration with Dorian Ulises Lopez, encapsulating the issue's playful yet thought-provoking exploration of queer narratives.[103, 104] The compact and understated composition of **THE BITTERSWEET REVIEW** transitions into the expansive, black-and-white visuals of **074 → 100FOR10 – ALIEN PLANET ERDE – EDITION NO. 087, Ramon Keimig, Melville Brand Design, 2018, 106 pp., 14.8 × 21 cm,** where intricate patterns and a cloaked figure create an enigmatic contrast. Ramon Keimig draws on influences from subculture, the psychedelic movements of the 1970s, and his personal history. His work combines traditional drawing techniques using ink and pencil with digital elements, referencing aesthetics of photocopy culture from the 1970s and 1980s, including tape culture, underground comics, and concert flyers.[105, 106, 107, 108] The bold yellow of **075 → FLASH – THE GARDEN AND THE CAVE, Tim Best, Pack Peel Pour, 2017, 24 pp., 13,4 × 21 cm** **(↦ see № 163)** creates an electrifying contrast, turning the spotlight onto a vivid and playful aesthetic. In **FLASH**, Tim Best captures what others want to show and what he wants to see, creating charged memories—emotional, socio-political, and sexual—beyond mere documentation. By including himself, the work reflects his identity, telling the viewer: "This is me. This is where I want to be." The design, by Katharina Nicole Stowe, and the writing, by Sesthasak Boonchai, enhance the narrative, adding layers to this exploration of self and perception.[109] The polished simplicity of **FLASH** transitions into the raw and candid photography of **076 → BUTT MAGAZINE 34, Andrew Pasquier, Jop van Bennekom, Gert Jonkers, & Nathaniel Feldmann (eds.), 2024, 104 pp., 17 × 24 cm** **(↦ see № 154 & 155).** The 34th issue of **BUTT MAGAZINE** continues its daring exploration of queer culture with a mix of candid interviews, bold photography, and provocative themes. Since its return in 2022, **BUTT** has become a vital platform amplifying diverse voices. This issue highlights themes like queer humor, intimate expressions, and contemporary dynamics. Founded in Amsterdam in 2001, **BUTT MAGAZINE** carved its niche with its iconic pink paper, pocket-sized format, and raw, unfiltered conversations about identity, art, and sexuality. It has long served as a unique space for the queer community to share their stories, blending raw honesty with a vibrant cultural lens. **077 → PINUPS, NO. 16 Christoph Schulz (ed.), 2012, 56 pp., 20.5 × 25.5 cm, Xerox print** **(↦ see № 156)** shifts focus to a rugged, natural setting, emphasizing the interplay between the human form and raw landscapes. Each **PINUPS** issue comprises images from a single photo shoot, usually of a single subject. Each magazine can be disassembled and the loose pages tiled to form a large image of the subject. The magazine has 20 issues to date (all photographed, edited, designed by Christopher Schulz).[110] The personalized intimacy of **PINUPS** evolves into the conceptual satire of **078 → FOOD, SEX AND TV, Robert Heinecken, Edition Fotoforum Kassel, 1983, 24 pp., 24 × 16,4 cm,** where everyday imagery critiques consumer culture with a humorous edge. Known for blending photography with pop culture, Heinecken's work explores the intersections of desire, consumption, and the pervasive influence of advertising and television. By projecting light through magazine pages to merge images from both sides, Heinecken exposed the constructed nature of desire and the cultural narratives embedded in advertising.[111, 112, 113, 114, 115] From this satirical critique of consumer culture, **079 → NEWDS #06, Sal Nunkachov, Paper View, 2017, 44 pp., 14 × 19 cm, laser print** shifts humor inward, using playful gestures and minimalist compositions to explore the body with a raw yet lighthearted lens. **NEWDS** explores the simplicity and raw beauty of monochromatic nudes, showcasing Nunkachov's dedication to the art of minimalist photography.[116] The subdued tones of **NEWDS** contrast with the provocative cover of **080 → KONKRET SEXUALITÄT, Hermann L. Gremliza (ed.), Konkret-Verlag, 1981, 98 pp., 20.2 × 29.7 cm** where bold typography and stark imagery provoke immediate attention. The special issue **KONKRET SEXUALITÄT** controversially argued that pedophilic desires are not inherently criminal and that those experiencing them should receive help to avoid committing crimes.[117, 118] The bold design of **KONKRET SEXUALITÄT** flows into the visceral and ritualistic imagery of **081 → HERMANN NITSCH: DAS ORGIEN MYSTERIEN THEATER. FOTOS FRÜHER AKTIONEN, Hannah Stegmayer (ed.), Kunstverein Rosenheim, 2004, 96 pp., 15.8 × 24.2 cm.** This catalog accompanies the exhibition *Hermann Nitsch: Das Orgien Mysterien Theater* at Kunstverein Rosenheim. It features photographs documenting various early actions by Hermann Nitsch, providing a visual insight into his groundbreaking and controversial performances.[119] These works under the theme of "Fetischistisch Subversiv" challenge conventional narratives through their raw, provocative, and often taboo-breaking aesthetics. Though unified in their exploration of fetishes and subversive themes, each publication approaches these ideas with distinct perspectives and methodologies. From Nitsch's immersive rituals, **082 → NEAPEL 1974 HERMANN NITSCH 45. AKTION, Allerheiligenpresse, 1980, 78 pp., 14.9 × 20.8 cm** narrows the lens to a single performance, delving deeper into the fetishistic interplay of bodily materials and subversive actions, highlighting both personal and political provocations. This publication contains numerous photographs documenting Hermann Nitsch's 45th ("neapolitan") action in 1974, along with texts by Nitsch and Peter Weiermaier.[120, 121] **083 → RUDOLF SCHWARZKOGLER KONZEPTUELLE PHOTOGRAPHIE – CONCEPTUAL PHOTOGRAPHY, Hannah Stegmayer (e.d), Kunstverein Rosenheim, 2002, 92 pp., 24x17 cm** marks a move from external spectacle to internalized, meticulously staged imagery. The book delves into Schwarzkogler's unique approach to art, highlighting his preference for mediated representation through photography, a cornerstone of his conceptual and performative oeuvre.[122, 123] In **084 → SEX & CRIME. VON DEN VERHÄLTNISSEN DER MENSCHEN, Dietmar Elger, Ulrich Krempel, Gabriele Sand & Thomas Weski (eds.), Sprengel Museum, 1996, 64 pp., 23.8 × 27.7 cm,** the theme of taboo continues but broadens its scope, juxtaposing individual transgressions with societal aggression. The catalog **SEX & CRIME. VON DEN VERHÄLTNISSEN DER MENSCHEN** is introduced with a passage from the Haarmann protocols, where early 20th-century serial killer Fritz Haarmann recounts his crimes. This serves as a poignant entry point for a broader exploration of the themes of sexuality and violence, which have long been used to reflect the state of human civilization. Through diverse media it examines contemporary artistic perspectives on the intersection of eros and violence, addressing internal struggles, societal aggression, and the human condition. By juxtaposing sexual obsession and violence, the catalog offers a critical lens on the cultural boundaries and contradictions shaping modern society.[124, 125] **085 → VILE: VOL. 3, NO. 1, CHRISTMAS SPECIAL Banana Productions, 1975, 66 pp., 21 × 28 cm** disrupts the solemnity of earlier publications, replacing critique and introspection with irreverence, humor, and chaotic visual experimentation. This issue of **VILE** magazine is an early Mail Art publication. Bursting with humor and absurdity in the spirit of Alfred Jarry, **VILE** stands as a parody of *FILE Magazine* and embodies the disruptive and playful energy of the mail art movement.[126, 127, 128, 129] **086 → 100FOR10 – NOTHING TASTES QUITE LIKE IT – EDITION NO. 070, Simon Lohmeyer, Melville Brand Design, 2018, 106 pp., 14.8 × 21 cm** **(↦ see № 148 & 213)** shifts the fetishistic gaze to stark monochromatic photography, blending raw eroticism with a reverence for natural human form. The minimalist aesthetic amplifies the underlying subversion of societal expectations about nudity and intimacy. The photographs, blending authenticity with an artistic vision, depict a lifestyle influenced by travel, fashion, and meaningful encounters. The book conveys Lohmeyer's belief in the natural human state, using the nude form to evoke intimacy and connection while exploring themes of freedom and authenticity.[130, 131] In **087 → MANN & FRAU – ÜBER DIE VIELFÄLTIGKEIT DER MÄNNLICHEN UND WEIBLICHEN GESCHLECHTSTEILE, Luca Feigs (ed.), Lieschen Montag Verlag, 2012, 74 pp., 14.8 × 21 cm** the fetishistic lens turns clinical yet provocative, using unfiltered images of genital diversity to deconstruct stereotypes and challenge societal discomfort with the natural body. Its bold straightforwardness adds to the subversive narrative. Feig focuses on the diversity of male and female genitalia. For this work, he used Facebook to invite people to submit photographs of their genital areas—explicitly aiming to avoid any erotic or pornographic context. The objective was to highlight natural diversity without judgment or media-influenced stereotypes.[132] The experimental intimacy of **088 → THE BERLIN CHAMELEON – ARCHIVES 01, The Berlin Chameleon, 2024, 56 pp., 14.8 × 21 cm** **(↦ see № 161)** continues this trajectory, embracing fetish culture directly. The Berlin Chameleon is a Berlin-based artist whose work in photography delves into themes of gender, love, sexuality, fetishes, identity, and the photographic medium itself. **THE BERLIN CHAMELEON – ARCHIVES 01** is a curated selection of 46 photographs created over six years, described as a "melodic pile" of contrasting tones—shiny and rough, soft and filthy, melancholic and ecstatic. As a sex-positive and kink-friendly artist, The Berlin Chameleon collaborates with open-minded individuals willing to document and share their authentic selves.[133] Finally, **089 → X FILES, Stephanie Falcione, 2023, 19.0 × 25.6 cm** **(↦ see № 176)** elevates the subversive narrative with a feminist critique of fetishization. The experimental body of work explores themes of femininity, intimacy, nudity, eroticism, beauty, and body image through self-portrait photography as a medium of expression. The visuals capture the beauty and sensuality of femininity, intertwining the author's personal interpretation of the sensory experience of her body and the sensitivity of her mind with a critique of societal perspectives over the last hundred years.

From the fetishistic and subversive intensity of **X FILES**, we move into a new realm of photography defined by spontaneity, everyday intimacy, and a raw, unfiltered look at the world. These shapshot-like covers capture fleeting moments and personal narratives, creating a bridge between documentation and artistry. This gives way to **090 → DAS SOFORTBILD POLAROID, Gerhard Johann Lischka, Der Löwe, 1977, 128 pp., 14,5 × 19 cm,** where the immediacy of the Polaroid format takes center stage. The immediacy of the Polaroid image became a core element of performative practices and a visual reflection of the ideologies behind these artists' work.[134, 135, 136] The exploration of overlooked niches continues with **091 → USEFUL PHOTOGRAPHY #013, Erik Kessels, Hans Aarsman, Julian Germain, & Frank Schallmaier (eds.), KesselsKramer, 2015, 240 pp., 21 × 29.7 cm** **(↦ see № 185)** humorously dissecting male anatomy through a "day in the life" of intimate imagery. The thirteenth installment of the **USEFUL PHOTOGRAPHY** series, titled *Enjoy a Day in the Life of Dick,* ventures into the surprising, humorous, and occasionally educational world of male anatomy photography. This issue focuses on an unconventional subject: the global obsession with photographing the male phallus. These intimate and inventive portraits, shot by men around the world, explore a wide variety of perspectives on male vanity, creativity, and humor. This edition bundles years of "flesh photography" into a cohesive volume, creating what the editors describe as a "monument to male vanity."

From this cheeky anthropological study, we enter the personal yet detached world of **092 → RICHARD KERN POLAROIDS, Art Paper Editions, 2023, 176 pp., 22 × 30 cm** **(↦ see № 162 & 170),** where Richard Kern has explored and illuminated the complex and often darker sides of human nature. With his dry approach, Kern emphasizes the absurdity of truth and objectivity in photography while challenging our reliance on taxonomies of sexual representation. Designed and edited by Jurgen Maelfeyt, **POLAROIDS** offers a striking compilation of Kern's work, reflecting his enduring fascination with human complexity and his unique artistic vision.[137] Kern's introspective lens opens the door to **093 → PICK – ERICA LOU, Pickpocket Gallery, 2014, 20 pp., 13.7 × 19 cm,** where Erica Lou's black-and-white photographs take an even more stripped-down approach. The only black-and-white zine-series contains only photographs, with no accompanying text, and are produced in a limited edition of 100 copies.[138] The minimalism of **PICK** evolves into the historical and political narrative of **094 → DIK FAGAZINE NO 11 – HOMOSEXUALITÉ COMMUNISTE?, Karol Radziszewski, Queer Archives Institute, 2017, 98 pp., 28.5 × 21 cm,** blending archival images with contemporary queer art. This shift expands the snapshot concept beyond the personal into a broader, cultural context, documenting queer experiences and identities with both immediacy and depth. Founded in 2005 by Karol Radziszewski and currently designed by Martin Falck, **DIK FAGAZINE** is a groundbreaking art magazine from Central and Eastern Europe that explores homosexuality and masculinity through a combination of archival research and contemporary art. This edition examines the complex relationship between communism and queer experiences, offering historical insights and artistic reflections.[139, 140] From **DIK'S** socially charged content, we pivot to the diaristic chaos of **095 → BRIAN SERGIO – DIOS MIO!, dienacht Publishing, 2021, 86 pp., 16 × 25 cm (↦ see № 177 & 178),** where Brian Sergio's transgressive snapshots piece together fragments of a turbulent personal life. As Sergio himself says, "There are personal stuff, pictures of Christian devotees practicing their penitence, behind the scenes pictures of porn shoots, and my mislabelled Kinbaku sessions. There is something in them, a pattern of some sort that suggests how I instinctively map my memory through pictures. Giving it a diaristic take of my transgressive personal life." Bound in soft cover with Japanese binding stitched in burgundy thread, the book features two real photos attached to the cover and includes five fold-out pages.[141] **096 → A TIME, TOO GOOD TO BE TRUE, Lina Marie Ritthammer, 2023, 28 pp., 16 × 14 cm** takes the snapshot category to its most intimate extreme. Ritthammer created this photobook as a personal project. On the 2nd of October 2022, the artist's ex-boyfriend suffered a near-fatal accident, which profoundly altered her world. After this life-changing event, she turned to photography as a means of coping with sorrow and loss. This photobook offers an intimate glimpse into their cherished time together, serving as a tender and emotional exploration of memory and love.

Moving on to more detail- and haptic-oriented covers, where visual perfection takes precedence, this section highlights works that emphasize beauty through precise composition, lighting, and harmony. Themed around tension, **097 → SOMESUCH STORIES 8 – THE TENSION ISSUE, Suze Olbrich (ed.), Somesuch, 2024, 256 pp., 17 × 23.5 cm (↦ see № 159)** explores sex, suspense, danger, fantasy, and transgression through 19 captivating contributions from writers and artists. This edition is designed by Thomas Coombes of Guest Editions for **SOMESUCH STORIES 8** and examines how tensions spark emotions, compel actions, and lead to outcomes ranging from the tragic to the comic, horrific, ominous, and explosive. **098 → CUNTS, Betty Tompkins, Innen, 2018, 24 pp., 19 × 13 cm** is marked by a shift from a conceptual and layered aesthetic to an intimate, body-centric design. Published on the occasion of the Printed Matter NY Art Book Fair at MoMA PS1 in September 2018, **CUNTS** is a monochrome collection printed on colored paper, featuring reproductions of Betty Tompkins's iconic cunt paintings.[142, 143, 144] The stark visuals of **CUNTS** pave the way for the glossy and vibrant design of **099 → STRAP ISSUE 1, Ben Saunders, 2023, 208 pp., 21 × 29.7 cm (↦ see № 214). STRAP** is a magazine brimming with trans masc erotic artwork, photography, writing, and interviews. It celebrates trans masc bodies and sexuality, offering a safe and empowering space away from the fetishization that many in the community face. Created by and for trans people, the magazine is a proud declaration of identity.[145, 146] Moving into **100 → ERIC CARSTENSEN. TESTSIEGER, Fotogalerie Alte Feuerwache, Das Wunderhorn, 2001, 108 pp., 17 × 12 cm,** the focus pivots to a deliberately chaotic yet controlled aesthetic. Eric Carstensen's **TESTSIEGER** is a small-format catalog book presenting an absurd collection of found images that challenge notions of individual morality and societal norms. The photographs range from mundane to provocative, including motifs from pornography, the media appearances of the Pope, and idealized visions of beauty and cars.[147] **101 → MULIERIS MAGAZINE ISSUE 4 – BELT OF VENUS Greta Futura Langianni (ed.), Mulieris, 2022, 224 pp., 16.8 × 23.7 cm (↦ see № 171, 173, 191, 192 & 221)** explores femininity and mythology with a polished and editorial style. This issue delves into sexuality, power, lust, love, and everything in between. It explores the transformation of the female figure and examines what femininity means today. Desire, sensuality, and sex remain strongly associated with femininity, along with the power—or absence of power—linked to them. This issue was edited by Greta Futura Langianni (Editor in Chief & Founder), with creative direction by Sara Lorusso (Creative Director & Co-Founder) and graphic design by Chiara Cognigni (Art Director & Graphic Designer). With **102 → MISMATCH, Auriane Loctaelli, 2024, 9 pp., 21 × 29.7 cm,** the narrative narrows to a more intimate, tactile level. The booklet consists of loose A3 sheets folded in the middle and held together with a red bra strap. It is enclosed in a letter-like cover and completed with an original bra clasp, enhancing its thematic connection to the subject matter. The uncoordinated, second-hand underwear pieces shift the focus from the body itself to the objects that interact with it. **103 → A TIME TO PLANT AND A TIME TO DESTROY, Maryna Shtanko, 2023, 40 pp., 20.6 × 27.2 cm** turns the visual narrative more poetic and abstract. In this book, Maryna Shtanko uses flowers as symbols to explore gender roles in the context of war. Women have traditionally been seen as preservers of life, while men are often associated with destruction. Through her photography, Shtanko highlights this dichotomy, illustrating how these archetypes persist even as societal roles shift. The imagery reflects both historical stereotypes and modern complexities, where women now serve in the military and men increasingly engage in childcare. **104 → THE OPÉRA VOLUME XI. THE PHOENIX ISSUE, Matthias Straub (ed.), Kerber Verlag, 2022, 224 pp., 24 × 31 cm (↦ see № 153, 167 & 168)** shifts the focus to a refined and contemporary aesthetic, celebrating the elegance and artistry of the human form. **THE PHOENIX ISSUE** emphasizes a predominantly female perspective on the human body, authentically conveyed through the works and statements of numerous female photographic artists.[148] **105 → LIEBE, SEX & AIDS II, Mike Meiré & NEO NOTO, 2001, 61 pp., 19,6 × 32,8 cm** pivots to an artistic commentary on societal issues, maintaining a strong focus on visual storytelling and aesthetic impact. The publication **LIEBE, SEX & AIDS II** is an artistic exploration of love, sexuality, and the societal impact of HIV / AIDS. Central to the publication is a striking crocheted object—a condom—designed by avant-garde fashion designer Bernhard Willhelm. This object became the centerpiece of a photo series by Kira Bunse, capturing bold and authentic interactions. While **LIEBE, SEX & AIDS II** utilizes bold objects and contextual imagery, **106 → ZINE, Lina-Marie Ritthammer, 2024, 28 pp., 21 × 15 cm (↦ see № 166)** distills its aesthetic into subtle, emotionally charged portraits. The collection highlights individuals with whom the artist shares a special connection. Ritthammer's work often centers on capturing women in intimate and personal ways, emphasizing the emotional depth and unique essence of her subjects.

087 088 089 090 091

092 093 094 095

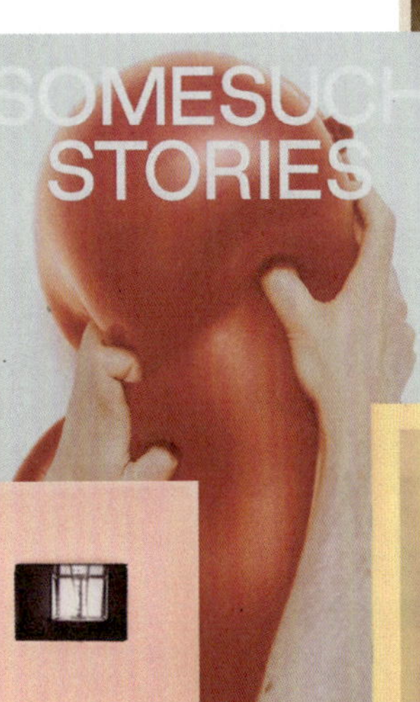

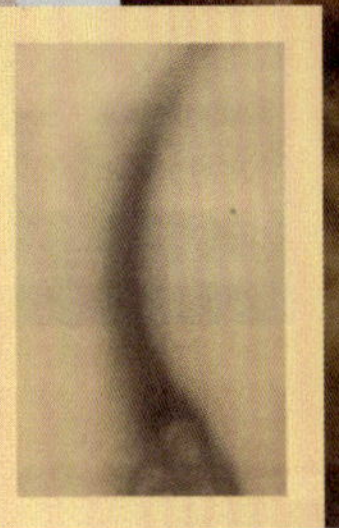

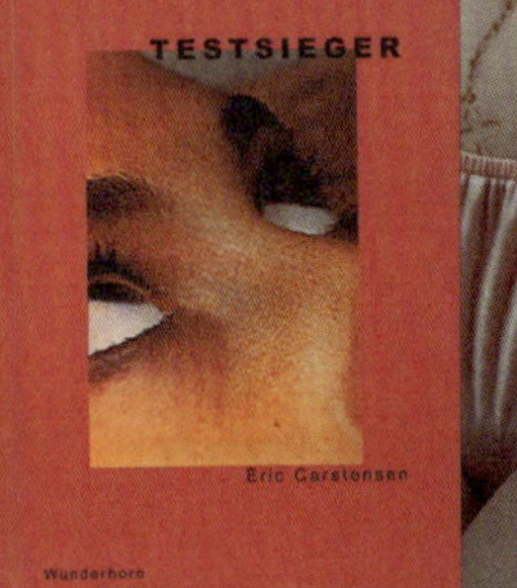

MULIERIS

096 097 098 099 100 101

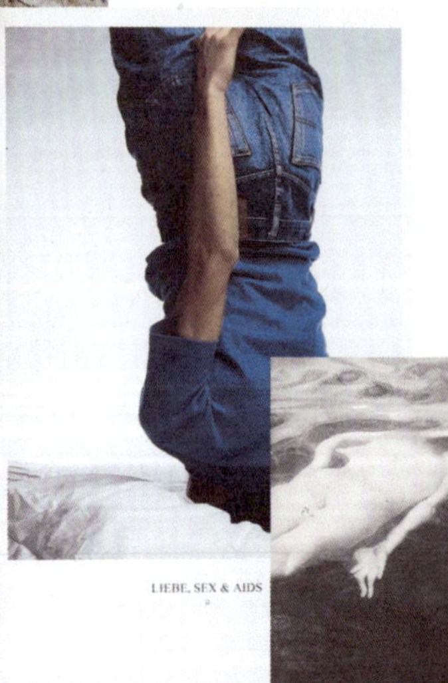

102 103 104 105 106

cover/ graphics.

The term graphic design was virtually unheard of in the 1920s. Even though in 1922 W.A. Dwiggins referred to it, it was not a generally accepted term. How could one know about Jan Tschichold in Pratt Institute, or in Brooklyn, or in Brownsville, or in East New York? One knew about "pool sharks" and icepick murders but not about Tschichold or the "new typography."

At the beginning of design history, it ordered and systematized. Design was seen as a system. If you don't build a thing right, it's going to hell. Some apply this philosophy to graphic design. Fortunately, nobody's going to die if you do the wrong thing.

Nowadays, besides order, chaos is possible. Design experimentation became a strategy. If it fails, you learn from that failure. Today's challenge: How do we create something new? We no longer need to redesign what's already been done–but we will always crave exploring the new and unfamiliar. That's human nature. As Steven Heller says: "For me, it all has a political underpinning in the sense that we are driven–at least, I am driven–by political forces. I'm particularly interested in design being an effective tool one uses to convey information, messages, and sermons too."

When something becomes appealing, a lot more of it gets produced by others, which often diminishes the originator's work in comparison to the copycats'.

107 → **CONCRETE NR. 06 2017: FRÜHLINGSERWACHEN, Marlene Neumann (ed.), FormatWorks, 2017, 56 pp., 25.8 × 35 cm** is a free Munich-based city magazine focused on culture, lifestyle, design, and art. The sixth issue, themed **FRÜHLINGSERWACHEN** ("spring awakening"), delves into topics such as love, sex, bondage, prostitution, aphrodisiacs, the red light district, music, poetry, photography, and shunga. **CONCRETE** prides itself on doing what others dare not, staying free of conventional trends and commercial constraints. As a self-described "analog blog for Munich," it offers a glimpse behind the city's facade, capturing its true essence with a fresh, unfiltered perspective.[149, 150, 151] With its clean layout and bold colors, **CONCRETE NR. 06** flows naturally into 108 → **PROLOG 6: "LIEBE, SEX, SUCHT," Anton Schwarzbach (ed.), Prolog, 2010, 21 × 29.7 cm,** where minimalist design enhances emotional depth through simplicity. The sixth issue of **PROLOG** focuses on the themes of love, sex, and addiction. Founded by Anton Schwarzbach in 2007, the magazine combines works of drawing and text, offering a platform for a diverse range of contributors.[152, 153] The controlled energy of **PROLOG 6** shifts smoothly to the stark minimalism of 109 → **100FOR10 I WANT YOUR CANDY EDITION NO. 019, Florian Brugger, Melville Brand Design, 2017, 106 pp., 14.8 × 21 cm** which is the 19th edition in the **100FOR10** series, featuring black-and-white prints by Florian Brugger.[154, 155] From the stripped-down aesthetic, 110 → **I WANNA GIVE YOU DEVOTION, Philipp Gufler, Hammann von Mier Verlag, 2017, 112 pp., 17 × 24 cm** (↦ see № 219), adds layered content while maintaining a clean, minimalist design. Philipp Gufler realized the installation *I Wanna Give You Devotion* in collaboration with Forum Queeres Archiv München, a self-organized archive dedicated to queer history.

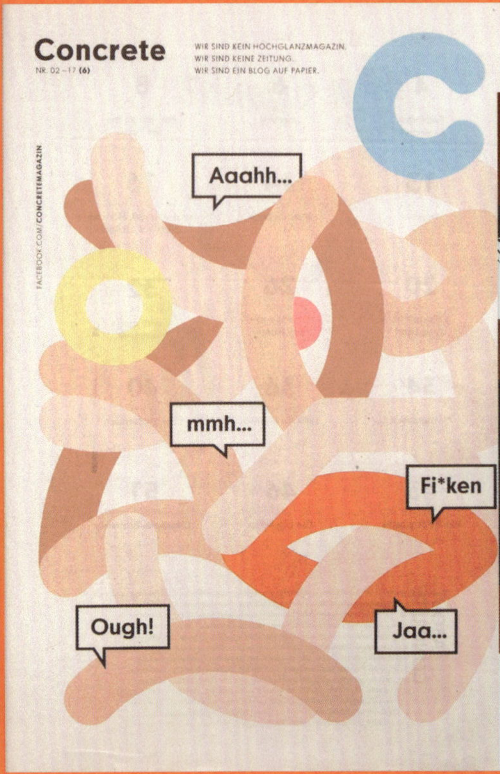

107

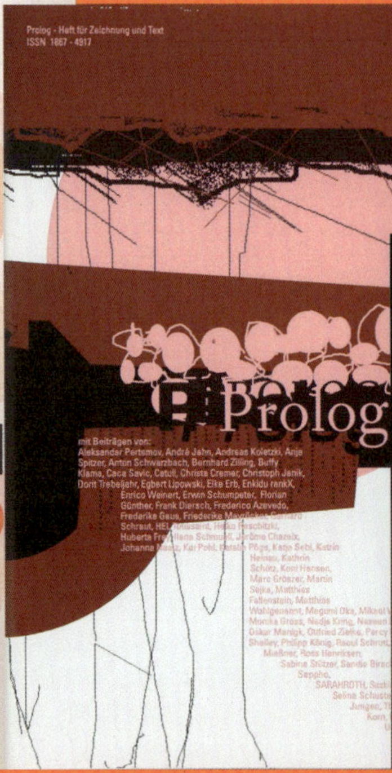

108

109

113

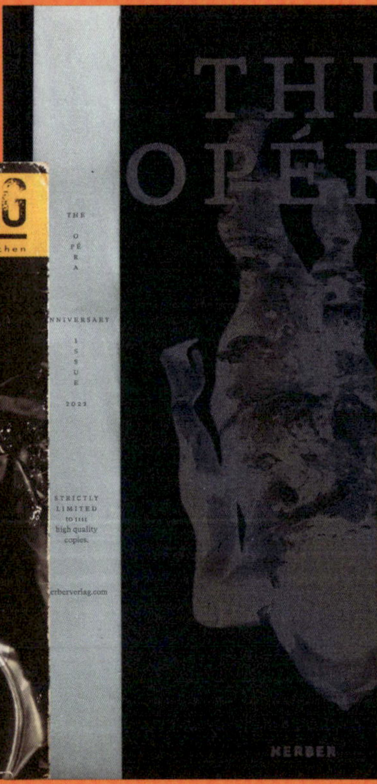

114

115

110

111

112

116

117

118

119

This artist book was created alongside the exhibition, presenting posters and other works that reflect the intersection of queer history, art, and activism. This publication with text contributions by Kerstin Stakemeier, Philipp Gufler & Laura Lang, and members of the forum, combines historical posters and flyers with new contributions from 29 artists and collectives, invited by Gufler to engage with and reinterpret the archive's materials.[156, 157] The curated simplicity of **I WANNA GIVE YOU DEVOTION** leads into the tactile and layered minimalism of **111 → FREIBORD – ZEITSCHRIFT FÜR LITERATUR UND KUNST, Gerhard Jaschke (ed.), Edition Freibord, 1984, 28 × 19 cm** where every element finds its place. The carton, bound with fasteners, contains eight morning editions. **FREIBORD** aimed to merge literature and art with cultural criticism and sociopolitical engagement. Quickly, it became a vital platform for underground authors and established itself as an avant-garde publication.[158] **112 → PIPS – ZEITSCHRIFT FÜR UNKOMMERZ & UNZEITGEIST 1/90 SEXTÜTE, Katharina Eckart, Claudia Pütz, et al. (eds.), Pips-Dada-Corporation, 1990, 35 pp., 21 × 29.7 cm** experiments playfully, yet still grounded in minimalist presentation. The **1/90** edition of **PIPS** is a zine held together with a plastic clip, comprising various papers and materials. Unlike later editions, which appeared in box formats, this early issue reflects the zine's experimental origins. Limited to 200 numbered copies, it included bizarre and provocative elements such as a real pubic hair, a "sex bomb," or a censorship postcard.[159] The handcrafted minimalism of **PIPS** transitions naturally into the ethnographic focus of **113 → DER ALLTAG. DIE SENSATIONEN DES GEWÖHNLICHEN. THEMA: SEX. NR. 1/89, Walter Keller (ed.), Der Alltag, 1990, 192 pp., 21.5 × 27 cm** which reflects on everyday life and aims to "intelligently accompany" it. This issue, centered on the theme of sex, caters to sociological interests through photography, interviews, reports, and essays. In the foreword, Michael Rutschky remarks that readers of **DER ALLTAG** can discover "what else they can be taught and delighted by—just while waiting at the crosswalk for the pedestrian light to change."[160] Straightforward design evolves into **114 → THE OPÉRA ANNIVERSARY ISSUE – BEST OF CLASSIC & CONTEMPORARY NUDE PHOTOGRAPHY, Matthias Straub (ed.), Kerber Verlag, 2022, 320 pp., 24 × 31 cm** **(↦ see № 152, 165 & 174)**, blending elegance and simplicity to celebrate the human form. The cover features textured linen with silver print and a banderole, adding a luxurious finish. Designed by Steffen Knöll and Sven Tillack from Studio Tillack-Knöll, Stuttgart, the **ANNIVERSARY ISSUE** is a strictly limited edition of 1,111 high-quality copies, offering a comprehensive celebration of classic and contemporary nude photography over the last decade.[161] The refined style of **THE OPÉRA** shifts to the intimate warmth of **115 → THE BOY IS BEAUTIFUL #3, Leonidas Liolios (ed.), The Boy Is Beautiful, 2024, 112 pp., 17 × 23 cm, lith print** where minimalist tones meet layers of meaning. **THE BOY IS BEAUTIFUL** unravels the thread of queer Greek chronicles, weaving together narratives from myth and history to contemporary life. Each issue illuminates the closeted history of a gay utopia while celebrating the work of contemporary artists, photographers, writers, and sex workers who engage with Greece as a symbolic and literal space for queer identities everywhere. The third issue, *Hyacinth,* continues this exploration with bold and unapologetically queer storytelling on its signature terracotta pages. It reimagines Greece as a haven for diverse expressions of identity, blending ancient mythological references with modern perspectives on sexuality, desire, and culture.[162] From this warm minimalism, **116 → GARAGE MAGAZINE NO. 1, Dasha Zhukova (ed.), garagemag, 2011, 274 pp., 26 × 34.2 cm** **(↦ see № 149 & 189)** shifts to bold simplicity, showcasing graphic design's power to create impact through experimental yet minimalist layouts. **GARAGE MAGAZINE** is a biannual print publication that brings to life the most original and ambitious collaborative projects across contemporary art and fashion. The magazine features an iconic butterfly-sticker cover, concealing a tattoo design by Damien Hirst, setting the tone for its innovative approach. **GARAGE MAGAZINE** fosters a dynamic dialog between emerging and established creators, uniting influential voices in art, fashion, and design. Mike Meiré and his editorial team have been responsible for the style-defining artwork since the very first edition.[163, 164 165] Boldly redefining visual storytelling, **GARAGE MAGAZINE NO. 1** flows seamlessly into the innovative design of **117 → TWEN 1969 NR. 3, Willy Fleckhaus & Udo Wüst (eds.), Kindler & Schiermeyer, 1969, 26.5 × 33.5 cm,** a magazine for young adults in postwar Germany, published from 1959 to 1971. Known for its bold coverage of political and societal topics, it stood out for its innovative design and striking visual storytelling. This 1969 issue highlights a shift toward vibrant use of color and a growing emphasis on themes like the human body, sex, and eroticism. **TWEN** embodied the controversial ideas and burgeoning freedoms of its time, often pushing boundaries with provocative content.[166, 167] **118 → FLUFFER EVERYDAY ISSUE NO. 6, Sotiris Trechas (ed.), Fluffer Everyday, 2024, 64 pp., 21 × 28.4 cm** **(↦ see № 215)** is an erotic publication that celebrates arousal in the everyday. Promoting body and sex positivity, the magazine challenges traditional notions of what is considered sexy and "normal," emphasizing moments over societal or gendered standards. Each issue delves into a specific kink, offering visual and mental stimulation that embraces diversity and inclusivity. This sixth issue highlights performers who inspire body and sex positivity. The issue is presented in two special-edition covers, each printed in a limited run of 500 copies. As a platform that combines print with an online blog, **FLUFFER EVERYDAY** aims to make the daily life feel more adventurous and provocative. By transforming fantasies into obsessions and finding erotic potential in mundane moments, it encourages readers to embrace a more open and diverse perspective on sexuality.[168] Building on the boldness of **FLUFFER EVERYDAY, 119 → OHNE PAUSE – EIN ÄSTHETISCHER GEGENSTAND, Erwin Puls, Edition Freibord, 1986, VHS cassette** introduces a layered and thought-provoking aesthetic. **OHNE PAUSE** ("without a break") is a compilation film by Erwin Puls that combines pornographic footage from the interwar period and postwar era with amateur recordings and unused material from Austrian director Michael Pilz. In addition to the visual material, a philosophical text runs at half reading speed, where Puls reflects on film, montage, aesthetics, pornography, art, and its reception. This interplay of visuals and text creates a dense aesthetic framework that examines the relationship between art and erotica.[169, 170] Puls broadens **OHNE PAUSE's** exploration of taboo themes, but here, the layered typography and the provocative image heighten the chaotic yet intentional aesthetic. **120 → PULS FÜR DEN INTIMBEREICH, Erwin Puls, 1975, 120 pp., 13.6 × 9.8 cm** is presented with a delicately illustrated dust jacket and features numerous black-and-white pornographic photographs. From the early 1970s onward, Puls worked predominantly with reproduced and found materials, often incorporating pornographic imagery into his montages. His provocative approach garnered significant attention and led to several legal disputes. **PULS FÜR DEN INTIMBEREICH** exemplifies Puls' exploration of art through a transgressive lens, pushing boundaries between aesthetic creation and societal taboos.[171] While Puls provokes through layered visuals, **121 → STELLUNGEN, Jesper Fabricius, Lubok Verlag, 2011, 24 pp., 14.8 × 21 cm (↦ see № 194 & 195),** takes this chaos further with cut-out windows and cubist-inspired layering. In **STELLUNGEN**, Jesper Fabricius reproduces a magazine that served as source material for his artistic process. Known for his collages, Fabricius frequently incorporates image and text fragments from 1970s porn magazines. This work features cut-out windows that reveal glimpses of subsequent pages, creating a unique interplay of form and content. The resulting layered visuals evoke an almost cubistic tension, blending provocative themes with experimental design.[172] The bold, collage-like layouts of **STELLUNGEN** evolve into the visual rebellion of **122 → SEX PRESS: THE SEXUAL REVOLUTION IN THE UNDERGROUND PRESS, 1963–1979, Vincent Bernière & Mariel Primois (eds.), Abrams, 2012, 240 pp., 22.5 × 34 cm.** This publication captures the vibrant and rebellious spirit of the sexual revolution as chronicled in underground press publications from 1965 to 1975. Covering a wide array of journals, magazines, and fanzines, **SEX PRESS** delves into the bold and provocative era when publications such as *Other Scenes, Yellow Dog, Actuel, Suck, The Body,* and *Screw* challenged societal norms. Illustrated with vivid full-page facsimiles, the publication traces the evolution of sexual expression from the exuberance of the 1960s to the codified forms of pornography in the mid-1970s. **SEX PRESS** offers a compelling visual narrative of this extraordinary period of experimentation, creativity, and freedom, celebrating the groundbreaking role of the underground press in shaping the sexual revolution.[173] **123 → SMILE ART-MAGAZIN AUSGABE 4, Josef Klaffki (ed.), Smile-Magazin, 1986, 51 pp., 30 × 21 cm** carries forward the chaotic energy of **SEX PRESS**, blending Mail Art aesthetics with provocative yet playful imagery to create a unique visual dialog. This fourth issue of **SMILE**, edited by Josef Klaffki (also known as "Joki"), features black-and-white photographs alongside orange-colored graphics. **SMILE** itself was conceived as an experimental, multi-origin publication by Monty Cantsin. Various contributors used the same title, with no fixed format or singular responsibility, fostering a unique collective creative endeavor.[174, 175] The bold experimentation of **SMILE** transitions into the raw, unapologetic documentation of Hamburg's nightlife in **124 → ST.-PAULI-NACHT-REVUE NR. 52, Peter Martens (ed.), HANSEATA, 1971, 39 pp., 23.5 × 32 cm.** The **ST.-PAULI-NACHT-REVUE** was a weekly publication released in Hamburg by the Hanseata-Zeitschriften-Verlag. The magazine documented nightlife and cultural themes of the St. Pauli district, reflecting its vibrant and notorious character.[176] **125 → PSYCHEDELIC SEX, Dian Hanson (ed.), Taschen Verlag, 2014, 408 pp., 25.5 × 21 cm** captures the experimental spirit of St. Pauli but elevates it with mesmerizing visuals, embodying the vibrant chaos of the 1960s counterculture. In a brief yet transformative period between 1967 and 1972, the sexual revolution and the rise of recreational drug experimentation converged, creating what is now referred to as "psychedelic sex." During this time, men's magazine publishers attempted to visually emulate the effects of LSD, using colorful, kaleidoscopic projections on nude bodies, often portraying the carefree and uninhibited lifestyle of hippies. These images were aimed at enticing a conservative audience curious about the promises of free love and the counterculture movement. **PSYCHEDELIC SEX** explores this fascinating era through over 400 pages of photographs and text, presenting naked figures with psychedelic designs on their bodies, surrounded by quintessential elements of the time—beaded necklaces, drug paraphernalia, and posters of bands like Led Zeppelin.[177, 178] From the psychedelic era, the layered visuals of **PSYCHEDELIC SEX** seamlessly transition into **126 → BI ALL MEANS, Julia Koschler, 2022, 46 pp., 14.8 × 21 cm,** showcasing a celebration of identity with bold, diverse graphics. **BI ALL MEANS** is a three-part zine exploring the bi+ spectrum, created in response to bi+ erasure and hostility in mainstream society and queer communities. It aims to provide a platform for sharing experiences, perspectives, anger, and joy, promoting visibility and connection. **BI ALL MEANS** celebrates the diversity and resilience of the bi+ community, fostering a deeper understanding of identity and relationships.[179] **BI ALL MEANS'** delicate florals transition into the striking typography of **127 → INSTANT NR. 12 – AMORE, Franz Aumüller, Thomas Feicht & James Nitsch (eds.), Trust, 1985, 29.5 × 42 cm**, blending intimacy with bold expressions of love. **INSTANT** is a magazine situated at the intersection of design, advertising, and art, with each issue centered on a specific theme. Issue 12, titled **AMORE**, explores the concept of love through a blend of numerous photographs. The magazine's mission is to dissolve boundaries between advertising, art, opinion, and self-expression.[180] Finally, **128 → ST. PAULI NACHRICHTEN NR. 130, Helmut Rosenberg (ed.), St. Pauli Verlag, 1970, 32 × 47 cm** pushes boundaries with provocative visuals and daring typographic elements. The **ST. PAULI NACHRICHTEN** was a men's magazine published in Hamburg, known for its mix of provocative content and, in its early years, politically left-leaning, ambitious, and sometimes controversial articles. Founded in 1968 by photographer Günter Zint and antiques dealer Helmut Rosenberg, the magazine combined explicit imagery, contact ads, and socio-political commentary. Rosenberg described the publication as fulfilling a "ventilation function" for its readership, evidenced by the weekly influx of postsacks containing personal ads and messages.[181, 182]

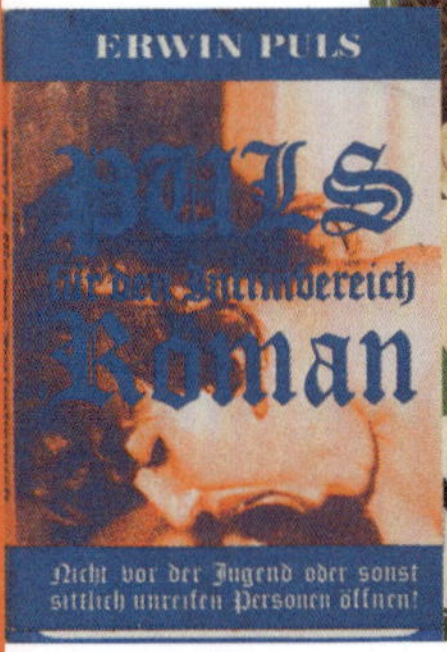

120

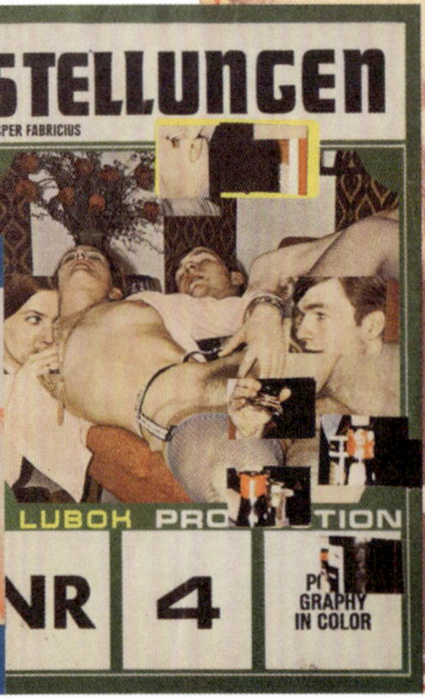

121

122

123

124

125

126

Deutschlands frechste Zeitung

St. Pauli Nachrichten

Über 5,4 Millionen Leser

C 20194 B

Nr. 130 • 2. Oktober 1970

informiert ❋ DAS LUSTBLATT DER WELTSTADT ❋ amüsiert

80Pf

Seitensprung zu Discount Preisen!

Die mit dem größten Heiratsmarkt „Seid nett aufeinander"

Aus dem Inhalt:

Reise ins Land der Gifte (S. 14)

Aus der Welt

Hamburg, 2. Oktober „Einheitliche Preise fürs bumsen, das fordert der „Club Hamburger Liebesdienerinnen CHL". Immer wieder gibt es Streit und eins auf die Nase unter den engagierten Damen. Daß eine Regulierung in dieser Sache aber nicht so einfach ist, mußten wir leider bei unseren Recherchen zu diesem Thema feststellen. Lesen Sie un- ...richt auf Seite 4.

Das Amt eines Richters ist nicht immer leicht. Diese Feststellung mußte ein New Yorker Scheidungsrichter machen, nachdem ein Ehepaar ihm seine ungewöhnlichen Liebespraktiken geschildert hatte. „Salomon ist tot, aber ein Urteil muß her", meinte der Richter: Lesen Sie Seite 24.

Scheidung von Tisch und Brett

Nachruf für JIMI SEITE 12

...ben? S.2

SCHWEIZER MORAL BEIM POP FESTIVAL SEITE 12

Dahinter steckt immer ein aufgeklärter Leser

...en beleben WIESO LESEN SIE AUF SEITE 3

mini r 4 25,– tag + mwst
tel 763 22 06
trend autovermietung
999 frei km
morris 1100 fiat 128 30,– tag + mwst

INSTANT AMORE
Nº 12 DM.6 $.2.50 £.2 Ff.14

127

128

cover / punk!

Punk rock, which emerged in the 1970s as a musical and cultural rebellion, had a lasting influence on graphic design, particularly in album art, magazine layouts, and DIY zines. Punk's ethos of subversion, anti-establishment values, and rejection of traditional norms reshaped the visual language of design, influencing both the style of its time and future generations of designers. Originating in New York and London, punk's aesthetic was defined by chaos, disorder, and a break from modernist formalism.

One of punk's most significant contributions to graphic design was its embrace of DIY ("Do It Yourself") culture, which manifested in album covers, zines, and promotional materials. Rick Poynor noted that punk design featured a raw, unpolished look, employing techniques like collage, hand-lettering, and Xerox copying to create fast, aggressive visuals. The punk aesthetic rejected the polished, mass-produced imagery of mainstream culture, opting instead for a direct, almost anarchic approach to design. Sarah Hyndman described this as part of a broader Postmodern rejection of Modernist principles, which had dominated graphic design with clean lines and neutral typography.

Central to this rebellion was the use of collage and cut-up techniques, which became iconic in punk graphic design. This method of remixing existing materials reflected punk's ideology that nothing was sacred and everything could be reinterpreted. Additionally, the punk aesthetic was heavily influenced by zines such as SNIFFIN' GLUE and PUNK MAGAZINE. These self-published magazines embodied the movement's anti-consumerist stance, featuring crude drawings, rough typography, and scrawled messages. Their raw style, made on minimal budgets with basic materials, reinforced the idea that anyone could create culture.

The legacy of punk's aesthetic persists today, visible not just in music but across various forms of visual culture. By rejecting clean, corporate aesthetics, punk paved the way for contemporary practices that celebrate imperfection, spontaneity, and rebellion. As Rick Poynor stated, "Punk's image is anything but ambiguous" (Budrick, 2019), and this clarity of purpose remains central to its identity in graphic design.

Ultimately, punk's contribution to graphic design was not just a visual style but a defiant attitude. It challenged norms, embraced unconventionality, and empowered a generation of designers to subvert the visual language of the time.

129 130 131 132

129 → FUCK UP MERZ – 40 JAHRE PROSTITUTION PURE, Michael Ried, Panik Verlag, 2019, 28 pp., 14.4 × 21 cm has been published regularly in Haidhausen since 1980 under various titles. Michael Ried's life and work reflected a blend of art and personal experience, often revealing themes of alcohol, drugs, and sex. His creations were entirely handmade, showcasing his commitment to craftsmanship, even as he faced challenges in earning a living from his art.[183, 184] **130 → LA STRADA, Michael Ried, Free Sahara Publishing Company, 2000, 14.8 × 21 cm** continues to explore the raw, handmade creativity of Michael Ried. "Ich kopiere alles, was ich in die Finger kriege," ("I copy everything I can get my hands on") said Michael Ried about his distinctive technique. His process involved making a photocopy of the original, overlaying tracing paper, and then redrawing the lines with a thick felt pen. Each issue featured handwritten content or drawings, primarily consisting of comic-style nude sketches.[185] Michael Ried's raw, handmade world gives way to the collaged irreverence of **131 → MR. EDWARD'S POP TARTS, Neil Edwards, 2012, 28 pp., 19.8 × 14.8 cm,** where found imagery is rearranged with a playful and anarchic spirit. A collection of found texts and images from magazines and newspapers, extracted from their original context and rearranged to create new meanings.[186, 187] Neil Edwards's playful deconstruction of media in **MR. EDWARDS POP TARTS** sets the stage for Erik Steinbrecher's **132 → ERIK STEINBRECHER: HALLI GALLI, Nieves 2011, 16 pp., 11.5 × 17.0 cm,** where the gritty allure of Zurich's red-light district is captured and reimagined through photographic interventions. After work artist Erik Steinbrecher every now and then takes a stroll around town. For this project he explored Zurich's red-light district around Langstrasse with his camera in his pocket. He took photos of the advertising vitrines around the erotic-dance scene located there. A selection of these photographs of artistic dancers were then printed out and overworked by Steinbrecher.[188] From this voyeuristic exploration, the focus shifts to the collaborative rebellion of **133 → COMMONPRESS 39 – HOMOSEXUALITÄT, machArt (ed.), Selbstverlag, 1981, 22.3 × 31.3 cm,** where global mail art networks unite to confront societal taboos with dissident creativity. This issue of **COMMONPRESS** was created for an exhibition at the KCR Kommunikations-Centrum-Ruhr in Dortmund-Dorstfeld. The publication consists of loose sheets presented in a file folder, bound with a cord and hole-punched in the top left corner. Paweł Petasz, a key figure in the Mail Art movement, created collages, visual poetry, and handmade art objects that reflect the charm of dissident production. His initiative with **COMMONPRESS** aimed to bring together artists worldwide, creating a unique platform for artistic collaboration and exploration of socially relevant themes.[189, 190] In contrast, **134 → COMMONPRESS 18 NUDES ON STAMPS E. F., Higgins III (ed.), DOO-DA Postage Works, 1979, 20 pp., 14 × 21.8 cm, Xerox print** expands this collaboration with a focus on visual miniatures, offering a playful and conceptual twist. This rare issue of **COMMONPRESS** showcases the innovative concept of rotating editorship. Edited by E. F. Higgins III, a prominent artist known for his prolific creation of artist stamps, this issue explores the theme of

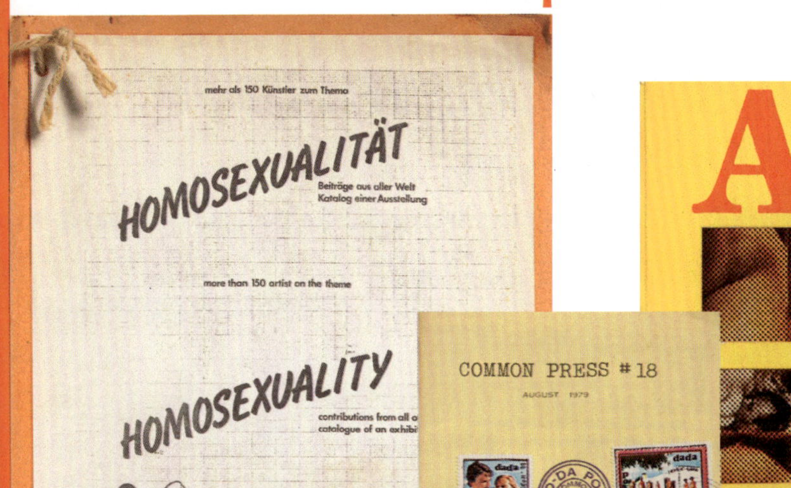

133

134

135

140

141

142

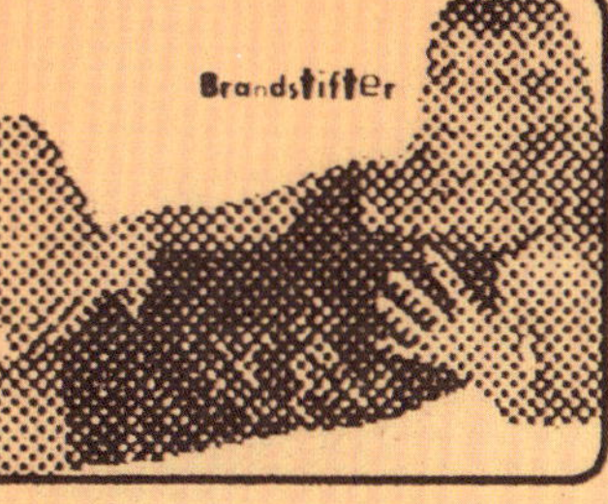

136 137 138 139

143 144 145

NUDES ON STAMPS. Higgins invited contributions of stamp-sized images from the global mail art community, resulting in a visually rich collection of xeroxed illustrations and eight perforated leaves.[191, 192] 135 → **ACID. NEUE AMERIKANISCHE SZENE, Rolf Dieter Brinkmann & Ralf-Rainer Rygulla (eds.), März Verlag, 1969, 422 pp., 21 × 27.4 cm** takes this bold energy further by showcasing the radical spirit of the era through its vivid exploration of American subculture and countercultural design. The volume features works by prominent figures such as William S. Burroughs, Charles Bukowski, Diane di Prima, Andy Warhol, Frank Zappa, and many others. The title **ACID** reflects both the counterculture's radical ethos and its association with the psychedelic experience.[193, 194, 195] 136 → **MANI-ART NR. 4, Pascal Lenoir (ed.), 1984, 18 pp., 15 × 21 cm** returns to the raw, photocopied punk zine format. Remaining true to the ethos of mail art, Mani-Art was neither sold nor purchased but distributed freely to its contributors, fostering an inclusive and non-commercial artistic community. This fourth issue, like others in the series, embodies the spirit of creative exchange and showcases the experimental and diverse nature of mail art.[196, 197] Building on this collaborative energy, 137 → **KROMIX NR. 8, Ralf Palandt & Stefan Riedl (eds.), Totenkopf-Verlag, 1995, 84 pp., 29.7 × 21 cm** explores satire and societal critique through experimental comics and punk-inspired aesthetics. **KROMIX NR. 8** is an adult-oriented comic anthology that blends satire, experimentation, and entertainment. This issue prominently features a reprint of a safer-sex educational comic by renowned US artist Dave McKean. To emphasize the comic's educational intent, the album includes a condom. 138 → **KONTAKT PUNKT, Brandstifter, V.E.B. Freie Brandstiftung, 2005, 14.8 × 21 cm** distills punk's raw edge into abstracted copy art, transforming sex ads into provocative visual statements. **KONTAKT PUNKT** is a photocopied zine featuring copy art works created using printed sex ads from a local weekly paper. By enlarging the photos with a xerox machine, the small screened black points are magnified, causing the naked bodies to lose all sexual attraction. Expanding on the fragmented, xeroxed aesthetic, 139 → **LOST & FOUND HYSTERIA GRAZ, Brandstifter, V.E.B. Freie Brandstiftung, 2014, 16 pp., 14.8 × 21 cm** turns urban ephemera into collaged narratives, preserving punk's spontaneity. **LOST & FOUND HYSTERIA GRAZ** is an art zine created during Stefan Brand's 2014 artist residency in Graz, Austria, as part of his long-term project *Asphaltbibliotheque*. The zine features lost and found sheets of paper, hand-collaged and xeroxed into a limited, signed, and numbered edition of 40 copies. The cover displays a photocopied ad with female sex workers and typewriter font, aligning with the raw, ephemeral aesthetic of the project. From urban chaos to playful provocation, 140 → **WHAT DOES THE BIBLE SAY ABOUT SEX?, Brandstifter, V.E.B. Freie Brandstiftung, 2014, 20 pp., 14.8 × 21 cm** merges irreverent humor with subversive commentary on cultural and religious norms. The cover shows a keychain sex toy from a vending machine in 90s Vienna with a rudimentary male and a female body. The bodies are connected with a chain long enough to stick the plastic penis in one of three holes of the female toy figure. They keychain was photocopied and collaged with text from the Old Testament's command of female submission. Continuing the punk-driven critique, 141 → **ANTIPODES 010 – NO ART MOVE STUDIES, Brandstifter, V.E.B. Freie Brandstiftung, 2016, 24 pp., 14.8 × 21 cm** fuses collage and mail art to confront themes of gender, exploitation, and rebellion. It is a Mail Art collaboration between a Belgian collagist and performer with the editor thematizing the beauty of women, politics, and human exploitation. 142 → **SEX, PERFORMANCE, AND THE 80'S – FRANKLIN FURNACE – THE FLUE – DOUBLE ISSUE, Martha Wilson (ed.), Franklin Furnace, 1982, 56 pp., 21 × 27 cm** bridges punk's DIY ethos with feminist-driven explorations of sex and social dynamics. This double issue of **THE FLUE** presents a unique format with two front covers: one side titled **SEX, PERFORMANCE, AND THE 80S** and the other **L.A. LONDON CATALOG**. This issue of **THE FLUE** exemplifies the intersection of performance, feminist critique, and cultural innovation in the 1980s, serving as both a testament to and a critique of its era's evolving artistic and social landscapes.[198] 143 → **VIRGEN HASTA EL MATRIMONIO NO.1, Innana, 2017, 8 pp., 14.8 × 21 cm** blends punk visuals with political and cultural critique, sharpening its message through stark imagery. The title **VIRGEN HASTA EL MATRIMONIO** translates to "Virgin Until Marriage" in English. The cover features a provocative illustration characterized by clear, simple, sketch-like lines. 144 → **COMING ATTRACTIONS. BEAT PRESSER, InterArt Corporation Basel, 1984, 21 × 30 cm** captures punk's disruptive essence with ironic, philosophical visuals. The photographic sequences blend an avant-garde flair with a commitment to exploring the realities of contemporary life, presenting a mix of irony, philosophy, and artistic provocation.[199] In the same disruptive style, 145 → **EDITA – SELF-PUBLISHING PRACTICES IN CONTEMPORARY MEXICO, Bernhard Cella (ed.), 2013, 40 pp., 15.5 × 29.6 cm** celebrates the diversity of self-publishing, aligning punk's independent ethos with Mexico's vibrant sociocultural narratives.[200] 146 → **(S)EXPLORATION TIMES, Maya Warthon, 2022, 28 pp., 35 × 50 cm** (↦ see № 150, 187 & 217) reimagines punk's raw openness through a broadsheet format focused on sexuality and intimacy. At its heart, the newspaper serves as an invitation to engage in a deeper exploration—both of oneself and of connections with others—encouraging open conversations about intimacy, desire, and human relationships. Finally, 147 → **PLASTIC INDIANER NO 04 HOL DIR EINEN RUNTER, Wolfgang L. Diller & Bernhard Springer (eds.), bspr Werkstatt, 1982, 24 pp., 21 × 29.7 cm** channels Munich's punk energy with its provocative DIY approach. **PLASTIC INDIANER** is the punk and art fanzine of the former Munich artist group EX-Neue Heimat. Published since 1981 by Wolfgang L. Diller and Bernhard Springer, the zine captures the raw, rebellious spirit of the time. Issue No. 4, titled **HOL DIR EINEN RUNTER** ("jerk yourself off"), was released in April 1982. It is heavily themed around sex and emerged as a reaction to a visit to a lost exhibition. The zine features loose black-and-white photocopied pages, with a hand-stamped cover.

(S)exploration Times

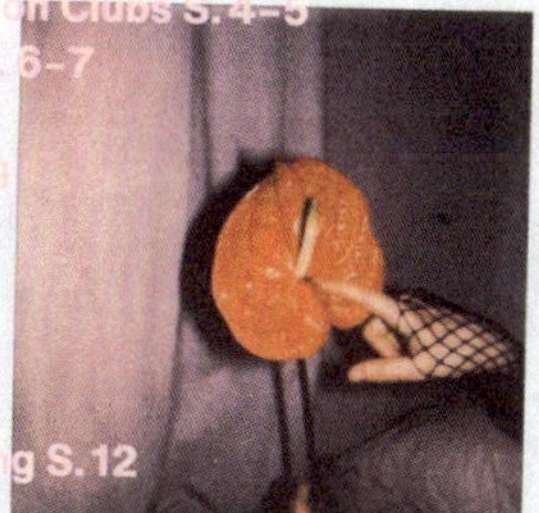

Free poster inside!
aphrodisisches Rezept
und Shibari Anleitung!

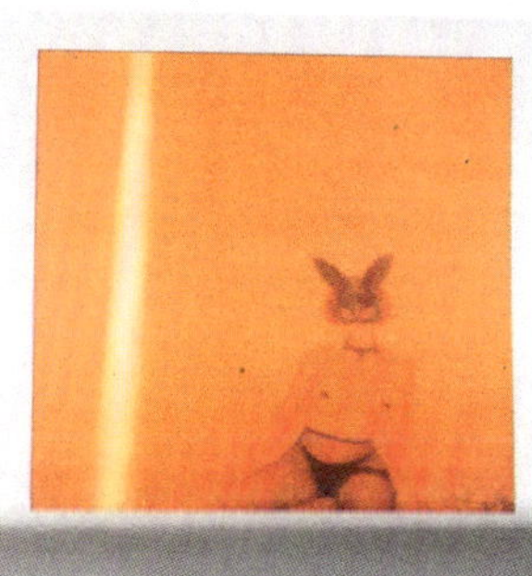

!

Achtu
HO

!
Content Warnin
Inhaltswarnu

Diese Zeitung behandelt
zu Sexualität, Kink und
Es werden über explizite
lungen in diesen Bereich
richtet.

plastic indianer no 4

bspr Werkstatt anglerstr 12

„Ein leichtes Kribbeln,
mehr war da nicht...“

plastic indianer

collages. # /&

Printed media has long served as a platform for examining and redefining sexuality. From underground zines to commercial magazines and radical manifestos, editorial design has shaped how sex is visualized and understood. This chapter presents a selection of posters, zines, and magazines that engage with sexuality—not as isolated artifacts but as interconnected compositions contributing to evolving cultural dialogs.

Each publication employs distinct aesthetic and conceptual strategies, using photography, typography, illustration, and design to explore themes of desire, identity, and power. Some take a direct, confrontational approach, addressing taboos head-on, while others rely on abstraction, symbolism, or humor. When juxtaposed, these works generate new interpretative connections—overlapping bodies, fragmented headlines, and layered material textures that challenge and recontextualize their original meanings.

Sexuality in editorial design is not merely a subject but a site of visual experimentation, continuously negotiating social norms and reclaiming marginalized narratives. Beginning with a survey of visually striking covers, this chapter further examines selected magazines, analyzing the conceptual and aesthetic frameworks they construct.

148 → 100FOR10 – NOTHING TASTES QUITE LIKE IT – EDITION NO. 070, Simon Lohmeyer, Melville Brand Design, 2018, 106 pp., 14.8 × 21 cm (↦ see № 086 & 213)

149 → GARAGE MAGAZINE NO. 1, Dasha Zhukova (ed.), garagemag, 2011, 274 pp., 26 × 34.2 cm **(↗ see N° 118 & 189)**
Nudes, Max Farago (Photography), Olympia Scarry (Creative Direction), Tamara Rothstein (Stylist), Sarah W. (Model), Wendy Nichol (Product)

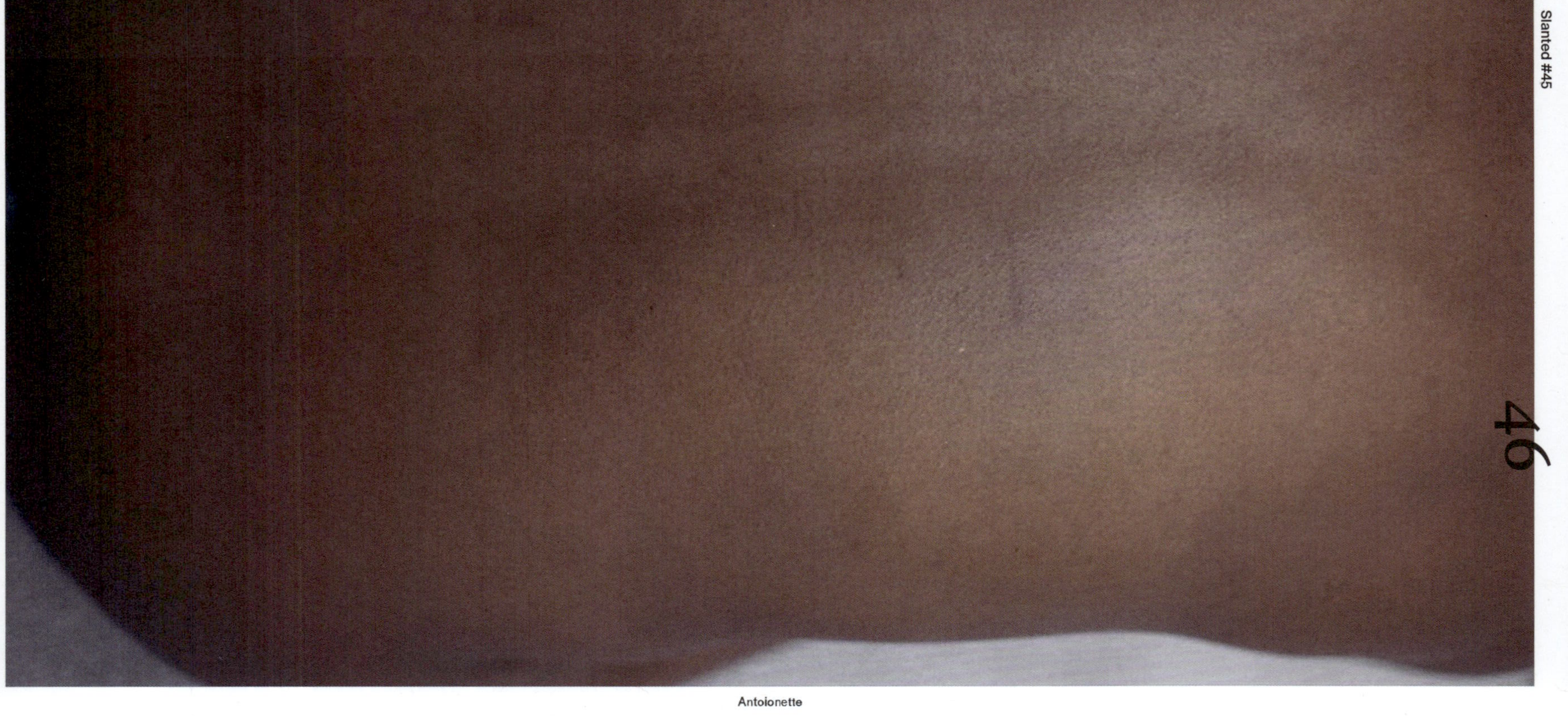

Antoionette

Sarah W wears custom-made

NUDE

Photographer
MAX FARAGO

Creative Direction
OLYMPIA SCARRY

Stylist
TAMARA ROTHSTEIN

JOIN THE
JOIN THE
PLORATION

150 → (S)EXPLORATION POSTER, Maya Walthoh, 2022, 59.4cm x 84.1cm (→ see № 146, 187 & 217

The (S)Exploration Club invite
you to go on an adventure:
Go and discover yourself and y
opposite and you will find a
new world of pleasure awaiting
you.
Read the latest issue of the
(S)Exploration Times and buckl
up for the ride!

Have fun!

151 IT'S NOT GETTING ANY BETTER Simon Becker Studio B2302 2021 30 x 40cm

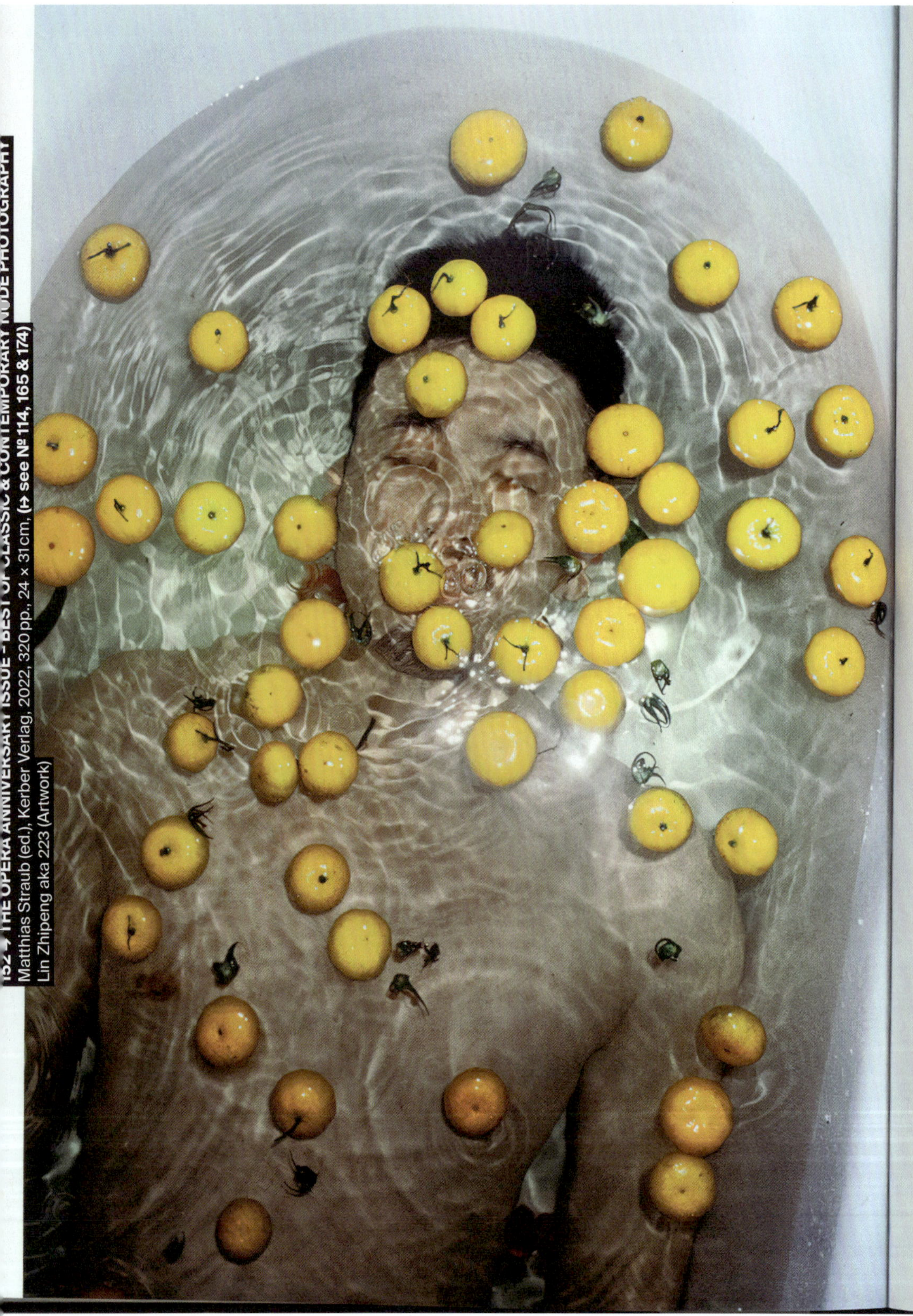

152 → THE OPERA ANNIVERSARY ISSUE – BEST OF CLASSIC & CONTEMPORARY NUDE PHOTOGRAPHY
Matthias Straub (ed.), Kerber Verlag, 2022, 320 pp., 24 × 31 cm, **(↦ see № 114, 165 & 174)**
Lin Zhipeng aka 223 (Artwork)

153 → THE OPÉRA VOLUME XI. THE PHOENIX ISSUE, Matthias Straub (ed.), Kerber Verlag, 2022, 224 pp., 24 × 31 cm **(↦ see № 104, 167 & 168)**
Men Are Made to Reproduce, Milena Schilling & Fiona Mentzel

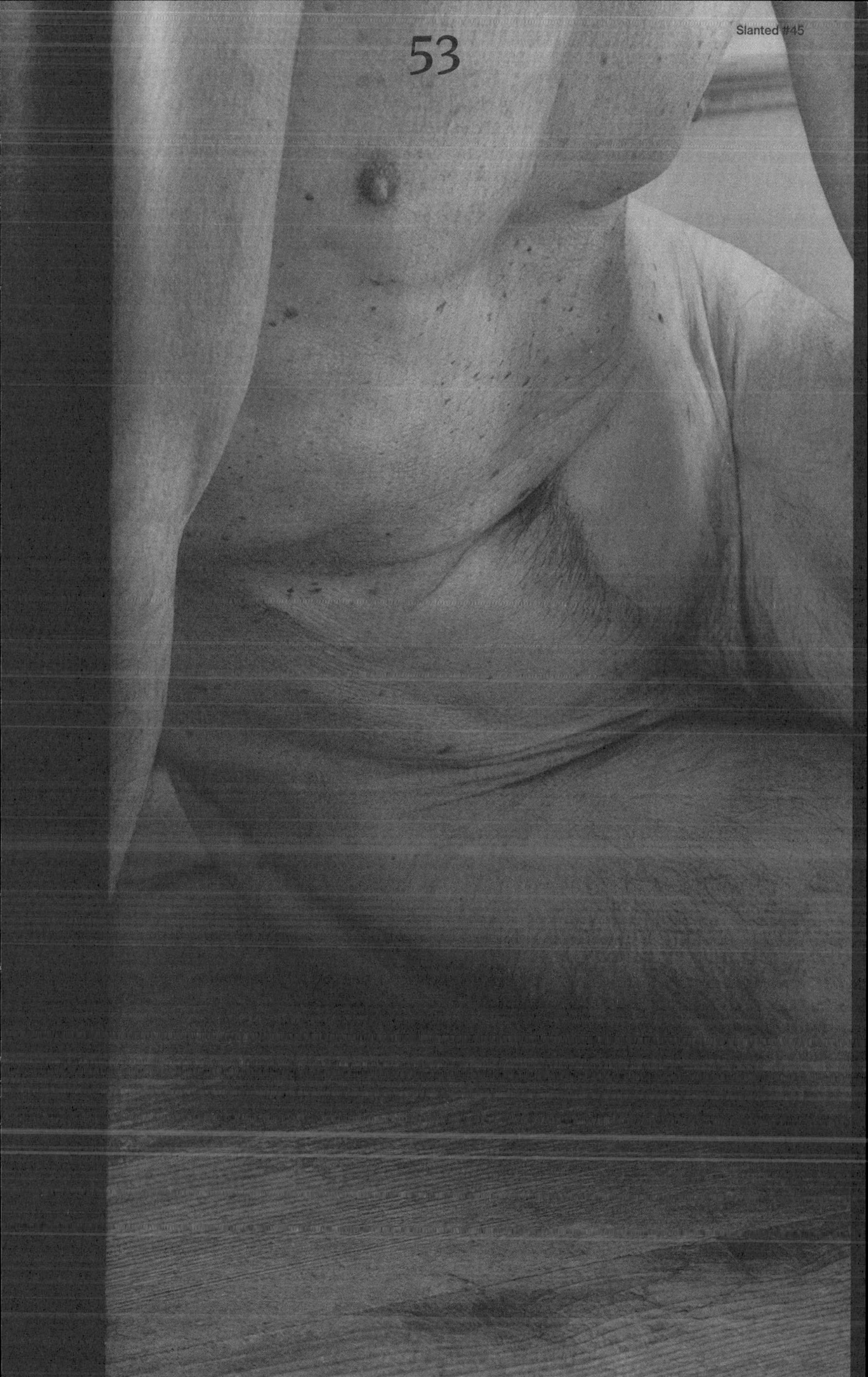

154 → BUTT MAGAZINE 34, Andrew Pasquier, Jop van Bennekom, Gert Jonkers & Nathaniel Feldmann (eds.), 2024, 104 pp., 17 × 24 cm (↦ see № 076 & 155)

42

● FICKEN 3000

SEX

BERLIN'S FINEST COCK-SUCKING WATERI HOLE

Frank Redieß, the 60-something founder of Ficke much a participant in the bar's nightly fun as its Popular both with the Berlinale crowd and father the street, Ficken 3000's silly vibes and endless will suck you in until 7AM, seven days a week.

● Interview and photography by Matt Lambert

● EXPOSÉ

Hari Nef

- Literally a doll
- 31 years old
- Beefy IMDB credits
- Downtown troublemaker
- LA starlet
- Occasional art writer
- Damn!
- Hot coffee, hotter chat
- Hollywood Diner, 6th Avenue, NYC

● Interview by Zak Stone
● Photography by Collier Schorr

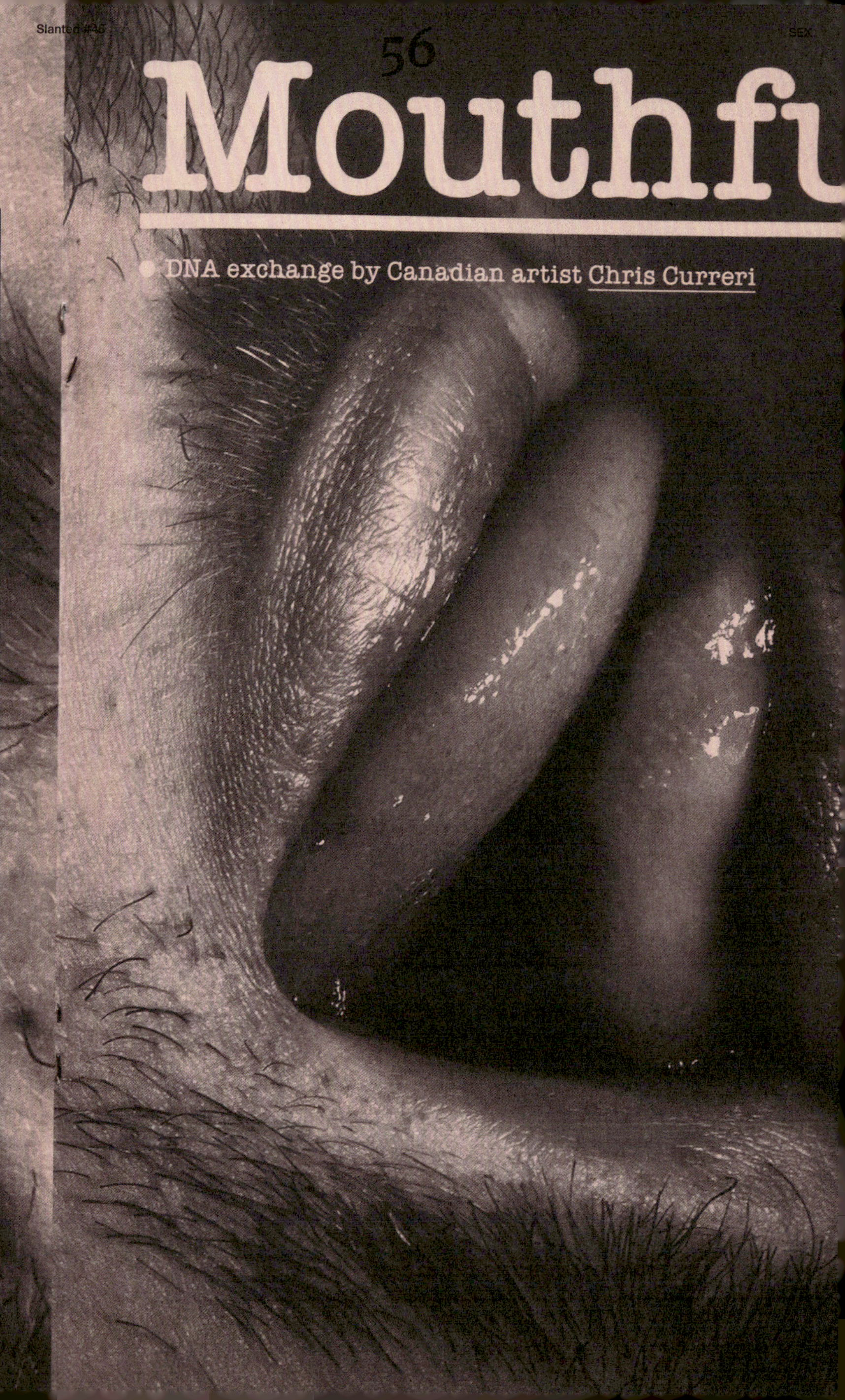

Mouthfu

DNA exchange by Canadian artist Chris Curreri

153 / BUTT MAGAZINE 34, Andrew Pasquier, Jop van Bennekom, Gert Jonkers & Nathaniel Feldmann (eds.), 2024, 104 pp., 17 x 24 cm (↳ see N°076 & 154)

158 → PINUPS, NO. 15, Christoph Schulz (ed.), 2015
56pp, 20.5 x 25.5cm, Xerox Print

157 → PINUPS, NO. 13, Christoph Schulz (ed.), 2010
56pp, 20.5 x 25.5cm, Xerox Print

156 → PINUPS, NO. 16, Christoph Schulz (ed.), 2012,
56pp, 20.5 x 25.5cm, Xerox print (→ see № 077)

159 → **SOMESUCH STORIES 6 – THE TENSION ISSUE,** Suze Olbrich (ed.), Somesuch Editions, 2024, 256 pp., 17 × 23.5 cm, Printed by Colt Press UK **(→ see N-097),**
Design: Thomas Coombes; Product Images Marloes Haarmans; Copyright: © Somesuch Editions.
PLEASE, Birk Thomassen, 2024

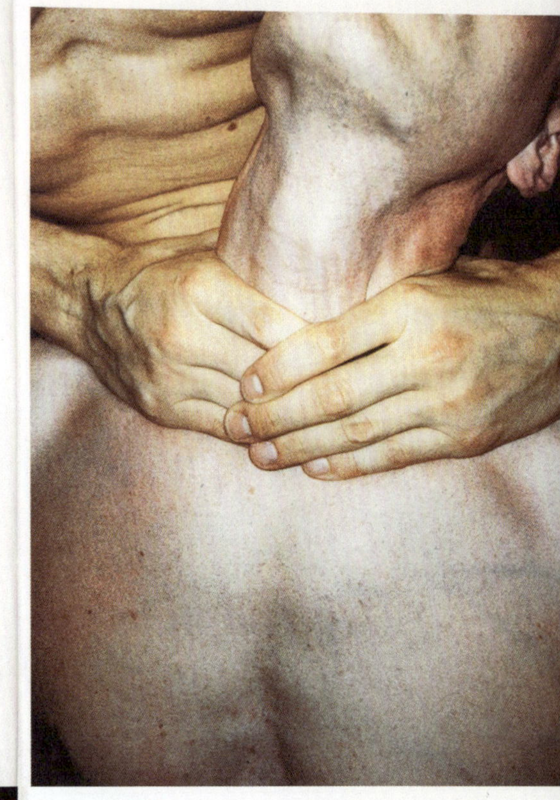

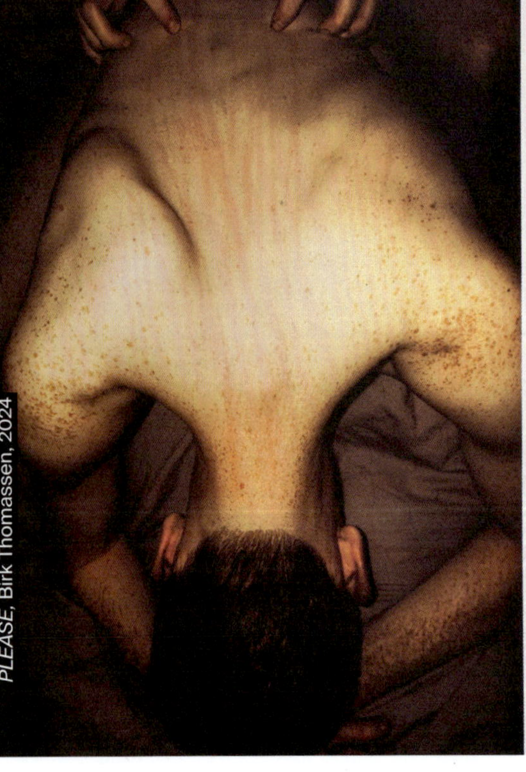

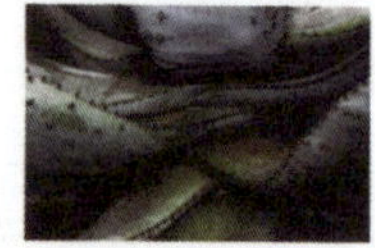

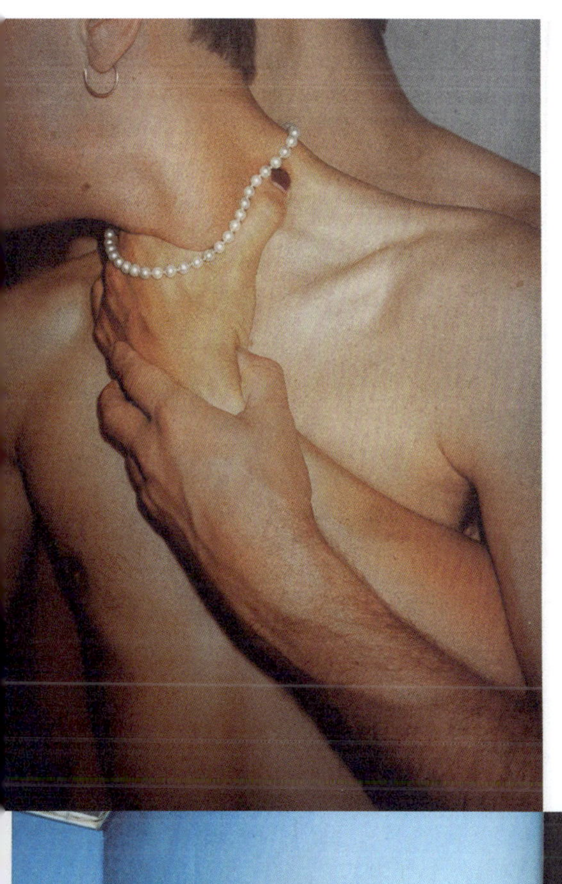

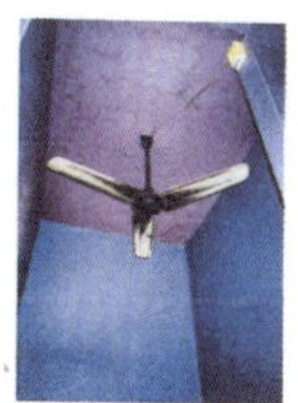

PEGGING TRUDEAU

Priya Guns

PEGGING

Pedro & Francisco, Juan Antonio Papagni Meca

038

160 → BOYS! BOYS! BOYS! THE MAGAZINE – VOLUME 8, Ghislain Pascal (ed.), The Little Black Gallery, 2024, 160 pp., 20 × 27 cm (↦ see № 001)
Twins Dancing On The Beach, Pancho Assoluto

161 → THE BERLIN CHAMELEON – ARCHIVES 01, The Berlin Chameleon, 2024, 56 pp., 14.8 x 21cm (→ see № 068)

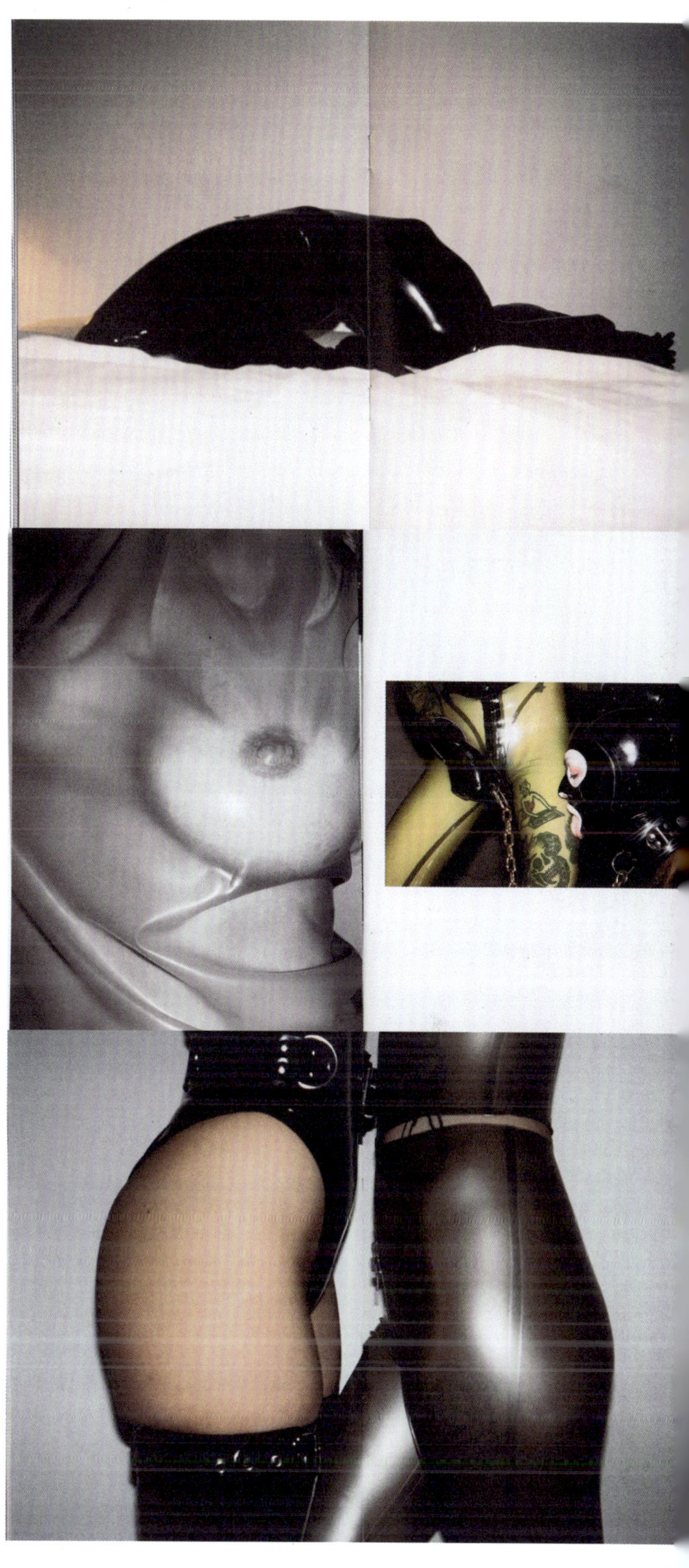

64

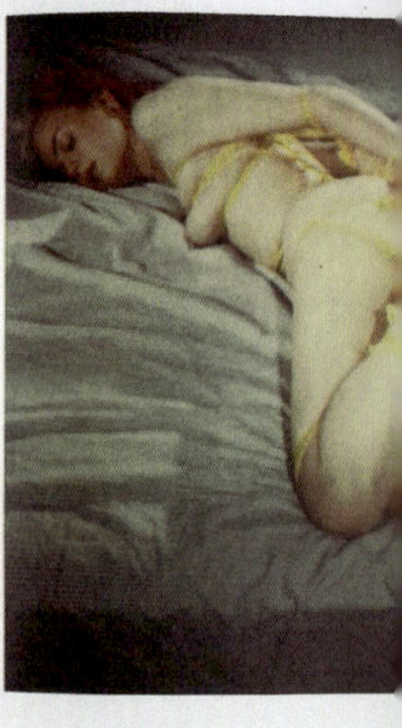

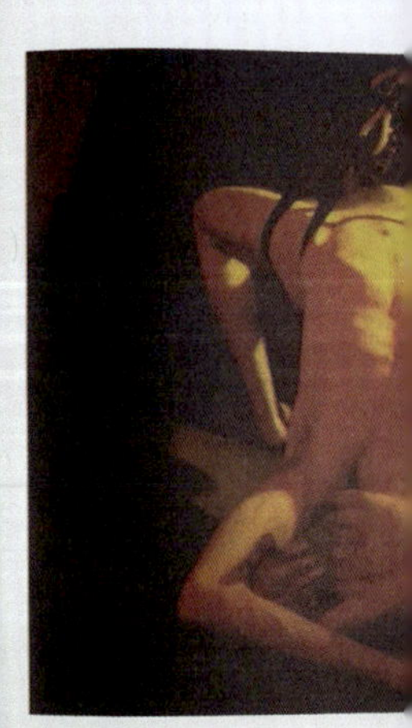

162 → RICHARD KERN POLAROIDS, Art Paper Editions, 2023, 176 pp., 22 x 30 cm (→ see Nº 092 & 170)

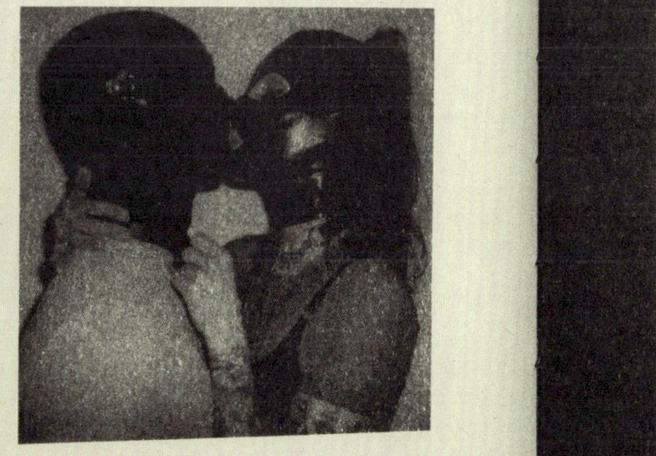

164 → MOAN ZINE ISSUE 5, Moan, 2024, 98 pp., 13 × 18 cm, riso print by Dizzy Ink, The Berlin Chameleon **(↦ see № 033 & 196)**

163 → FLASH – THE GARDEN AND THE CAVE, Tim Best, Pack Peel Pour, 2017, 24 pp. 13,4 × 21 cm **(↦ see № 075)**

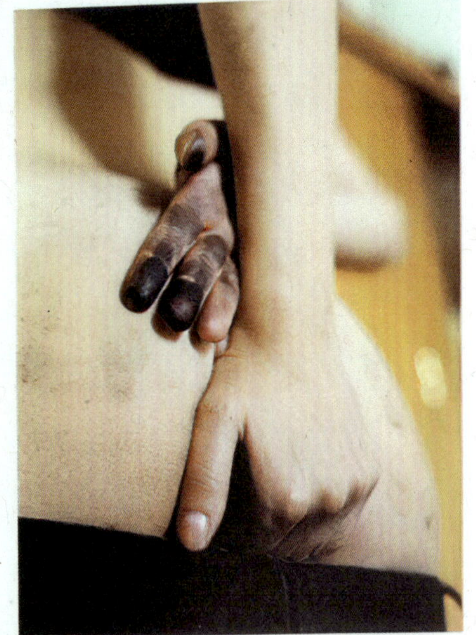

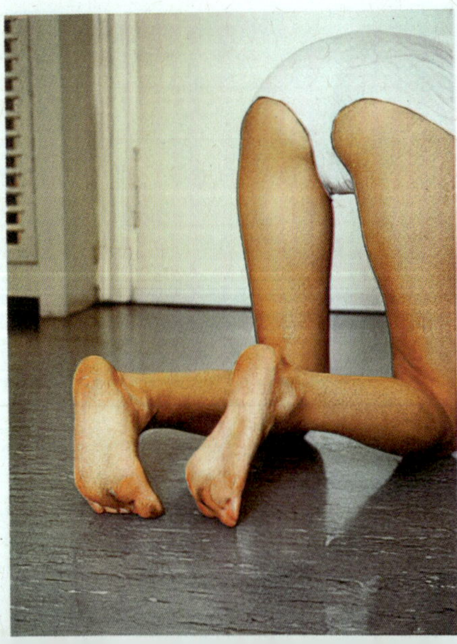

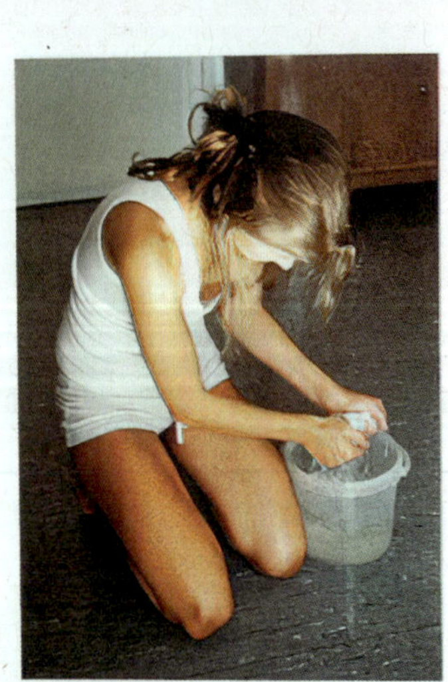

165 → THE OPERA ANNIVERSARY ISSUE – BEST OF CLASSIC & CONTEMPORARY NUDE PHOTOGRAPHY, Matthias Straub (ed.), Kerber Verlag, 2022, 320 pp., 24 × 31cm, **(↦ see № 114, 152 & 174)**
Thomas Sing (Artwork)

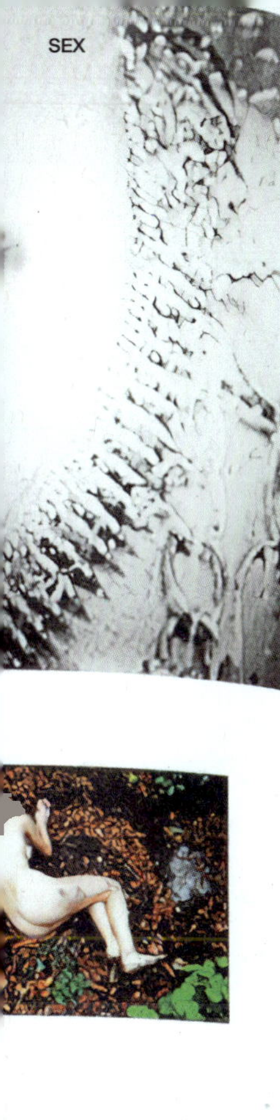

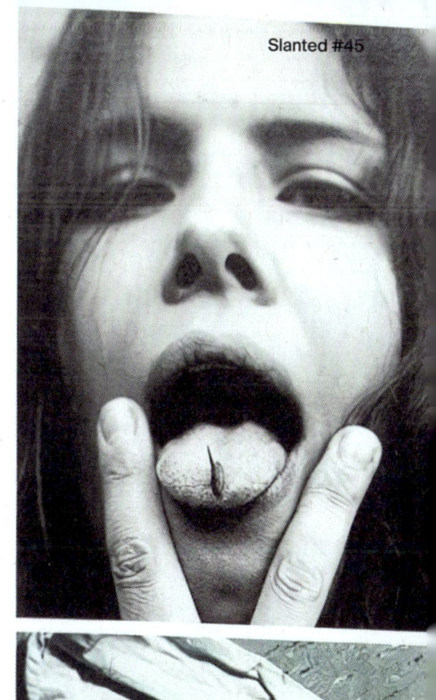

Madita in the shower, 2023

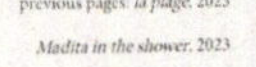

previous pages: *la plage*, 2023

Madita in the shower, 2023

6

Sophie underwater, 2023

25

168 → ZINE, Lina-Marie Ritthammer, 2024, 28 pp., 21 x 15 cm, **(→ see № 106)**
Sophie Underwater, 2023

(Thomas Sing)
ctures were originally shot for my 3rd photo
. "Liminal", which has been photographed
ore than a year in 3 different countries with
Teresa Del Sole. The whole book explores
spaces of the body and the mind, a dimension
nothing is fixed and anything is possible
could say it is where life really takes place.
inal step in the project, this series was shot in
studio with special high speed techniques
ate multilayered effects in camera. It is an
ation to consider how we are not one fixed
ut rather a multiplicity constantly rearrang
g itself, and in this multiplicity lies our
ity to connect with the world around and
within us.

167 → THE OPÉRA VOLUME XI. THE PHOENIX ISSUE, Matthias Straub (ed.), Kerber Verlag, 2022, 224 pp., 24 × 31 cm, **(↦ see № 104, 153 & 168)**
Thomas Sing (Artwork)

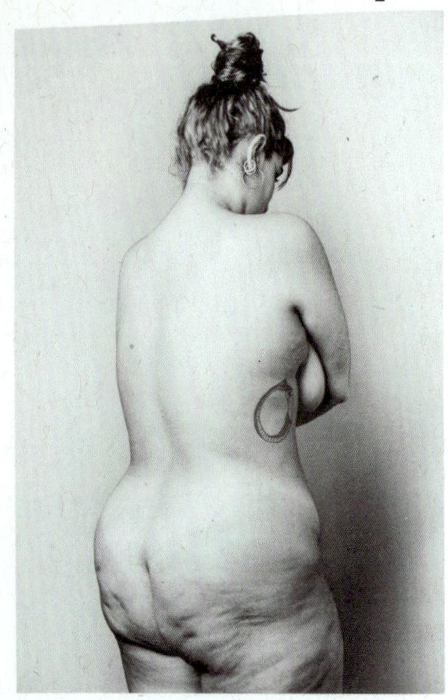

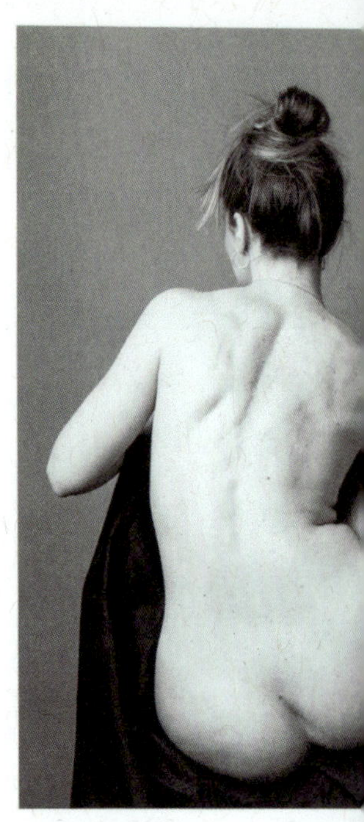

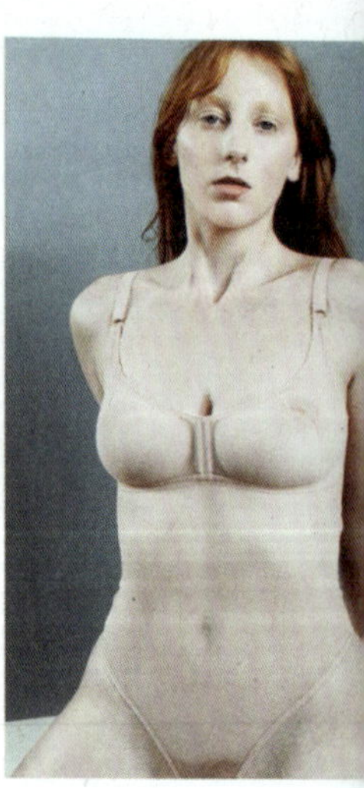

168 → THE OPERA VOLUME XI. THE PHOENIX ISSUE, Matthias Straub (ed.), Kerber Verlag, 2022, 224 pp., 24 × 31 cm, (→ see 11–104, 153 & 167) Camila Asaf (Artwork)
Ginger, Bruno Clement

169 → AUS DEM RAHMEN GEFALLEN, Ursula Scherrer, 2020, 72.5 x 72.5 cm, Flo Kaufmann (Photography)

170 → RICHARD KERN POLAROIDS, Art Paper Editions, 2023, 176 pp., 22 x 30 cm (→ see N°-092 & 162)

171 → MULIERIS MAGAZINE ISSUE 4 – BELT OF VENUS, Greta Futura Langianni (ed.), Mulieris, 2022, 224 pp., 16.8 × 23.7 cm (↦ see № 101, 173, 191, 192 & 221)

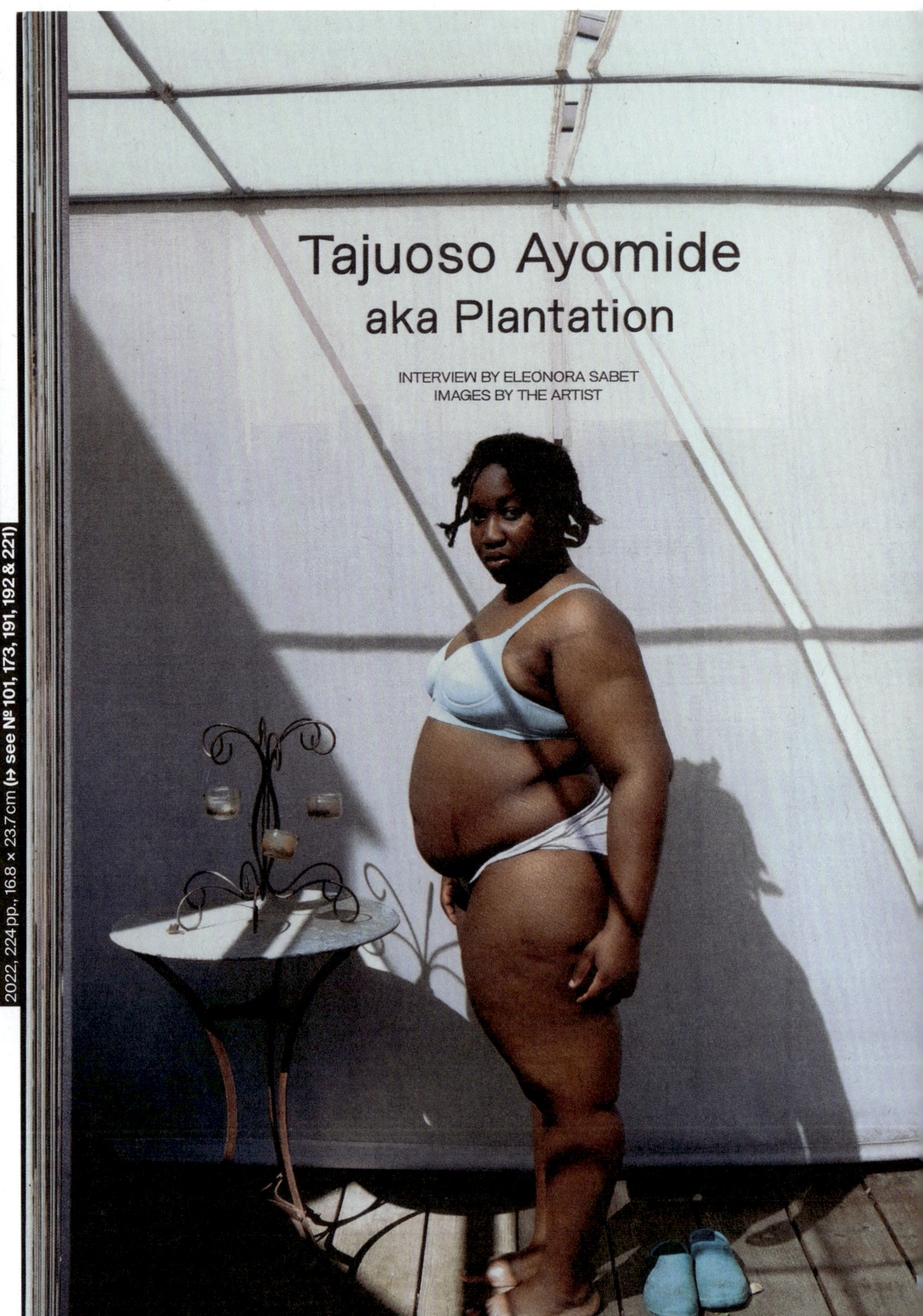

172→181, Art Paper Editions, 2024, 48pp., 23 x 30cm [→ see N° 012]

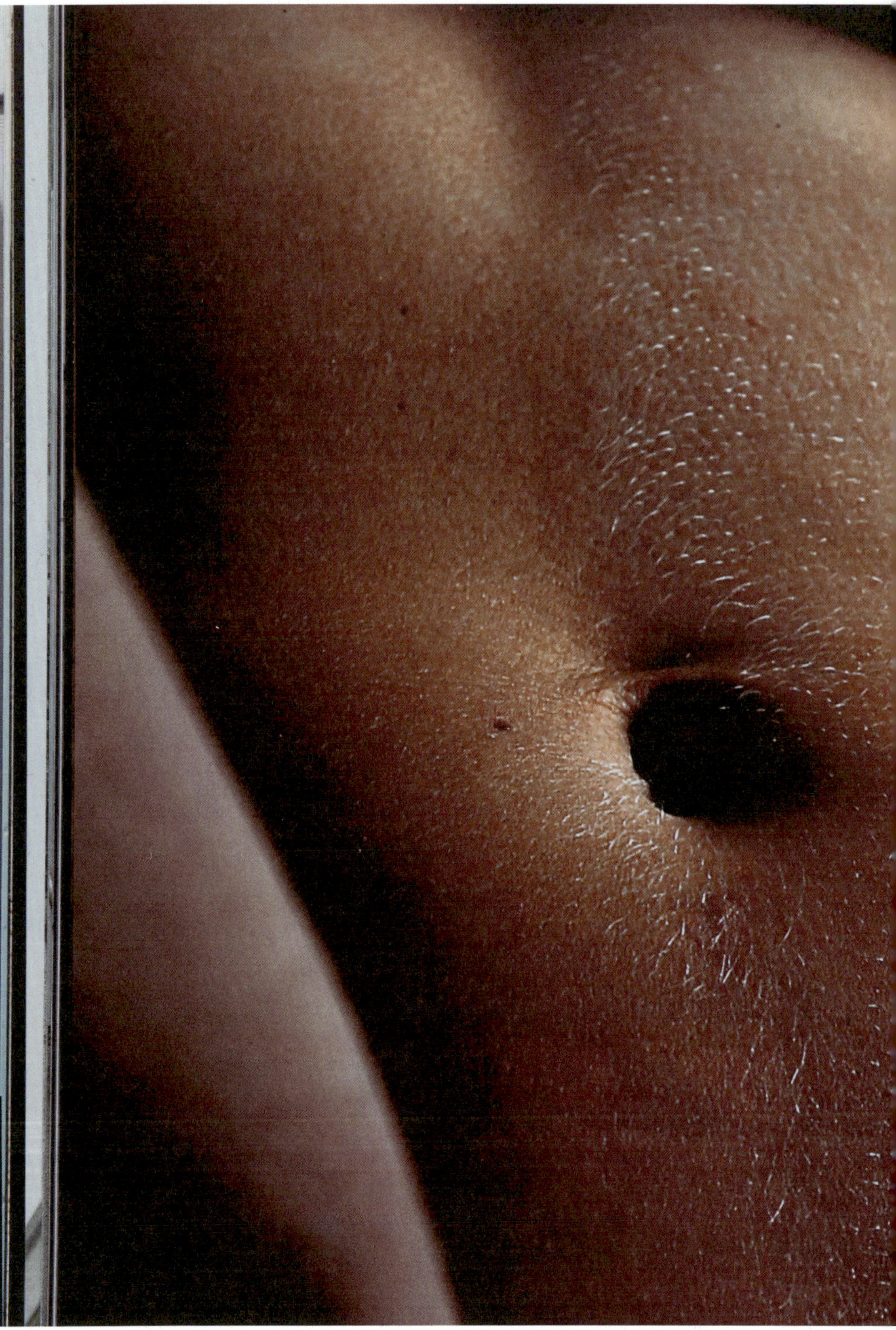

173 → **MULIERIS MAGAZINE ISSUE 4 – BELT OF VENUS,** Greta Futura Langianni (ed.), Mulieris, 2022, 224 pp., 16.8 x 23.7 cm (→ see N° 101, 171, 191, 192 & 221)
Sara Scanderebech (Artwork)

174 → THE OPERA ANNIVERSARY ISSUE – BEST OF CLASSIC & CONTEMPORARY NUDE PHOTOGRAPHY, Matthias Straub (ed.),Kerber Verlag, 2022, 320 pp., 24 × 31 cm, (↦ see № 114, 152 & 165)
Manon Ouimet (Artwork)

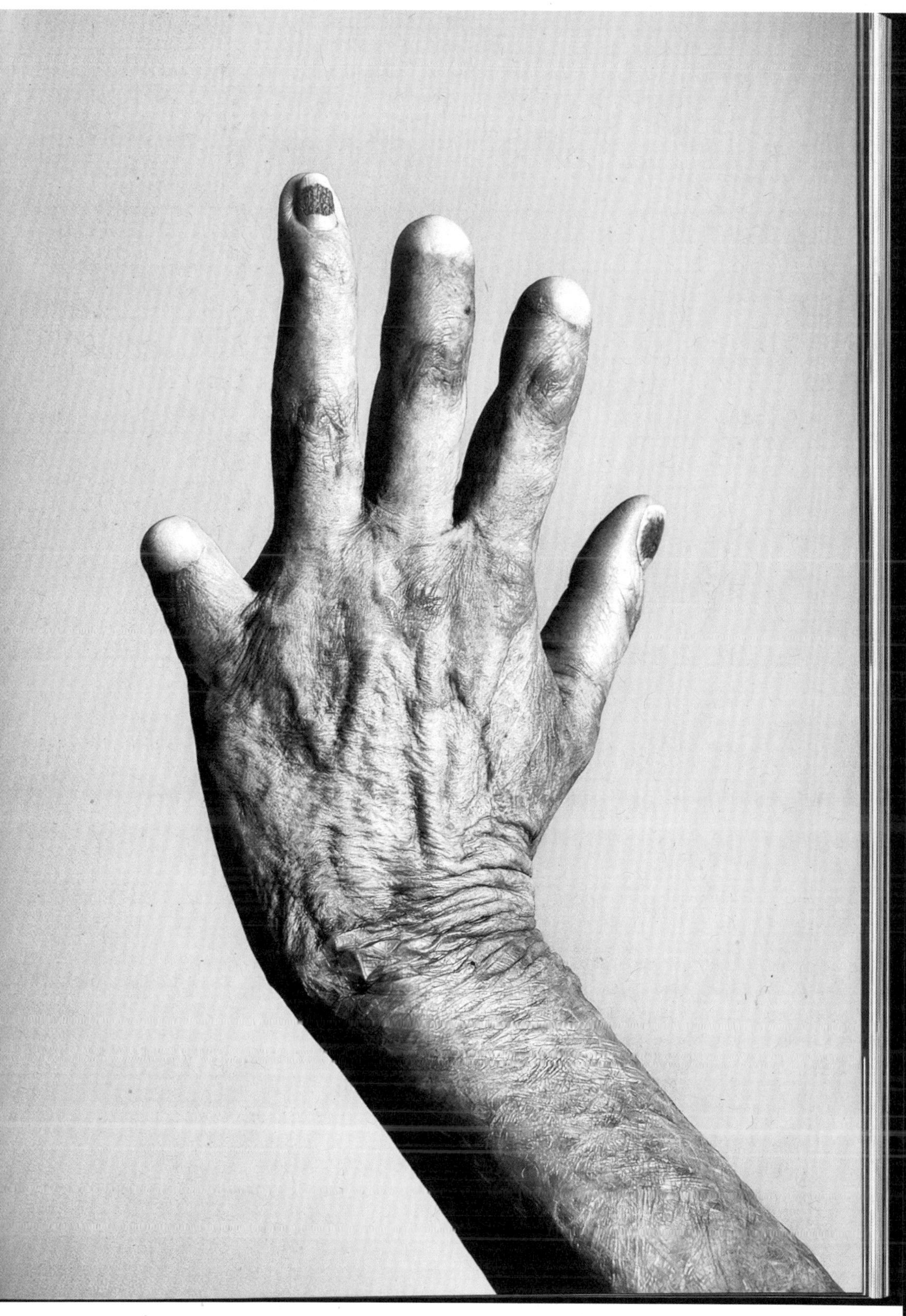

175 → LOST OPFER, Volker Derlath, Buchendorfer Verlag, 2002, 78pp., 30.5 x 24.5cm (→ see N°015)

Du
bist
mein
Traum

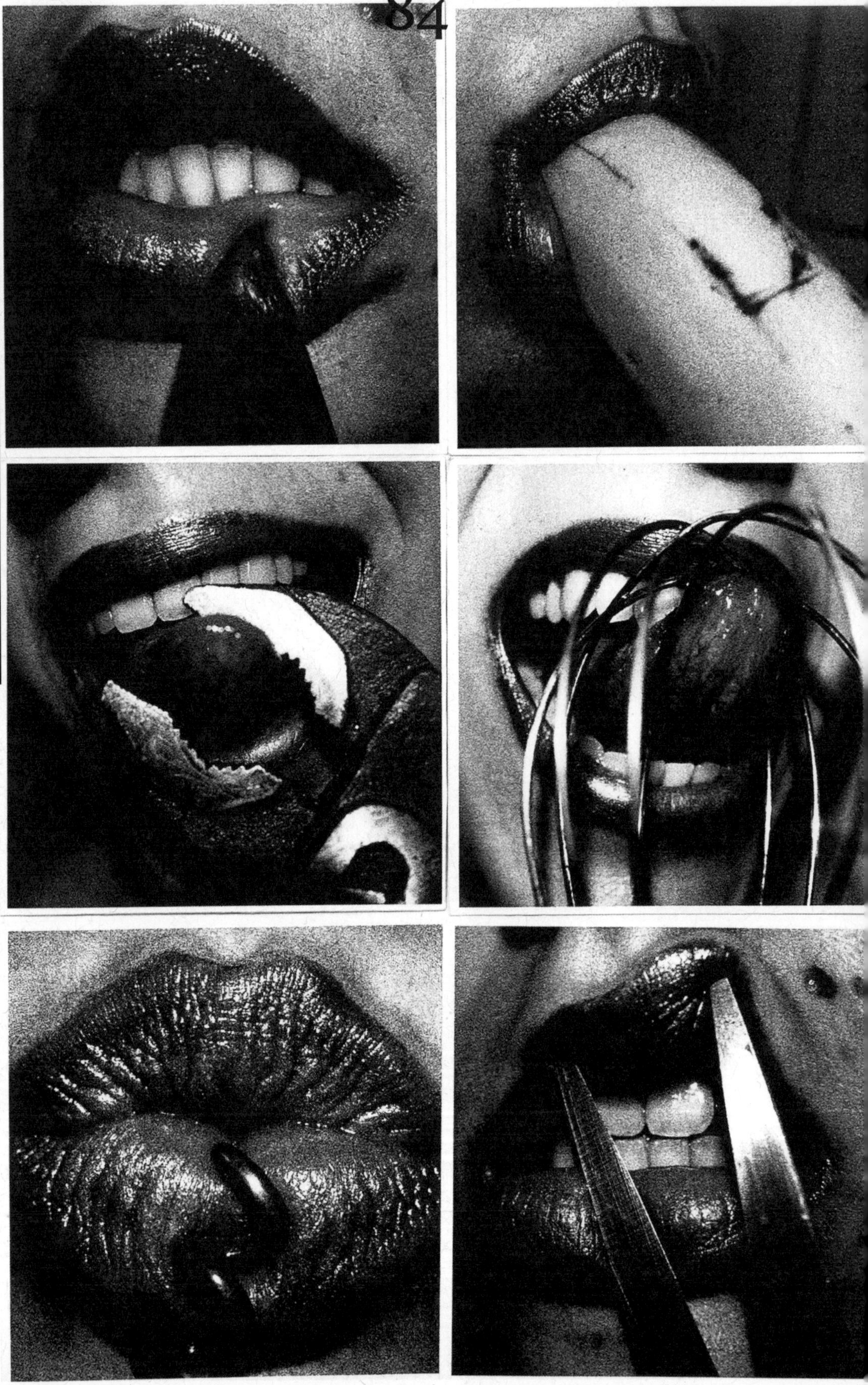

176 → X FILES, Stephanie Falcione, 2023, 0.75 x 0.75cm (→ see N° 089)

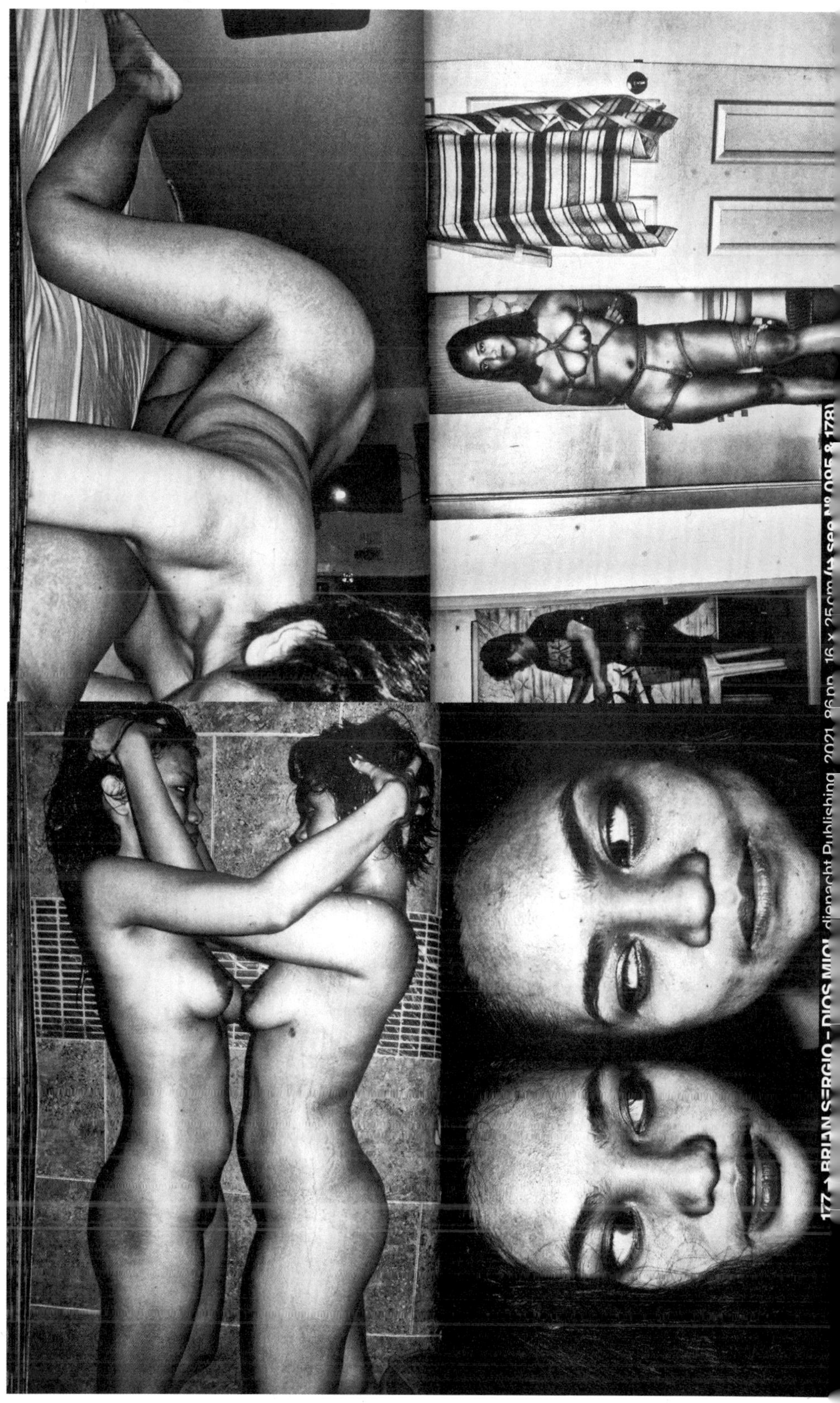

177 → BRIAN SERGIO – DIOS MIO | diepacht Publishing, 2021, 86 pp, 16 x 25 cm (→ see N° 095 & 178)

178 • BRIAN SERGIO – DIOS MIO!, dienacht Publishing, 2021, 86 pp, 16 x 25 cm (↳ see Nº 095 & 177)

180 / THE COMPLETE COLLECTION OF NUDISTS, Gerhard Theewen, Salon Verlag im Verlag Kretschmer & Großmann, 1982, 160 pp., 14.8 x 21cm (→ see N-070 & 182)

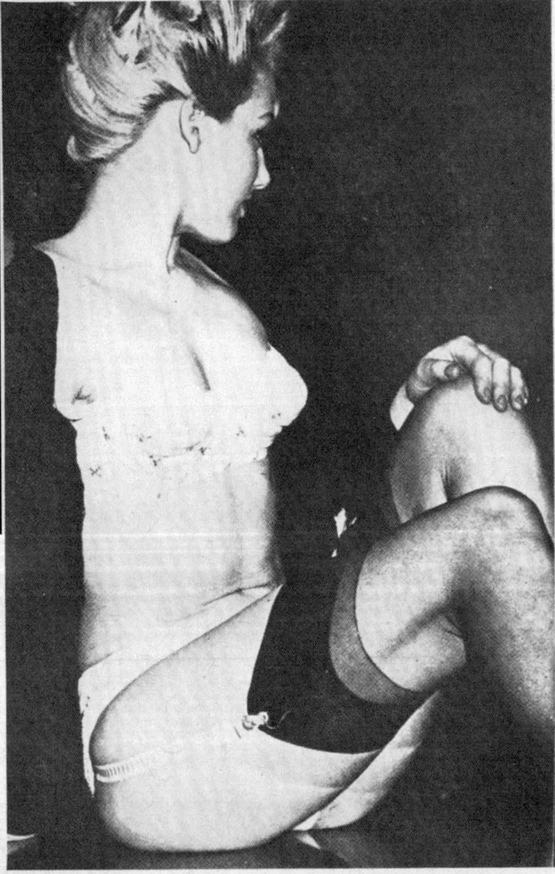

161 → THE COMPLETE COLLECTION OF PIN-UPS, Gerhard Theewen, Salon Verlag im Verlag Kretschmer & Großmann, 1981, 160pp., 14.8 x 21cm

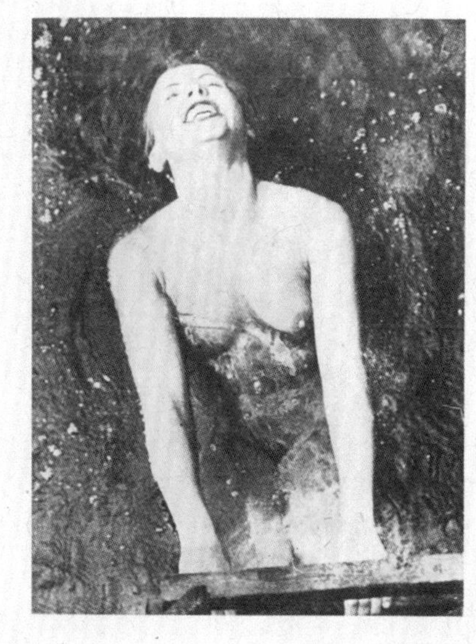

182 THE COMPLETE COLLECTION OF NUDISTS, Gerhard Theewen, Salon Verlag im Verlag Kretschmer & Großmann 1982, 160 pp, 14.8 x 21 cm (see № 070 & 180)

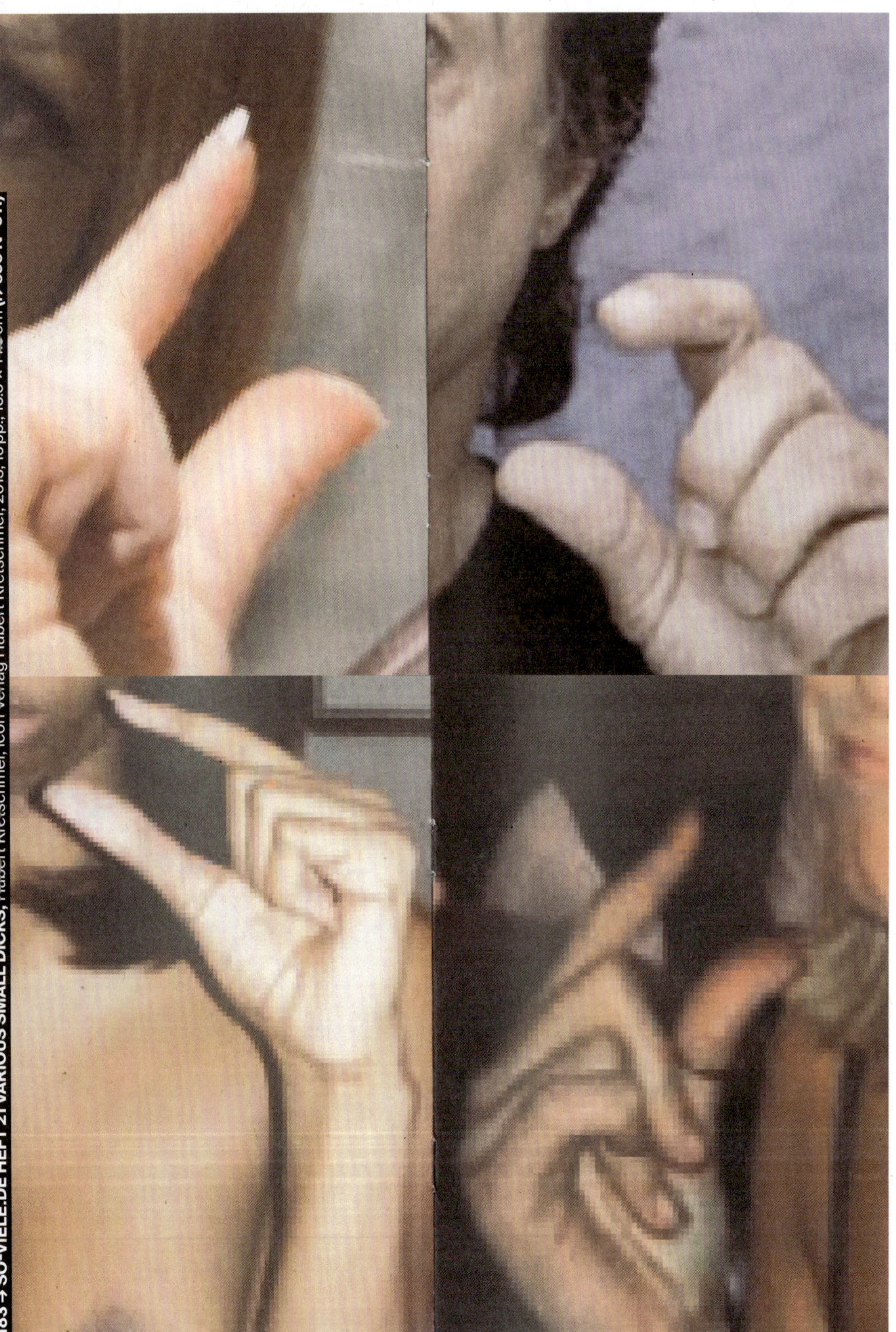

183 → SO-VIELE.DE HEFT 21 VARIOUS SMALL DICKS, Hubert Kretschmer, Icon Verlag Hubert Kretschmer, 2015, 16pp,

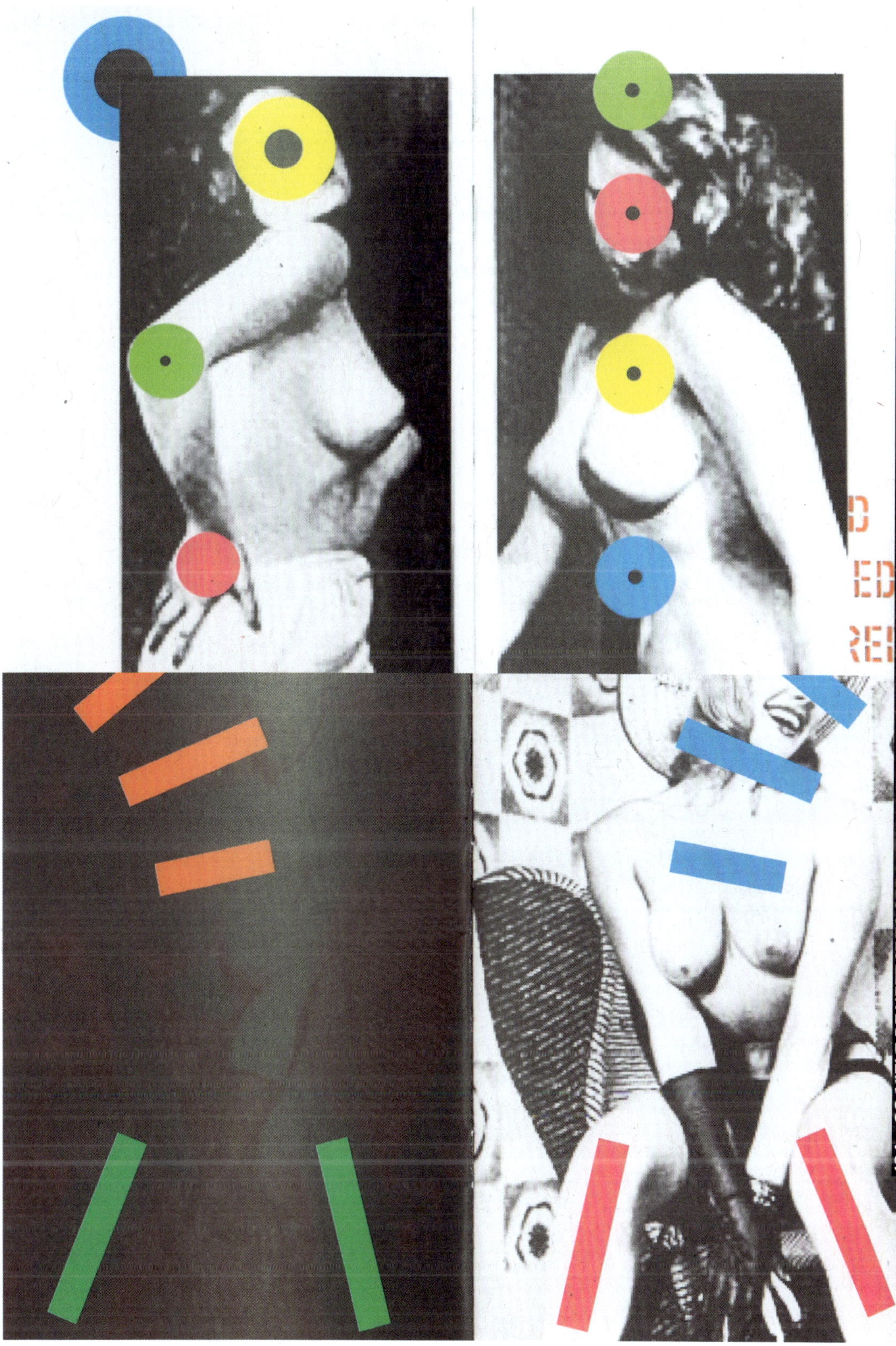

184 / SO VIELE DE HEFT 27 TO SEE AND NOT TO SEE, Hubert Kretschmer, icon Verlag Hubert Kretschmer 2014, 16 pp, 10.5 x 14.5cm

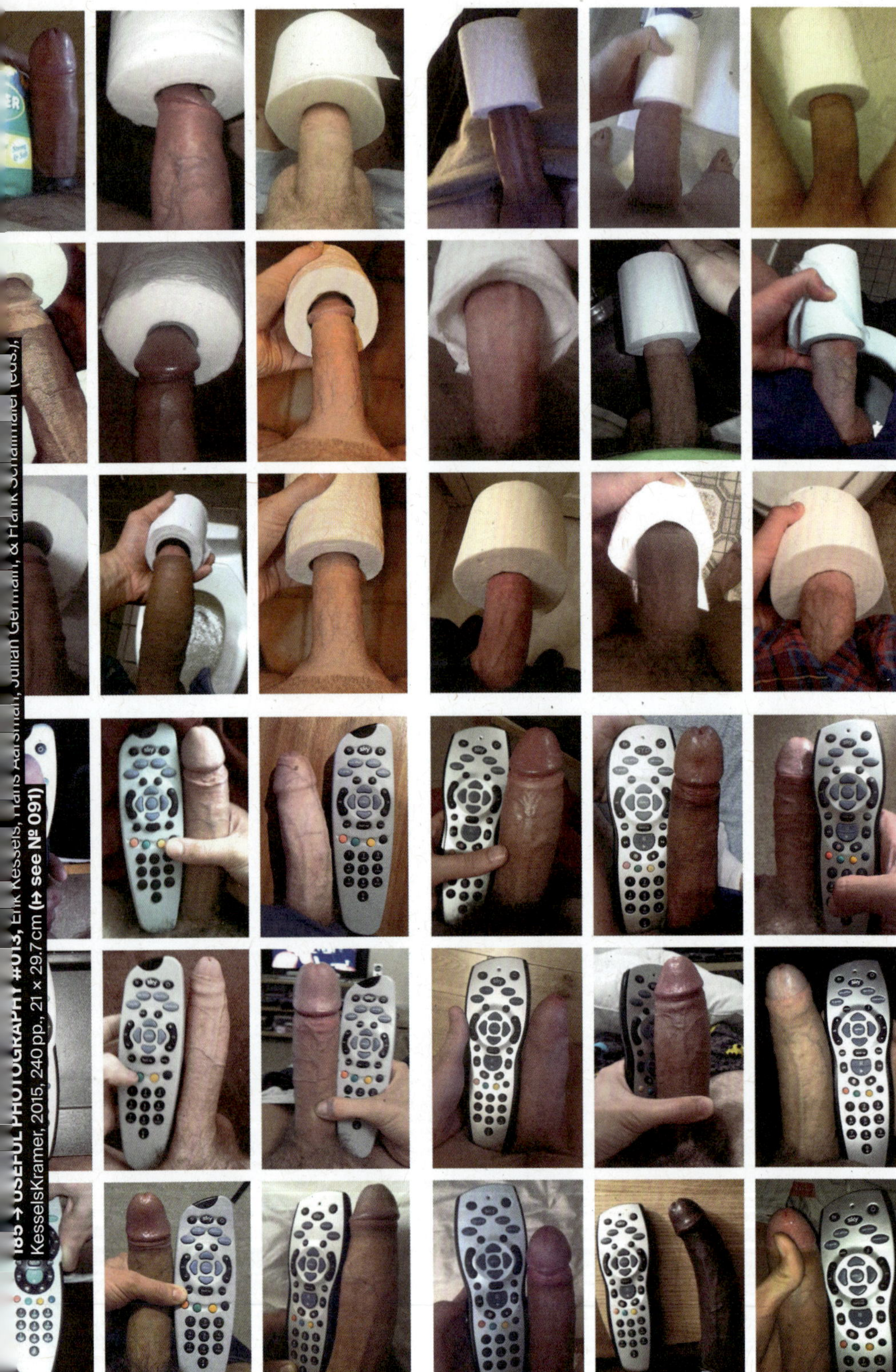

185 → USEFUL PHOTOGRAPHY #013, Erik Kessels, Hans Aarsman, Julian Germain, & Frank Schallmaier (eds.), KesselsKramer, 2015, 240 pp., 21 × 29.7 cm **(↦ see Nº 091)**

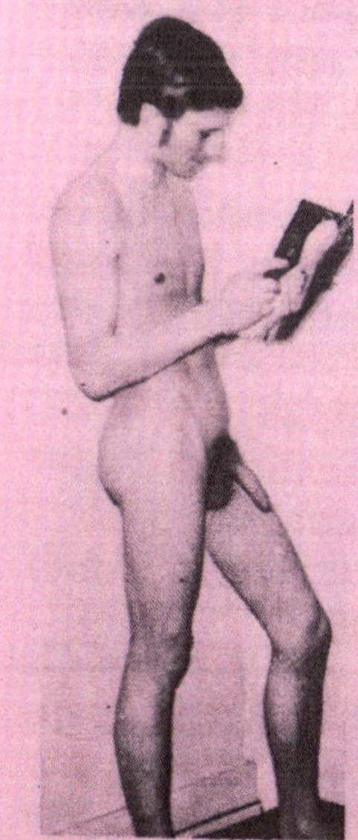

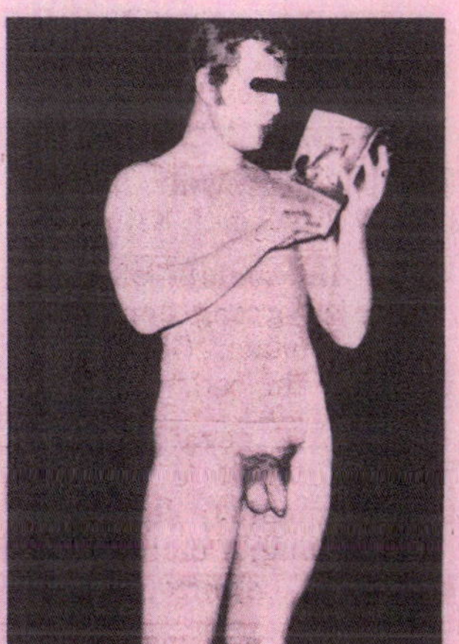

186 ↘ READ NAKED Erik Kessels Skinnerboox 2019 148 pp 16 x 24 cm (↳ see № [illegible])

187 → (S)EXPLORATION TIMES, Maya Walthon, 2022, 28 pp., 35 x 50 cm (→ see N° 146, 150 & 217)

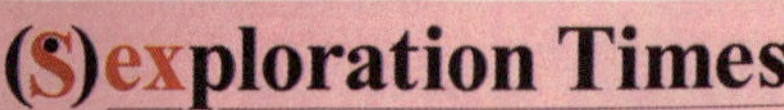

(S)exploration Times

On Consent

Eine Simple Shibari Fesselung

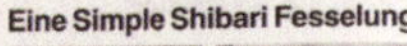

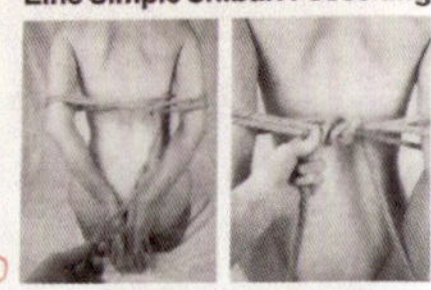

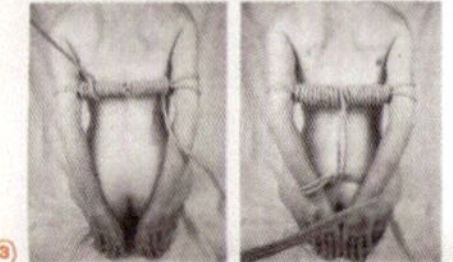

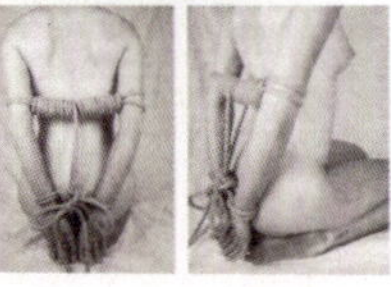

Suspension

Shibari

Anleitung:

12

(S)exploration Times

Lets talk about sex, baby.

Was

2

Sextalk Section

Lets talk about sex, Girls.

Oder die Entstehung des (S)Exploration Clubs.

Aphrodisierende Plätzchen, Schätzchen

Die Vorbereitung auf das Erste Meeting

3

189 → GARAGE MAGAZINE NO. 1, Dasha Zhukova (ed.), garagemag, 2011, 274 pp., 26 × 34.2 cm **(↦ see Nº 116 & 149)** Optiv Fiber, Ding Yilaqan & Margherita Missioni (Artwork)

188 → OUTSIDE THE BOX – HAAR, Silke Jaspers & Ludmilla Bartscht (eds.), ILLU Freiburg e.V., 2024, 24 pp., 15 × 21 cm, riso print **(↦ see Nº 059)** Elena Bal-es (Illustration)

191 → MULIERIS MAGAZINE ISSUE 4 – BELT OF VENUS, Greta Futura Langianni (ed.), Mulieris, 2022, 224 pp., 16.8 × 23.7 cm, **(↦ see № 101, 171, 173, 192 & 221)**
X IV & X X, Vivian Greven (Artsit), Ivo Faber (Photos), Laura Rositani (Interview)

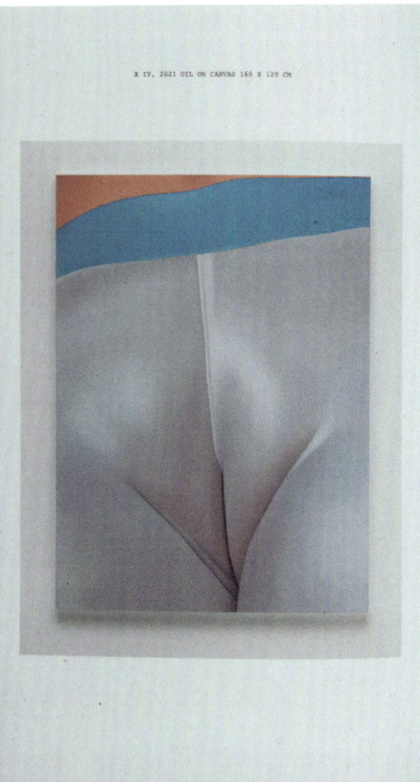

190 → EROTIC REVIEW ISSUE 2, Lucy Roeber & Saskia Vogel, (eds.), 2024, 168 pp., 17 × 24 cm, Litho Print **(↦ see № 029, 193 & 218)**
Peresphone & Peresphone and Demeter, Marie Howe

192 → MULIERIS MAGAZINE ISSUE 4 – BELT OF VENUS, Greta Futura Langianni (ed.), Mulieris, 2022, 224 pp., 16.8 × 23.7 cm **(↳ see № 101, 171, 173, 191 & 221)**
XII Vivian Greven (Artsit), Ivo Faber (Photo)

Point of Entry (Lingam Between Teal Circles), Loie Hollowell (2017)

193 → EROTIC REVIEW ISSUE 2, Lucy Roeber & Saskia Vogel, (eds.), 2024, 168 pp., 17 × 24 cm, Litho Print **(↦ see № 029, 190 & 218)**

Full-Bodied, Loie Hollowell (2024)

Incoming Tide, Lois Hollowell (2016)

194 → STELLUNGEN, Jesper Fabricius, Lubok Verlag, 2011, 24pp., 14.8 x 21cm (→ see N°121 & 159)

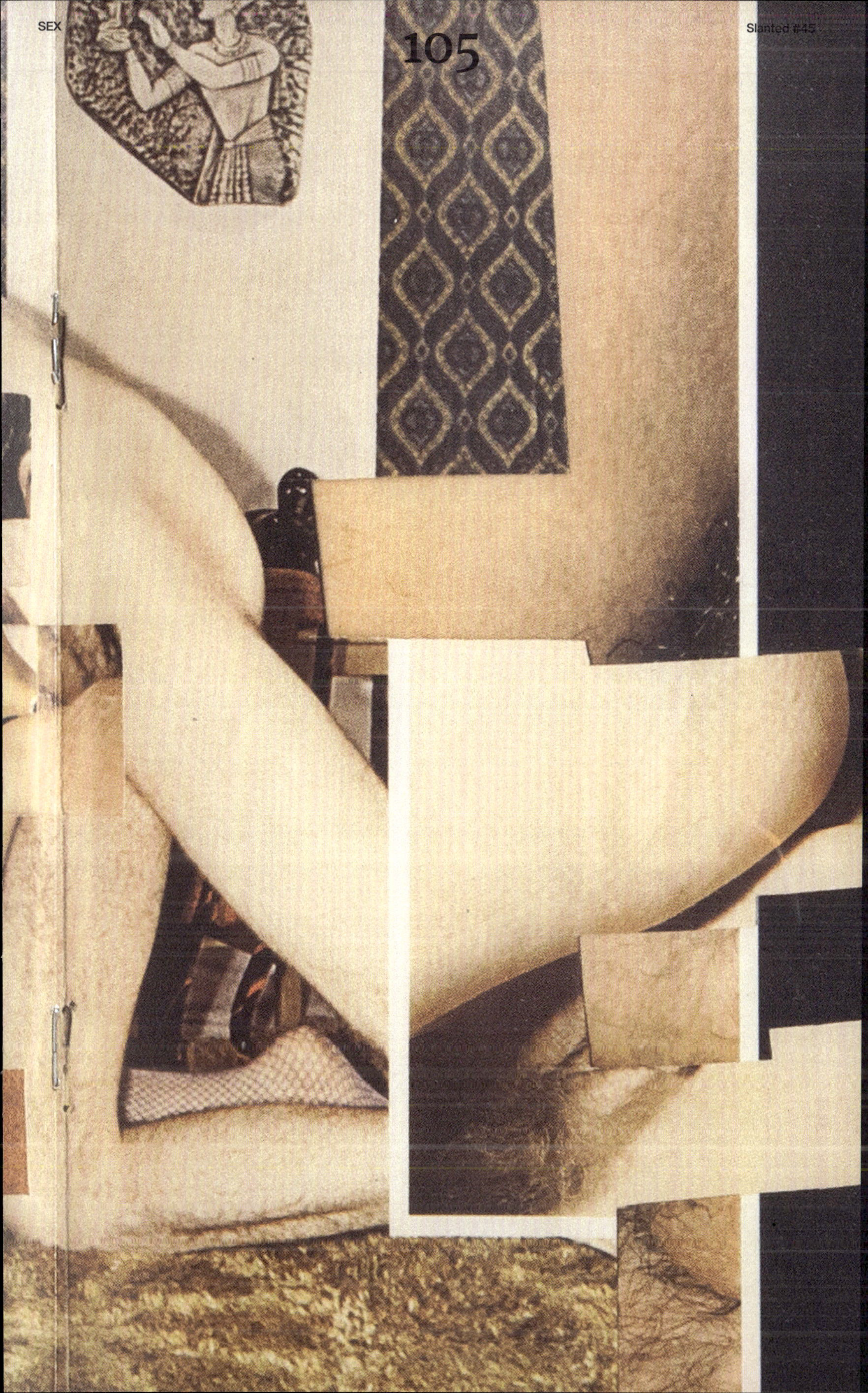

195 → STELLUNGEN, Jesper Fabricius, Lucky Verlag, 2011, 24pp., 14.8 x 21cm (→ see N° 121 & 194)

197 → MOAN ZINE ISSUE 4, Moan, 2023, 94 pp., 13 × 18 cm, riso print by Dizzy Ink **(↦ see № 198)**

196 → MOAN ZINE ISSUE 5, Moan, 2024, 98 pp., 13 × 18 cm, riso print by Dizzy Ink **(↦ see № 133 & 164)**

198 → MOAN ZINE ISSUE 4, Moan, 2023, 94 pp., 13 x 18 cm, riso print by Dizzy Ink (→ see № 197)
"Adults can play, too," Alice Ní Conchobhair (Photography), Byela (Nail Collaboration)

199 → POSTERS FOR CASANOVA LOVE AND EROTIC FESTIVAL IN VRSAR, Studio Sonda, 70.7 × 100 cm, Jelena Fiskus & Sean Poropat (Creative Direction), Aleksandar Živanov (Design & Illustration)

Paris, Ser Serpas
154

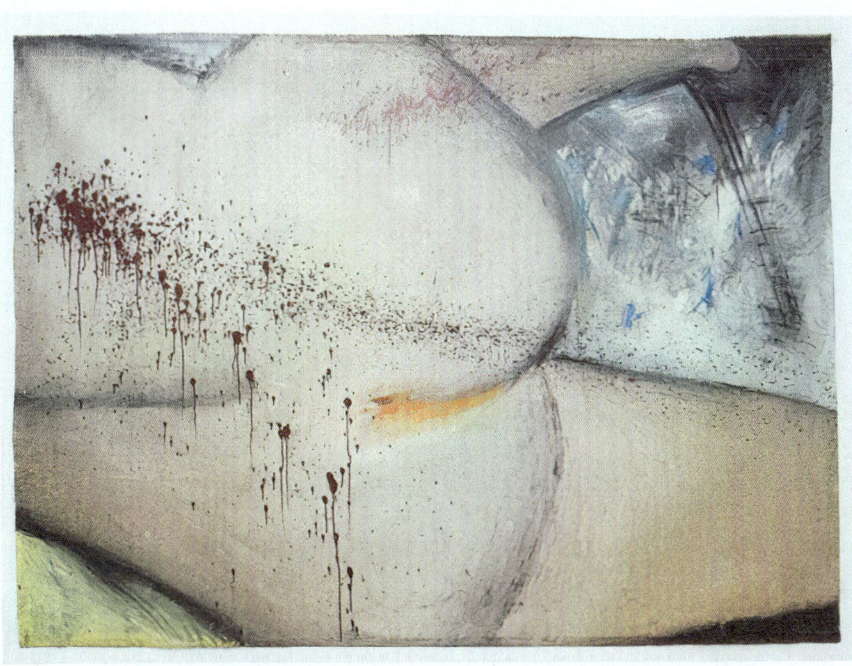

Ser Serpas

201 → B.L.A.D. HEROES II NO.11, Fett Burger, Sex Tags & Blank Blank, 2013, 52 pp., 9.5 × 13.5 cm
(↦ see Nº 016 & 204)

202 → MINI ZINE – NEEDLER, Mike Diana, Re:Surgo!, 2014, 16 pp, 10.8 x 14.8 cm, screen print

203 | LIEBESLEXIKON, Foris Hickmann, Martin Conrads, Franziska Monok, Verlag Hermann Schmidt Mainz, 2016, 64 pp., 10.7 x 15cm

L

Lecken, das: bei Säugetieren ist ein in der Mundhöhle liegender, schleimhäutiger, länglicher Muskelkörper – die Zunge – ein elementares Sinnesorgan mit einer hohen Dichte an Nervenzellen. Das gegenseitige Durchspeicheln dieses Muskelkörpers ist eine bei Menschen praktizierte Liebkosungsform, die sich – je nach Intensität der Zusammenkunft – auf weitere Körperregionen ausdehnen kann.

Libido, die: wird als der Trieb bezeichnet, der eine sexuelle Befriedigung zum Ziel hat und bei Menschen wie bei Tieren vorkommt. Aphrodisiaka sind Mittel zur Steigerung der Libido und finden sich bereits in der Antike. Da der Hirsch zur Brunftzeit einen besonders ausgeprägten Sexualtrieb hat, wurde dem Hirschgeweih oder auch dem Hirschhoden eine aphrodisierende Wirkung nachgesagt. Durch diese Hilfsmittel wurde auch die menschliche Begattung sichergestellt.

Liebeskummer, der: (veraltet: *Herzeleid*) bezeichnet jene psychischen oder psychosomatischen Schmerzen, welche bei Zurückweisung durch eine geliebte Person oder andere Formen von Unerfüllbarkeit einer angestrebten Liebesbeziehung auftreten können.

Liebesschloss-Ständer, der: eine amtlich aufgestellte, freistehende Vorrichtung, an der Liebende Vorhängeschlösser als Symbol ihrer Liebe anbringen sollen: häufig auf Brücken oder Aussichtspunkten zu finden. Fragwürdiger Versuch zum Schutz dortiger Geländer vor Einsturz und Korrosionsschäden.

Groupie, das: etwas mehr als ein Fan, etwas weniger als ein *Stalker*, schwebt das G. knapp unter dem Limit der Illegalität. Hinterhertouren und alles sammeln, was von seiner Ikone stammt oder über sie geschrieben wird, gehört für das G. zum Tages- und Nachtprogramm. Nach Konzerten, Reden oder Ausstellungen (je nach Fachbereich der Ikone) versucht das G., mit dem Künstler, Musiker, Politiker oder Star in oft auch sexuellen Kontakt zu kommen.

Großzügigkeit, die: bezeichnet als charakterliche Qualität einer Person die Freude daran, anderen eine Freude zu machen, und nicht zu erwarten, im Gegenzug etwas zu erhalten. Weitaus tiefgründiger als der ökonomisch gedachte Geschenkaustausch, zeichnet sich die G. dadurch aus, dass man versucht, seinen Mitmenschen etwas Größeres als sich selbst zu bieten.

Gruppensex, der: Sexualpraktik, bei der mehr als zwei Partner beteiligt sind. Zum G. als Form der gemeinschaftlichen sexuellen Vereinigung zählen der auch als *Ménage-à-trois* bekannte Dreier sowie Orgien, Bukkake, Gangbang, Reverse Gangbang oder Blowbang. Keine Bedingung, aber eine gute Voraussetzung für sexuelles Gruppenverhalten ist die Polyamorie, da es bei monogamen Paaren durch Partnertausch zu Eifersucht oder emotionaler Umorientierung kommen kann.

205 → **MINI ZINE – HOCKNEY ON STELLA,** Too Bob, Re:Surgo!, 2015, 16 pp., 10.9 x 14.7 cm, screen print **(↦ see № 055)**

204 → B.L.A.D. HEROES II NO.1, Fett Burger, Sex Tags & Blank Blank, 2013, 52 pp., 9.5 x 13.5 cm **(↦ see № 016 & 201)**

206 → MASTER FLAME, Patrick Rieve, Bone Response Publications, 2015, 8pp., 17 x 10cm (→ see N-0371)

WAS REDE ICH DA?

GIB MIR

PLEASE ME GIVE ME

HAK IHN AB WIE EINEN TERMIN!

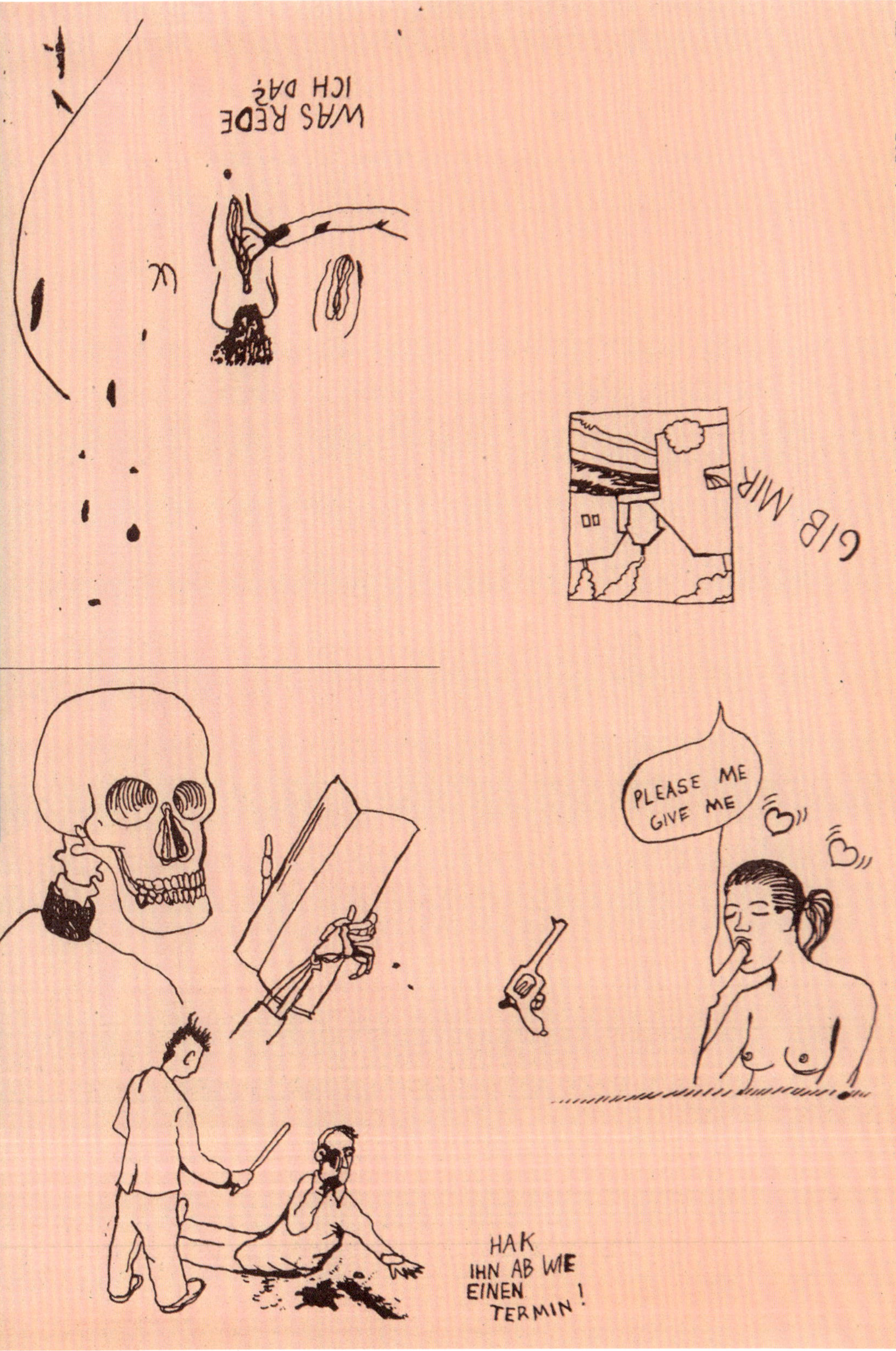

207 ↑ MINI ZINE – FRANCIS BACON ON MUSHROOMS, Fuzz Chriss, Re:Surgel, 2019, 16 pp, 10.8 x 14.8 cm, screen print (↓ see № 050)

209 → **SPRING #16 SEX,** Mairisch Verlag, 2019, 256 pp., 20 × 24 cm, neon print, (↦ see Nº 048)
Stephanie Wunderlich (Illustration)

DAS MUTTERMAL AUF MEINER BRUST SIEHT AUS WIE EINE NACKTE FRAU.

208 → **SPRING #12 PRIVEE,** Mairisch Verlag, 2015, 200 pp., 24 × 20 cm, **(↦ see Nº 049 & 210)**
Katrin Stangl (Illustration)

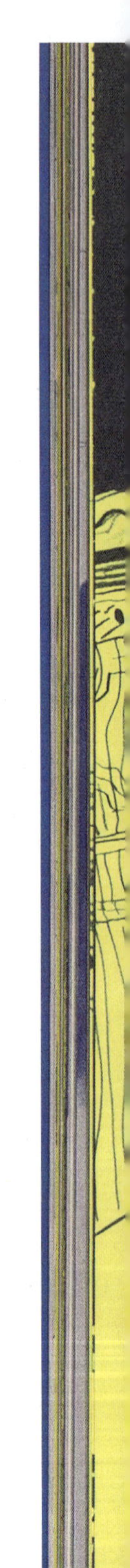

210 → SPRING #12 – PRIVÉE, Mairisch Verlag, 2015, 200 pp., 24 × 20 cm **(↦ see Nº 049 & 208),**
Ulli Lust (Illustration)

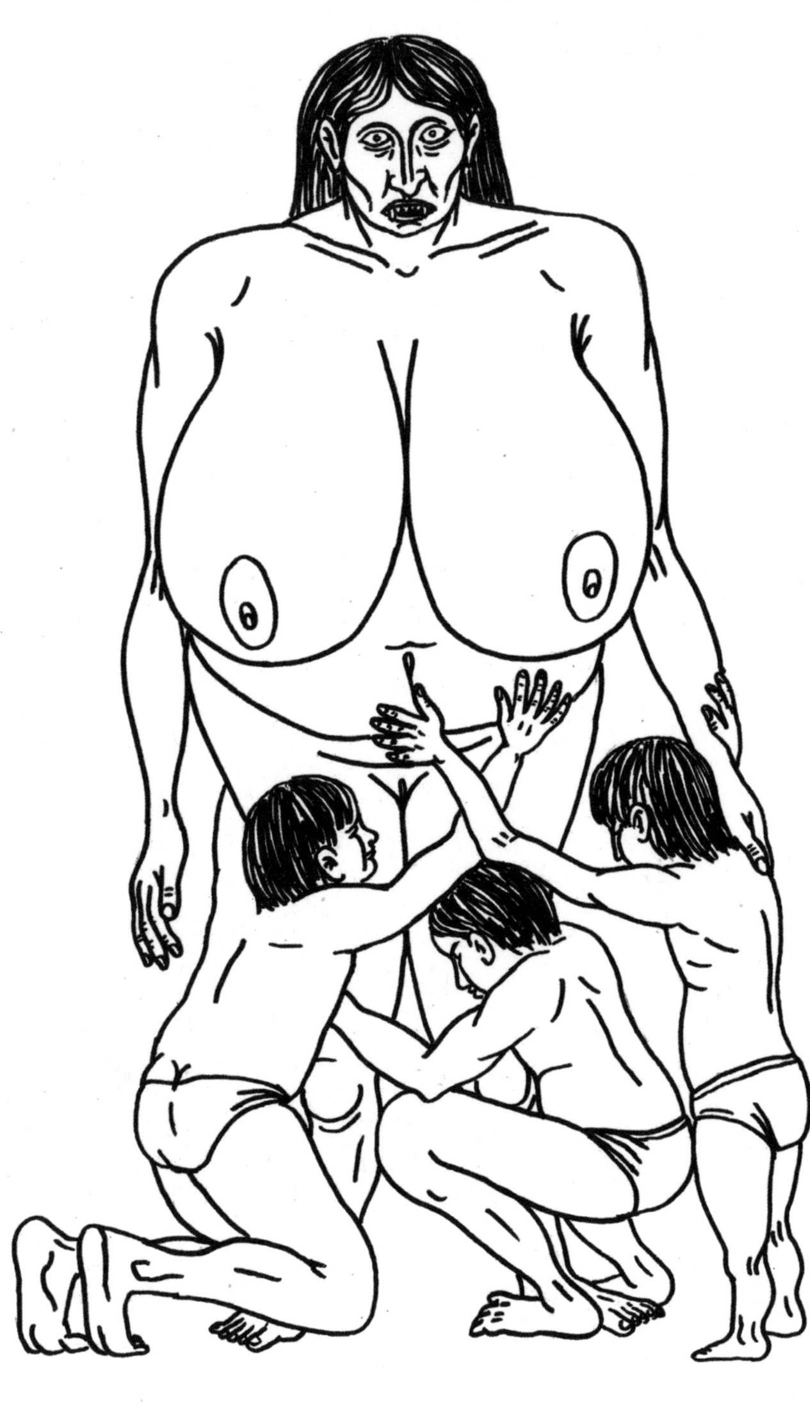

2H – 100FOR10 – 101 MAGICAL MOVEMENTS – EDITION NO. 052, Mono… 10, Melville Brand Design, 2017, 100 pp., 14.8 x 21 cm (→ see N° 058)

212 \ VON VORNE IS AUCH ALLES SCHICK Franziska Schaum Re:Surgel 2011 20pp 12 x 23cm (LSQ № 036)

213 → 100PORTO – NOTHING TASTES QUITE LIKE IT – EDITION NO. 070, Simon Lohmeyer, Melville Brand Design, 2018, 168pp., 148 x 210mm

Transexual feels right, if I have to define my individual trans I am hairier and between my legs smells different. Things that used to send me under for days I can now brush off. Is this chemical or the first time I am at ease?

Artwork by Nicholas (he/him) @nicosulliam

Work by Robin (they/he)

214 → STRAP ISSUE 1, Ben Saunders, 2023, 208 pp., 21 × 29.7 cm (↦ see Nº 099)

SEX AND EVERYDAY LIVING

www.fluffereveryday.com

113/500

215 → FLUFFER EVERYDAY ISSUE NO. 6, Sofia Trechas (ed.), Fluffer Everyday, 2024, 64 pp., 21 x 28.4 cm (→ see № 118)

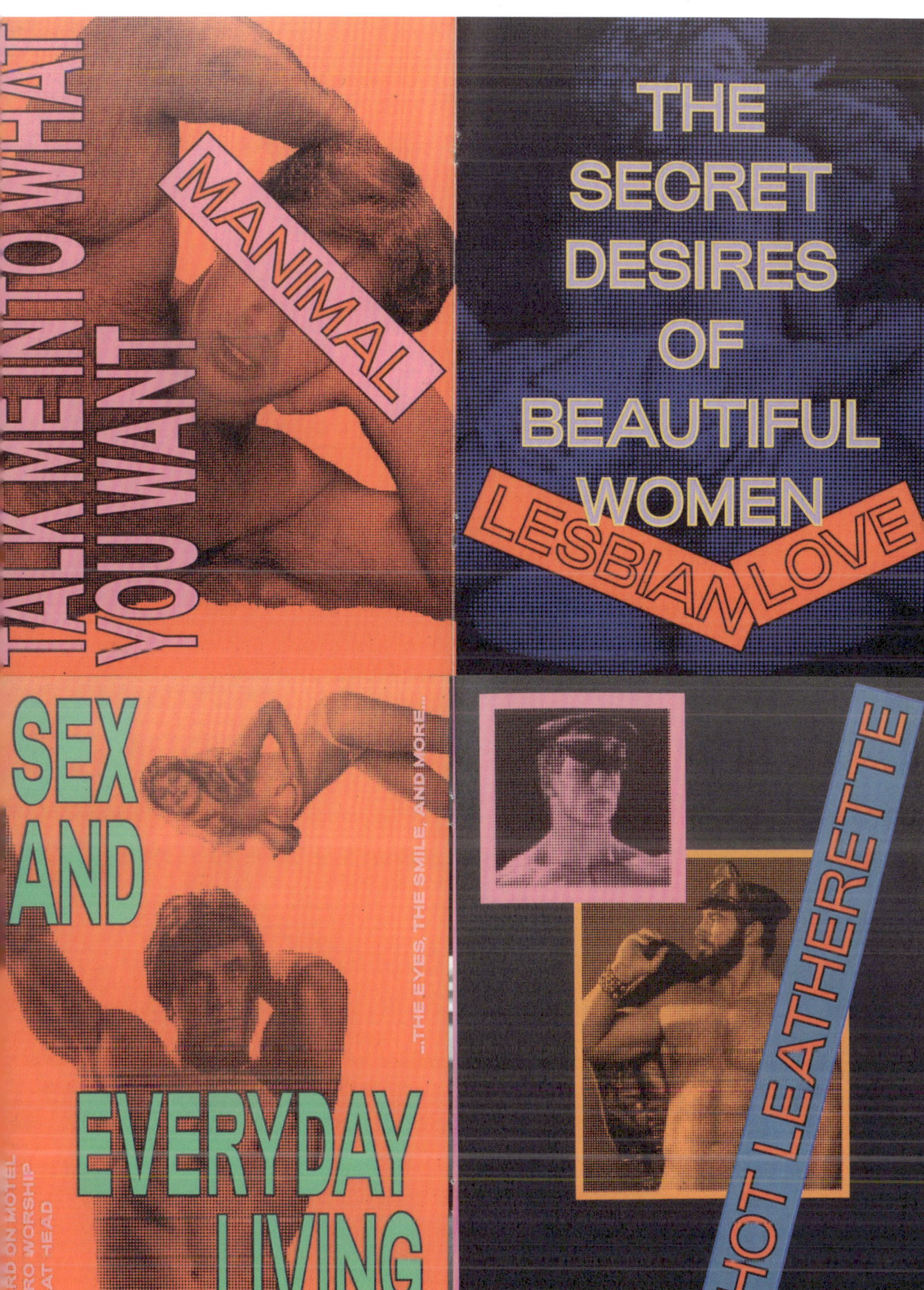
TALK ME INTO WHAT
YOU WANT
MANIMAL
THE SECRET DESIRES OF BEAUTIFUL WOMEN
LESBIAN
LOVE
SEX
AND
EVERYDAY
LIVING
...THE EYES, THE SMILE, AND MORE...
HARD ON MOTEL
HERO WORSHIP
MEAT HEAD
HOT LEATHERETTE

I want
a president
that had
an abortion
at sixteen
and

I want a
candidate
who isn't
the lesser
of two
evils

I want
a person
with
aids for
president

and I
want
a fag for
vice
president

216 → I WANT A PRESIDENT, Zoe Leonard, Gato Negro Ediciones, 2017, 32 pp., 8.5 x 10.5 cm, 1150 print (→ see N-062)

HOPP HOPP, GO PEE AFTER SEX, BABY.

217 (S)EXPLORATION TIMES Maya Warthon 2022 28pp 35 × 50cm (→ see № 146, 150 & 187)

218 → **EROTIC REVIEW ISSUE 2**, Lucy Roeber & Saskia Vogel (eds.), 2024, 168 pp., 17 x 24 cm, litho print (→ see N-029, 190 & 195)

Erotic Review

ART

Introductory essay by guest art curator, Enuma Okoro

Loie Hollowell Yulia Mahr Firelei Báez
Ana Prvački

POETRY

Juliana Huxtable

Marie Howe

Carmen Sànchez Ramos
trans. Judith Kerman

Margaret Ross

SHORT

I, Supernova
by Brian Lin

Namio Harukawa
by Sulaiman Addonia

Erotic Moment
by Claudia Cravens

REVIEW

Next Chapter Please: Shame, Desire and Fanfiction
by Emily Waddell

Mapplethorpe Elegy
by Liara Roux

ESSAY

In Transit
by John Burnside

Turn-off
by Agri Ismaïl

The Dress
by Jessica Stoya

Wild Spring
by Geoffrey Mak

The Loving Tongue
by Kira Josefsson & Jacqui Cornetta

FICTION

The Goddess of Xishuangbanna
by Can Xue
trans. Karen Gernant

Mating Season
by Hanna Nordenhök
trans. Saskia Vogel

Another Chicken
by Frankie Barnet

ISSUE 2
AUTUMN/WINTER 2024

ermagazine.com
Cover Image by Loie Hollowell

UK £20

Exploring Desire

VI

56

Münchner Merkur
aktuell
Münchens Stricher-Szene: 700 Männer verkaufen ihre Körper
Täglicher Leser-Service: Verkehrslage in München, Luftqualität, Wetter, Finanzen, Termine, Kino, Theater

No 62

No 63

219 → I WANNA GIVE YOU DEVOTION, Philipp Gufler (ed.), Hammann von Mier Verlag, 2017, 112 pp, 17 x 24 cm (↳ Sec № 110)

TENTACULAR THINKING

Non-violence

by Lola Olufemi

TENTACULAR THINKING

86

87

[Extra Extra INTERVIEW]

...The parts of the body that carry more smell are those where more soul is collected...

In the 1980s, I was working with a company that made tests about choosing a colour, shape or smell from a library of categories divided by olfactory families in order to understand whether people were more extroverted or introverted. All the introverts went for a more floral chypre or floral animalic, and the extroverts for an oriental spicy, etc. It was interesting, but I don't really base my work on that sort of thing, or at least I have never done it so far. But it's all marketing in the end.

Michael: In your manifesto for Orto Parisi you write, 'The parts of the body that carry more smell are those where more soul is collected. The strong smells have become unpleasant to us, because the excess of soul is intolerable to the extent that our innate animalism is repressed and breaking from civilisation.' The line is dedicated to your grandfather's garden that he fertilised with his own waste. In thinking about the smells of the body and especially your new perfume Sadonaso for Nasomatto, do you think adding skank to the mix is some kind of universal law of art? Putting noise in, mistakes, distortion, dirtying up the canvas, etc.

Alessandro: I think good work always has strong contrasts. There is no beauty without ugliness. So I love raw material ingredients like animal musk, dirt, urine, horse hair and wet dog. I love these things because they are extremely powerful, very difficult to control and balance. But when you find a way to do it by working very hard or through mistakes, what comes out is always quite magnificent, and that's why those smells are extremely attractive. The manifesto of Orto Parisi for me is about how we've lost contact with our own body smells. Maybe men don't realise, but they're always touching their balls, and women do the same to their genitals, but we take two showers a day, we bleach our anus, we have to shave completely in order to put on deodorant. We don't allow ourselves to understand what our own smell is, and we deny our smell because of whatever society says. We're marketed products to stay clean and attract a partner, but the best attraction for someone else is your own smell. Sometimes I visit clients that sell my products, and the most successful employees are the ones who have an exaggerated body odour! Many people have a problem staying near them because of the strong smell, but they are the most successful in sales. You would think it should be the other way around, but it's not!

Michael: With Seminalis, Duro and Sadonaso, you dive head first into the erotic much more than a lot of other perfumers. Tell me about how your conception of the erotic relates to your perfume work.

Sadonaso by Nasomatto

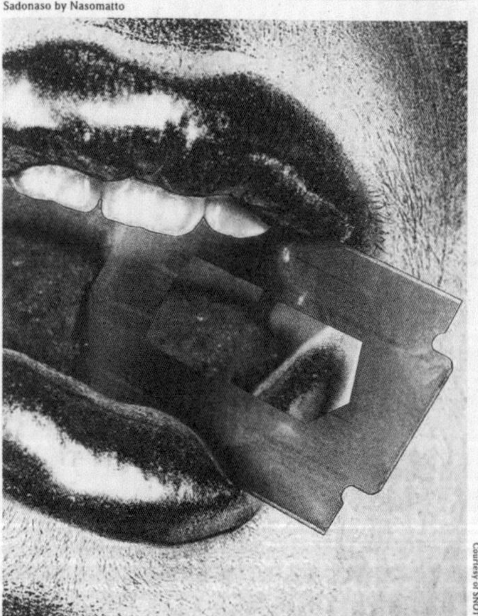

Courtesy of SNOTtv

Alessandro: Well, the erotic for me is the world of senses. You start with yourself, by finding your erogenous parts, and playing around with what you like as a sensation. You bring it to a certain limit and see how far you can go, and then when you are confident about your own eroticism, you share it with other people. Of course, this is strongly connected to smell, to the brain and

126

127

Alessandro Gualtieri

A perfume that encapsulates everything a human body releases in the throes of passion, Sadonaso is an oriental, musky, animalic tribute to the pleasures of the senses

20 ★ EXTRA EXTRA MAGAZINE ISSUE NO 23 URBAN EROTIC ENCOUNTERS Samira Benlaloua (ed.) Extra Extra 2024 210 p 17 x 24 cm (→ See Nº 062 & 200)

Slanted 45 printed on METAPAPER

COVER

CHROMO

White-Warmhite 300 gsm

The return of Chromo.

Available at Metapaper 1 May 2025.

TEXT

EXTRAMATT RECYCLING

White-Coldwhite 120 gsm

100% recycled with the highest possible whiteness.

Luxuriously matt. Blue Angel certified.

+

ROUGH AIR 1,5

White-Warmhite 100 gsm

The return of the wild surface.

Super rough. Extremely bulky. Best opacity.

STOBER
MEDIEN

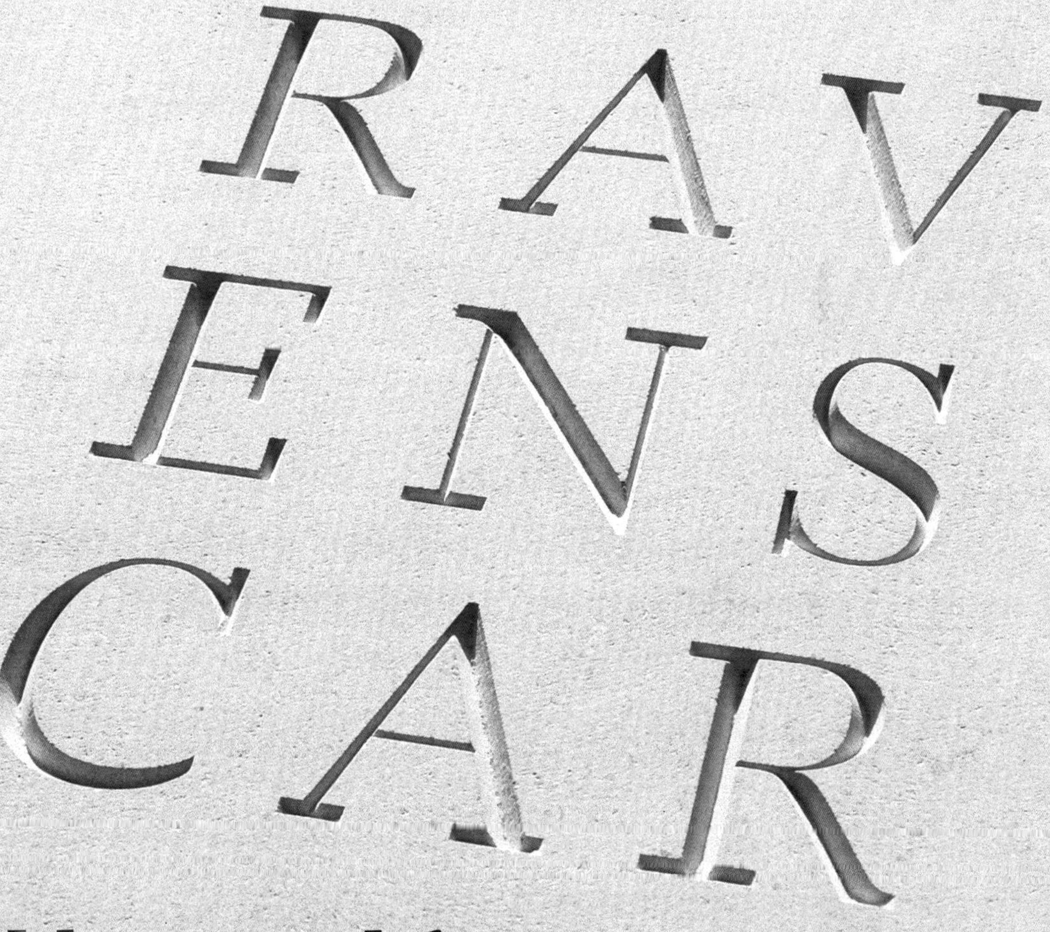

OF MILK?
YOU CEREAL?

*The % daily value (DV) tells you how much a nutrient in a serving of food contributes to a daily diet. 2,000 calories a day is used for general nutrition advice.

Go to Work
Have Attitude
Be Opulent

BUBBLE CORP.  

Polymode We approached XYZ with a question. It wasn't just 'we want a typeface,' it was more: How does, or can, a typeface dynamically express a point of view while also being able to remain 'neutral'? Ben and Jesse were phenomenal listeners and started by encouraging us to submit visual references that moved well beyond typefaces, consisting of personal and professional lineages—including BIPOC and LGBTQIA+ voices.

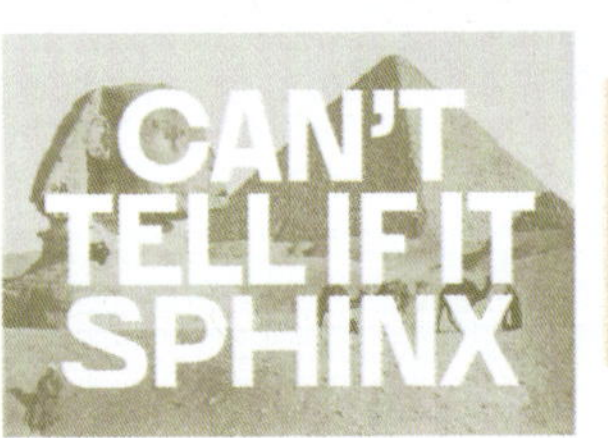

XYZ Type Once in a while, a project comes along that pushes our creative limits and commands personal and professional growth. We knew we were in for that kind of wild ride when Polymode asked us for a typeface that would reflect their design studio, represent their multifaceted identities, and be useful in their wide-ranging work.

Ceci n'est pas un spécimen.

Polymode supports many languages, which is why we haven't seen the *Missing Glyph* in a while. Have you seen it? If so, contact us and we would be happy to help with any expansion requests you may have.

Act Basic
Go to Work

XYZ.

XYZTYPE.COM

XYZ TYPE & POLYMODE

POLYMODESANS.COM

TP TQ
Zed Icons
TAXI
T3
2
tptq.com

Existentialist
Arbale Hairline

Métro Champs-Élysées
Arbitre Narrow Thin

Astrologically
Parisine Plus Clair Italic

Abstract Paintings
Altesse 38pt

KAFKAIENNES
Anisette ExtraLight

Distilled from 27 Botanicals
Alyssa Light

Objectivation
Astronef Base ExtraLight

Grande Vadrouilles
Alembert

SOLIDARITY
AW Conqueror Inline Regular

Fall Collection
Aukio

Gratuitement
Costa Light

Inspirations
Zingiber

TURQUOISE
AW Conqueror Sans Regular

Une Boutique Parisienne
Ambroise François Regular

CONSTRUCTIONS
Capek Bold

RAVISHINGLY
Retiro 24pt

Perfectionist
Aiglon Regular

Brainstormed
Deréon Italic 32pt

PÂTISSERIE
AW Conqueror Carved One + Two + Three + Four

MULTICOLORS
Retiro 24pt

DISTINGUISHED IMAGINATION
Arteria Compress Demi

L'Illustration
Le Monde Journal Bold Italic

KIMONO
Allumi Extended Inline Black 48a

Systematize
Caslonian S Heavy

Käsefondue
Prosaic ExtraBold Italic

ORIGINALLY
Mencken Heavy Italic

Tagliatelle alla Milanaise
Astronef Super Compressed

Newsletters
PS Fournier Black Italic

GEMINI SOCIABLE
Arteria Compress Black

PACKAGER
Arsen Display Heavy

NIGHTCLUB
Anisette Black

GROUNDWORKS
Arbitre Condensed Black

Tausend

n|w University of Applied Sciences and Arts Northwestern Switzerland
Basel Academy of Art and Design

Summer Workshops Basel 2025

June + July

- Generative Design
- UX/UI Design
- Tender Computing
- Poster Design
- Inquiry by Design
- Type Design
- Hacking Gutenberg

IDCE Institute Digital Communication Environments
www.baselsummerworkshops.ch

Merz Akademie
Hochschule für Gestaltung, Kunst und Medien • Stuttgart
staatlich anerkannt
Studieren in Stuttgart
Illustration • Fotografie • Grafikdesign • New Media • Film und Video • VR/AR/3D • Interface Design • Theorie
Bachelor
Master
merz-akademie.de

shop our publications at
slanted.de/shop
or support your local dealer
slanted

LUST UND MYTHOS: DIE ENTSTIGMATISIERUNG DES WEIBLICHEN ORGASMUS

Bachelorarbeit im Wintersemester 24/25
in Visuelle Kommunikation

Bachelor of Arts in Visuelle Kommunikation
An der Fakultät für Gestaltung der Hochschule Pforzheim

@design_pf & designpf.hs-pforzheim.de

Sharp

Sharp Type is a global type design studio that offers high-quality typefaces for retail licensing and custom client projects.

sharptype.co

! 10 × 10 “

BOYS! BOYS! BOYS!—Ghislain Pascal
EROTIC REVIEW—Lucy Roeber
EXTRA EXTRA—Linda Zhengová
FLUFFER EVERYDAY—Sotiris Trechas
MOAN ZINE—Moan
MULIERIS—Greta Futura Langianni
PLAYBOY—Florian Boitin
THE BITTERSWEET REVIEW—Kole Fulmine, Benoît Loiseau, Louis Shankar
THE BOY IS BEAUTIFUL—Leonidas Liolios
THE OPÉRA—Matthias Straub

1

Could you share your personal journey into the world of magazines? Was there a defining moment or influence that shaped your career path?

Ghislain Pascal, BOYS! BOYS! BOYS!

I fell into the world of magazines by default—as with most things in my career. My gallery, The Little Black Gallery, launched *BOYS! BOYS! BOYS!*, a program to promote queer and gay fine art photography, back in 2018. We had already published two *BOYS! BOYS! BOYS!* books and done several exhibitions when Covid hit in 2020. While in lockdown in the Canary Islands, I was talking to a photographer on Zoom who was showing me his pictures, and I thought they'd look really good in a magazine. That's when I had the idea to launch the *BOYS! BOYS! BOYS!* magazine. Little did I know it would take off in such a way, and we have just published our ninth volume. None of this would have happened without my amazing Art Director, Jeremy Kunze of Kunze Design, and our distributor, Ra & Olly.

Lucy Roeber, EROTIC REVIEW

I grew up in the 80s and 90s and magazines were very much part of youth culture then. Without the Internet, magazines were the way we thought about where we were, who we were, or wanted to be in the world. They were extremely influential. I edited my school magazine and had early ambitions to create and edit a magazine for women that didn't focus so much on the clothes, bags, and makeup we were supposed to be wearing.

Linda Zhengová, EXTRA EXTRA

My relationship with magazines goes way back. Even as a child, I was obsessed with them. I started by collecting cartoon magazines, but I'd also leaf through my mom's *Cosmopolitans,* even though I had no idea what they were about at the time. It was the glossy, shiny paper, and striking visuals that mesmerized me. Later, as a teenager, I fell headfirst into *BRAVO* and similar publications. I'll never forget the thrill of buying an issue, the excitement of shutting myself in my room to devour its contents. The extra bits inside—perfume samples, lip glosses, T-shirts, and, my god, the posters—felt like treasures. My relationship with magazines back then was almost obsessive. I'd anxiously wait for the next issue just to plaster a new poster of my platonic crushes on my bedroom walls.

That phase wasn't necessarily innocent, it became inherently voyeuristic and, strangely enough, sexual. Some of those magazines even had erotic comics that navigated me through my sexuality at a time when such discussions were completely off-limits at home. Now, as an adult, I rarely experience that same excitement when going through magazines. Everything feels too refined, overly serious, as though there's only one acceptable way to engage with them. The trashiness that made those old magazines so good, their irresistible charm, is missing. They were my guilty pleasure.

When I moved from the Czech Republic to the Netherlands. I kept checking out magazines in libraries but stopped buying them altogether. They'd become so expensive, and I didn't have the space to store them anymore. I always wondered: What would it take for me to buy one today? Eventually, I found myself on the other side of the equation when I got an internship at a magazine and had to figure out my relationship with the medium from a completely new perspective.

The Dreamer aka Sotiris Trechas,
FLUFFER EVERYDAY

I have been collecting magazines since I was a kid. I always found printed matter exciting, mostly because I understood early on the insane amount of work and talent needed to produce a publication. I was a creative child, always drawing, coming up with stories, and imagining fantastical worlds. When I was around 14, I got my first digital camera, nothing fancy. I would go around the house taking still-life pictures of what was getting my attention, and then I was creating covers for fake magazines on the computer. That's how I learned how to use editing software.

I always wanted to be an artist, but I was very afraid of deciding what kind of artist I should be—a painter, an illustrator, a photographer, and so on. The world loves labels, but I hated that so much. Then I realized that when creating a publication, I was able to use my creativity to the fullest without limiting myself. I could be the storyteller I needed to be, with the magazine as my medium of expression. That's when I decided what my dream job would be publishing my own magazine. So everything I did from that point on was about preparing myself, gaining the skills I needed to do this professionally.

Many years later, right after school, I found out about fluffers—people paid to help porn actors perform—and I was blown away by it. That's when I knew what my magazine would be about.

Moan, MOAN ZINE

Print was introduced to me during my time at university, where I studied Fashion Communication and Promotion. I began exploring printmaking and zine culture as powerful forms of visual communication, inspired by the endless possibilities for experimentation. Discovering the power of self-publishing and its social, cultural, and political impact sparked my deep-rooted passion for activism and continues to shape my work today. I became fascinated by how narratives could be told through elements like paper, binding, typography, layout, and imagery. Print feels inherently human; the touch and interaction with a physical item forces you to slow down, creating a more intimate and reflective experience. It's freeing, inspiring, and liberating—offering endless creative interactions while overcoming censorship and limitations that exist online.

A major influence on my career path has been my partner, now husband, who runs a print and design studio called Dizzy Ink. His passion for printmaking and our ongoing collaborations have been instrumental in shaping my journey. Developing ideas together and having a highly skilled printmaker and bookmaker bring them to life has been invaluable. We work on each issue of *MOAN* together, as well as other printed projects, which are always fun, exciting, and endlessly inspiring.

Greta Futura Langianni,
MULIERIS MAGAZINE

I studied photography and film at the Academy of Fine Arts in Italy, so this whole world related to magazines was never my main interest, until I kind of bumped into it.

I was spending a year abroad in Hamburg through a university exchange program and one night ended up at this final-year exhibition and party at University of Fine Arts Hamburg, which my boyfriend at the time was attending. I've never been to something similar, it was a party inside of the school. And by party, I mean a full on rave. At the same time, if you walked through the classrooms, you could see all the students' final projects, including the ones from the editorial, printing, and graphic design department.

I saw many magazines made by students and decided I wanted to work on something similar. I was probably just too high and tripped my way into the idea, but it ended up becoming what we have today—so I guess it was a good trip.

Florian Boitin, PLAYBOY

I have been fascinated by the medium of print since my earliest youth. As a teenager, I wrote my first stories on my father's typewriter and added my own illustrations. While studying communication design, I finally realized that I wanted to work with magazines professionally.

For one project, I set myself the task of photographically documenting poverty in Munich. That was a key moment for me. For my final-year project, I developed my own print magazine, and that was when I knew: That's it!

Benoît Loiseau, THE BITTERSWEET REVIEW

I remember making zines in my parents' basement as a young teenager. They were pretty bad and uninteresting, but I loved the process of putting text and images together and seeing how they looked on the page. I can't say there was a defining moment, but this original interest never left me.

At university, in my early twenties, I ran a journal of contemporary art and politics. We published six issues in total, I think, and got some surprisingly respectable people involved. Even in the age of social media and digital content, I find that self-publishing and printed matter is the ultimate punk combination.

Leonidas Liolios, THE BOY IS BEAUTIFUL

My mom is a hairdresser, so she would religiously buy *Elle,* which, at least in Greece, always came with big toiletry bags and things to organize her brushes and stuff. I always remember being fascinated by the fashion, the perfume samples, the idea that there would be another issue in a month.

Then there were indie titles aimed at teenage girls. I remember a poster of Felipe Colombo from *Rebelde Way* that made my heart beat faster. I wasn't sure of my sexuality at the time, but reflecting on it now ... the boy was always beautiful.

Matthias Straub, THE OPÉRA

I got into magazines in the late 80s and early 90s. Back then, skateboarding was my religion, and *Transworld* or the *Thrasher* skateboard magazine were my bibles. I ordered the issues by mail from the US—sometimes it took three weeks to get me the hot stuff. Then I would read every page, every article, and every line over and over again until I knew each issue by heart ... For me, magazines were—and still are—the door to another, yet better, world.

2

Do you remember your first encounter with an erotic / sex magazine? How did it challenge or shape your understanding of sexuality at the time?

Ghislain Pascal

I suppose the first magazine that falls into this category was the great Australian photography magazine *Black+White* which featured sexy pictures of men by famous photographers. I think it helped shape my understanding that it is possible to publish a magazine featuring beautiful pictures of men without being sleazy or pornographic.

Lucy Roeber

Probably the porn magazines that my mother's boyfriend kept tucked down the side of their bed. I can't remember the names now, but my friends and I would steal them and read through them to each other at night by flashlight. Pure, heterosexual male fantasy.

Linda Zhengová

Ah, those cheap gas station magazines, with their glossy covers featuring scantily clad women, all tucked away in a separate section ... As a child, I'd glance at them with a mix of curiosity and guilt, sensing they were something forbidden. I broke that taboo when I started visiting the local "trafika" (newsstand) near my apartment. While buying my usual magazines, I'd sneak peeks into these overtly objectifying publications. The man at the counter initially scolded me for looking, which, of course, made me want to look even more. Eventually, he gave up and let me browse freely.

The experience was anticlimactic. Those magazines had nothing to offer me as a young woman; they were made for heterosexual men, not me. I lost interest almost immediately.

In high school, *Playboy* magazines would circulate among the boys, pulled from under their fathers' beds. One time, I found a copy left in the corridor and snuck off to the bathroom to look inside. The women featured were stunning, but I didn't see myself in them. I just wanted to touch their skin—it looked so impossibly smooth—and imagined they probably smelled amazing, too.

The real game-changer for me was *Playboy* in Braille. I can't remember how I came across it, but I vividly recall the thoughts it sparked. It was the moment I understood erotica as something beyond the visual. The tactile nature of it—reading with your hands, letting the imagination take over—was transformative. It showed me how deeply personal and suggestive eroticism can be. Honestly, I still think it's one of the sexiest publications out there.

The Dreamer aka Sotiris Trechas

As a teenager I used to work in a video club. We had a big pornography section, and, as part of my job, I had to order new movies. From time to time, the distributors would send us catalogs presenting new releases or a new production house. That was the first time I came across erotic content that captured my attention on a deeper level.

Before that, like every teenager of the time, I would only come across mainstream, easily accessible, mostly straight erotic magazines at kiosks, and they never excited me. These catalogs were something special–somewhere between art and commerce, and I always found the professionalism that my boss had towards that so inspiring. The colors, the design elements, the language–everything felt so fresh compared to the overly saturated Hollywood stuff that would fill up the store's shelves.

Moan

Yes! The first sex-positive magazine I encountered was *Nin Magazine.* During Leticia's talk, I was blown away by her confidence and depth of knowledge on the subject. The way she spoke about sex, liberation, and womanhood was incredibly inspiring. She sparked a sense of feminism in me that has only grown stronger since!

Greta Futura Langianni

My first encounter with an erotic magazine was through more of a male lens I guess, which makes sense because my first approach to sex wasn't about what I wanted but about what I thought I should do to be wanted

A guy I was dating in my teens was into Milo Manara's work and showed me some magazines related to his artistic research. It's odd to think that at the time I was so deeply fascinated by what I was looking at, and now, many years later, I feel like that portrayal of women belongs more to a man's idea of what sex should look like rather than a woman's perspective. I think for women, a huge step is breaking free from being constantly sexualized in ways that don't represent us, shifting from objects of desire to humans who desire.

Florian Boitin

My first experience with erotic magazines was studying the sex education pages of *BRAVO.* Not only did they write about sexuality without taboos, but they also depicted the adolescent sexuality in very explicit photos. My mother found this much more offensive than the first *Playboy* she discovered when I was 15.

Benoît Loiseau

The first meaningful encounter I had with a sex-positive magazine must have been *BUTT* magazine in the mid-2000s. The fact that it featured interesting people, artists, and writers, but also hot imagery, blew my mind. I think for a long time I assumed these two things couldn't coexist in the same space. I also liked how DIY it looked.

Leonidas Liolios

It must have been a straight magazine that my cousins and I dug out of my uncle's basement. It felt like I was looking at something I wasn't supposed to see, and it was unlike anything I'd ever seen before. I felt like I had suddenly opened my eyes to this whole other side of the human experience–a collective horniness among all of us naughty kids flipping through the pages, as well as an obligation to engage and comment on the female parts shown because it was the "straight" thing to do.

When you're young, queer, and growing up in the suburbs of Athens in the 90s, access to gay erotica magazines or series like *Queer As Folk* is completely out of reach. It was the Internet that did for me what queer magazines did for previous generations. A chat with an emo on MSN or *abeardedboy's blog* on Tumblr. The Internet was interesting at the time because it was kind of like a locked drawer that our parents didn't have the key to because they didn't know how to use it.

In many ways, this meant that many of us queers were engaging with content relevant to us for the first time in our late teenage or adult years. It's like a second education. But hopefully things are changing for the better and now kids have access to shows like *Heartstopper* and queer children's books from the get-go–that is, if they live in a safe and supportive environment where watching or reading something like that is an option.

Matthias Straub

When I was a little boy of five years, my cousins used to show me a porn magazine. To this day, I still don't fully understand what I saw back then. I still think there's something pretty weird about what goes on in people's heads when they watch naked strangers having sex.

3

The sexual revolution was marked by bold liberation and breaking taboos, yet today's climate of political correctness and increasing prudishness seems to stifle open dialog. Do you think prudery is making a comeback, and how does this affect meaningful discussions about sexuality in your work?

Ghislain Pascal

I do think that we are entering a new era of conservatism, prudishness, and censorship. I think that this is particularly prevalent when it comes to anything queer or gay. It is virtually impossible to get anything related to queer or gay fine art photography published in the mainstream media. Similarly, social media platforms like Facebook and Instagram remove anything queer or gay, making it virtually impossible to post on their platforms. I fear we are regressing to the 1950s.

Lucy Roeber

I wouldn't call it prudery exactly. I mean, the UK has always had a heavy dose of prudishness and awkward humor, but generally, I think the world is far more open to different sexual inclinations than ever before, but the saturation of Internet porn has confused the concept of sexual liberation and all the other conversations are lost.

We are both trying to define everything and hide what is "inappropriate" rather than acknowledging the very gray area so many of our desires inhabit.

Linda Zhengová

The sexual revolution was critical because it gave people the freedom to talk about previously taboo topics without shame or guilt. But now we've reached a strange new point. In Europe, at least, there's so much openness around sexuality that explicitness has started to feel shoved in our faces, and ironically, this overexposure has led to a resurgence of prudishness.

I want to choose what I see, who I see, and what I find erotic. I don't need to be forced into witnessing everyone else's private lives. It feels like an obligation at this point. Kinks, fetishes, polygamy, and our sex lives have been mainstreamed into spectacles for entertainment, heavily monetized, and drained of mystery. And yet, it's mystery and connection that people are craving.

For me, the issue isn't prudery; it's the commodification of sexuality and desire. These "liberations" have become part of the same system they originally resisted. Michel Foucault's theories come to mind here–sexuality, once a site of resistance, has now been absorbed into the machinery of consumerism.

Sexuality is deeply personal. It's about intimacy, pleasure, and connection. I prefer to keep some things obscured, some desires unspoken, and some pleasures secret. Not out of prudishness, but because I value the power of subtlety and the sacredness of private experiences. The problem isn't openness, it's that we've lost the balance between what's shared and what's sacred.

The Dreamer aka Sotiris Trechas

Thankfully, society has made great strides forward, considering acceptance and sexual expression. Of course there is still a long way to go, but we should not forget the victories. Progress has helped us realize that there are better ways to address certain things, and I am totally on board with that. It is only limiting if you let it be. It's just another parameter to keep in mind.

There are a million ways to express yourself and your creative thinking. Many taboos still need to be broken, and many artists feel the need to break them. So I am positive that we will come up with bold new ways to do so.

The key to conveying the message you want to share and starting the conversation you want to have, is doing what you want in the most legal and professional way possible. If what you are doing is not a crime, then no one can stop you from creating the work you want to share with the world.

Moan

I'm not sure prudishness ever really left–yes, it seems to fluctuate alongside politics and social beliefs, but there's always an undertone of it. It always amazes me how much people shy away from talking about sex. It's something that touches all of us–it shapes our relationships, our identities, and our deepest experiences. But we're still scared to explore it openly. This saddens me because, for me, meaningful discussions and education on the topic are empowering.

Generally, it really depends on the community you're speaking to. Liberal, creative, and diverse spaces are often more open, accepting, and less judgmental, making room for meaningful discussions about sexuality. Outside of those circles, judgment remains a big obstacle, though I've had some interactions I approached with hesitancy that pleasantly surprised me. I've found prudishness often stems from fear or deeply internalized shame that gets projected outward. Since starting *MOAN*, I've watched societal attitudes shift back and forth. But these fluctuations only remind me how vital it is to keep these conversations going, especially from a female and queer perspective. Sexuality connects us all–it's a fundamental part of being human–and creating space to talk about it without shame is one of the most important things we can do.

Greta Futura Langianni

When breaking a taboo, the process often involves rejecting it so completely that we dive into the opposite extreme of the issue we're trying to address. However, in any quest, what we ultimately seek is balance–and achieving that often requires exploring both extremes

For instance, if you overindulge in sex simply because you feel socially pressured by the notion that it's "liberating," you're acting in much the same way as someone who avoids sex because they've been told it makes them more valuable. Both scenarios are driven by external expectations. This is the opposite of sexual freedom: in different ways, you're still confined, because what matters isn't the presence or absence of sex but how you approach it.

Any choice made out of fear of judgment isn't truly free and, therefore, it's never truly liberating. We can only speak of sexual liberation when the choice is fully our own–when I can freely decide to have ten partners in a week or only one in my entire life–and that decision reflects who I am and what I want, rather than how I'm expected to act.

I think many women are realizing this: "Maybe I wasn't free before, but I'm also not free now," because their actions are still shaped by what others expect of them. In this sense, I wouldn't describe today's trends as increasing prudishness; instead, we might be experiencing a new form of liberation, one that doesn't need to look the same for everyone.

Ultimately, the question we must ask ourselves is this: Am I choosing sex freely, based on my true self, or is someone else deciding for me what sexual freedom should look like?

Florian Boitin

I see contradictory trends today. On the one hand, sexuality and nudity are ubiquitous in our enlightened world, driven largely by digitalization of course. On the other hand, under the guise of so-called diversity, I see a new stuffiness—yes, a misunderstood political correctness that is nothing more than an increasing uptightness and inhibition in our society. Depictions of female nudity are now reflexively labeled "sexism."

But especially in *Playboy* photography, it is an expression of female autonomy. As successful actress Gisa Zach recently put it: "The *Playboy* pictures are my expression: 'Be what and who you want to be and do what you want to do,'" says the 50-year-old, cover star of the July 2024 issue. "They should be an impetus for women to free themselves from patterns that seem to dictate what's appropriate and what's not, what's beautiful and what's not."

Benoît Loiseau

I'm not sure prudery ever really went away. Prudery, the way I see it, is fairly harmless—everyone has their own boundaries, and if you're not into something, you don't have to engage with it. What bothers me more is having to justify why gender and sexuality are fields in their own right—whether in academia, art, or literature.

I think there's still a predominant belief that focusing on gender and sexuality is somewhat unserious, a sub-genre at best, a mere interest, when in reality, it is so consequential. Everyone has a stake in it, whether they are prepared to recognize it or not.

Leonidas Liolios

Prudishness is a plague, but one that has been around forever. I 100 % believe in the power of the individual to eradicate prudishness in a non-monitored context, whether it's a business meeting, a discussion about sex among friends, or a self-published historical text.

Speaking of monitoring, Meta took down our original Instagram account for *The Boy Is Beautiful* because of a Botticelli painting, but at the same time Twitter and, more recently, BlueSky have become these porn-safe havens years after Tumblr decided to censor itself into oblivion. Not to mention OnlyFans and other platforms that have revolutionized sex work and made it accessible to everyone.

I think it's important to remember that these are all products, and while they seem to take up a huge part of our lives, we always have the option to abandon them and find alternative ways to stay connected and share content.

Now, as a lecturer in graphic communication design, I often have to talk about my publishing practice to a room full of students and other academics whose practice is very different from my own, and in those moments I feel the least prude I could ever be—after all these years, I've managed to talk about Achilles and Patroclus fucking each other at school.

Matthias Straub

When I went to the sauna last Sunday, I noticed a young couple in their mid-twenties. They were wearing swimsuits—in the middle of naked grannies and grandpas. Yes, I think we are moving toward a much more conservative attitude toward the nude body—both in public and in private spaces. Publishing artistic nude photography is becoming increasingly scrutinized and judged through a "woke" perspective.

4

Has everything already been said and done? How have depictions of men, women, and sexuality evolved over the last two generations, and where do you see space for new conversations?

Ghislain Pascal

In the queer world, I definitely think we are just at the beginning of the conversation. It is only in the past decade that there has been an explosion of queer and gay photographers around the world expressing themselves and sharing their work without fear or persecution.

Lucy Roeber

Wow! Can we ever say and do everything that can be said or done? In anything? Our sexual selves have existed for so long behind closed doors, or in response to cultural expectations, that I think there are still so many voices, angles, and feelings that need to be heard, so many parts of ourselves connected to our erotic lives. If I'm honest, I sometimes wonder how we will coherently represent such a cacophony!

Linda Zhengová

I'm always searching for works, and trying to create works, that make me think, imagine, project, and feel something. If it's just beautiful, if it doesn't transport me anywhere, then it's ephemeral. It leaves no mark. The space for new conversations lies in the places where people are surprised, moved, pierced—where something resonates on a deeper level.

I also think there's an urgent need for more male erotica from female perspectives, more trans erotica, and more lesbian erotica. So far, we've been bombarded with female nudes and male gay narratives primarily from a Western perspective. While those stories matter, there's room for more diversity. At the same time, I don't think we need to universalize these experiences and depictions. Their power comes from their specificity, from their ability to feel deeply personal yet still move and affect us, even when they aren't our own.

Too often, I see repetition in art where images fail to go beyond the surface. It's frustrating when a piece doesn't push further, when it doesn't make me feel or imagine something bigger. I want to see art that uses bodies as portals, that takes me somewhere else, far beyond just shock or aesthetic pleasure. Fabricated intimacy doesn't interest me.

The Dreamer aka Sotiris Trechas

As a true millennial born in 1990, I have seen the world change over and over again. I do not believe that everything has been said and done before. But even if it has, there will be a million new ways to do it all over again.

We cannot predict how the evolution of technology will impact our lives. Take Instagram, for example—how different the life of a creative person was 15 years ago. Even 10 years ago! Gender expression and sexuality deeply reflecting the state of society, and as society changes, our views and actions will change as well.

Personally, I would like to reach a point as a society, where we refer to sexuality regardless of gender, but more as an energy. I truly believe that there would be fewer wars if everyone were pansexual.

Moan

Can anything ever be said enough? I often say that our rights—especially as women—are like thin glass, always at risk of shattering. Conversations about activism and feminism seem to move in cycles. Two generations ago, we were making strides toward reproductive rights, including access to abortion. Now, women are once again fighting for what should be basic freedoms, proving these conversations are far from over.

When it comes to sexuality, I believe women have never truly owned the space of eroticism in an authentic and empowering way. Mainstream depictions of sex have long been dominated by the male gaze—a perspective that benefits no one. This lens reduces sexuality to something performative rather than something intimate, equal, and multifaceted.

We need diverse perspectives where everyone's needs, desires, and pleasures are acknowledged. Moving beyond male-centric narratives, we must explore the erotic as deeply human—a space of creativity, connection, curiosity, and agency. Through *MOAN,* I aim to bridge this gap by creating a space for new conversations where pleasure isn't confined to stereotypes or societal expectations.

I strive to highlight equal desire and shared intimacy in ways that feel relatable and inclusive. We need more depictions of pleasure that reflect the full spectrum of human experiences, particularly from female and queer perspectives. These voices have been sidelined for far too long, and their inclusion isn't just important—it's essential to evolving how we think and talk about sexuality.

Greta Futura Langianni

There's always room for something more to say and do. As humans, we don't have the means to see and understand everything, we are not gods. We are flawed and will always fail to see all that needs to be seen. Through evolution new questions arise and new answers and debates emerge from them.

I feel like these last two generations tried to answer those questions creating a trail of change that we eventually followed, opening up new spaces by walking through them.

Some of those spaces made sense, some others are still trying to have a concrete shape. As long as we move forward and make room for new questions I think we will always find a new spaces to enter.

Florian Boitin

Of course, the representation of femininity and masculinity has evolved significantly in recent decades, both in textual and visual forms. The images and modes of representation have become more diverse, and I see this as a positive development and a real enrichment.

I believe we are in a constant dialog—women and men. But I think it is even more important now to foster an exchange between generations. That is where I see the greatest need for action.

Kole Fulmine

No, I don't think everything has been said and done, especially not for the QTIPOC community. I think maybe everything has been said and done for white cishet men! There are so many voices that have historically been underrepresented and we are only just getting started with prioritizing those voices. As a trans person, I do feel oversaturated with the binary depiction of oversexualized men and women. I think there is space in the erotic for fluidity, for gender non-conforming bodies and for pushing beyond the binary. Witnessing more bodies existing on a spectrum offers a different dimension to conversations around sexuality and those conversations pave the way for minorities to rise up.

Leonidas Liolios

To answer your first question: yes and no.

This is something we have asked ourselves as a team since the beginning of the project. Why retell queer myths if these are available for people to look up? Why explore the masculine form again? Why showcase practitioners who engage with ideas of queer Greece if they are already showcasing themselves through their own channels and other media? Why collect stories of ostracism and pleasure, aren't they always somewhat the same?

And yet, the more you read, the more you understand that it's all one big conversation that evolves and adapts to the context of its time—what's important is to keep that conversation going, and to contribute to it. For queer culture, publishing (including erotica magazines) is the single most important trace of our existence over centuries of bigotry and messianism. Whether it's an Attica vase, a Cavafy poem, a placard, or a fetish club leaflet, proof of our fabulousness is essential.

It's like questioning the importance of opening a new gay club in London because there have been so many before, when the tragic truth is that so many close year after year. Magazines, like venues, provide space for thoughts, ideas, and livelihoods to exist and ignite—so yes, it's all been said and done, but I'm happy to say and do it again and again.

In terms of how representations of men, women, and sexuality have evolved, our generation is much more sex-positive and open to how people choose to present themselves, and there are increasing numbers of magazines, online spaces and venues that cater to that.

This is an observation of my fellow queers—the straight world seems to be in a constant state of lag, but it's an intersectional issue that deserves much more space for analysis. In the meantime, we'll always have moments like *Barbie* and *The Substance* to hold on to.

Matthias Straub

Yes and no. Of course, there are limited ways of displaying the nude—but there are still new and unseen, sometimes very creative approaches to interpreting nudity.

5

How does design act as a lens through which we experience eroticism? What are the storytelling elements you prioritize to convey desire, intimacy, or provocation?

Ghislain Pascal

Design helps to bring the beauty of our photographers' work to the page. However, the true credit for the storytelling and artistic vision rightfully belongs to the photographers themselves.

Lucy Roeber

Design is fundamental to the entire *Erotic Review* project. We collaborated with Studio Frith to create a design that is modern and flashy but not gendered and expected. We have obviously done a good job because *The Guardian* named us a design highlight of 2024! We don't aim to prioritize any particular elements to convey a specific angle on desire. Instead, we strive to hold space for many voices—whether mundane or extreme.

Linda Zhengová

My experience with design mostly revolves around publications, so I'll speak from that perspective. I'm not a designer, but I'm very conscious of how design decisions can either elevate storytelling or completely destroy it. Design is a communication tool—it helps ideas come through clearly, making them resonate with an audience. It's the mediator between the artist and the viewer.

Things like paper choices, typography, the size of a publication, or the design of a cover are storytelling elements that can convey desire, intimacy, or provocation. They're as important as any other aspect of the work. I still think about certain papers I encountered while working on publications. Curious Matter, for instance, is a paper made of potato starch. Its texture is unforgettable, you just can't stop touching it.

These so-called minor decisions can elevate the experience in ways people often overlook. They transform a publication from a visual experience into a multisensory one. That's where design goes beyond decoration and becomes something tactile, emotional, and intimate.

The Dreamer aka Sotiris Trechas

Design is of great importance, especially when you're working on something that could be considered a taboo for many. When I came up with *Fluffer Everyday,* design was the way to communicate what I had in mind. A magazine with everyday people, in everyday moments, mostly with their clothes on, could not be perceived as an erotic publication by many. That's why I chose red as the primary branding element. Red is the color of sex—the moment you see red, you instantly think of something x-rated.

In addition, the paper I chose for the first format of the magazine was carefully selected to evoke the vintage porn magazines that we all have come across at some point. The same goes for the plastic bag the magazine is packaged in. Even if you don't immediately understand why this publication is sexy, you accept that it's erotic.

To emphasize the eroticism of the everyday—the whole point of the magazine—I decided that all the pictures should be as raw as possible: no flash, no black-and-white, no filters, as this isn't how the eyes naturally see. In the end, all these creative rules I established became part of the branding, making the project feel more cohesive and complete.

Moan

Design is a powerful lens through which we experience any form of communication, including eroticism. With *MOAN*, good design creates a space where sexuality can be explored in ways that feel empowering, and beautiful. When you play with print, the possibilities of design and storytelling become even more exciting—tactile materials and carefully considered processes can completely transform how a story is told and experienced.

Craftsmanship is vital because it has the power to reframe how we think about eroticism. Using luxurious paper, tactile embossing, and alternative printing methods such as Riso and screen printing turns each page into something intentional. It's about celebrating eroticism as something deserving of care, attention, and beauty.

I love using contrast in design to evoke emotion. Whether it's the juxtaposition of bold, female-made typography with delicate imagery, or the explicitness of a story paired with a uniform grid structure and minimal design choices, these elements create clarity—almost as if you're entering a silent, private, and intimate space with a feminine and activist touch. They allow intimacy and provocation to coexist in a way that feels genuine. For me, design is an invitation—it invites people to look closer, feel something, and engage with their own ideas about pleasure and connection.

Greta Futura Langianni

In our magazine, most of the elements we used to convey desire, intimacy, and provocation are shaped through women's perspectives—their bodies, their thoughts, almost in an excessively feminine kind of rhetoric that uses the oversexualization of women as a weapon to reclaim our sexuality. There's softness, aggression, something explicit, and other times sex is not even mentioned. A range of tools is used to say: "Sex isn't what you think it is—it's what I want you to want it to be."

Florian Boitin

Design in general, and photography in particular, serve crucial functions as communication tools. They are the language of eroticism. This is where I see the most significant developments in recent decades—especially in my work at *Playboy*.

It is very important for us to create intimacy and closeness in our visual language. However, the model should never be reduced to her pure physicality. Rather, each image should express the subject's self-determination. And, of course, many people find this self-confidence provocative

Kole Fulmine

Design is fundamental to eroticism, it's the gateway to seduction, and it's really easy to get wrong! You don't want to over egg the pudding—striking the right balance can be incredibly subjective.

Working with John's structure for the magazine is always our priority, as a collective, we rely on irony, humor, and an understanding that our reader comes from a queer perspective. Which means we don't have to work as hard to convey a rich history of diversity.

What is also important for us as editors is that we let our writers and artists provoke—we provide a platform, a net for their provocations. We then consciously curate their work to ensure that our collective message is communicated.

Leonidas Liolios

That's a great question for Dan Rhatigan of *The Hot Type Club*, but I'd like to answer it with a set of questions. What does the name of the magazine say about what awaits you inside? How does the cover relate to the title? If there is an image on the cover, how does it relate to the title? Are the materials, colors, and typefaces used to convey an idea? What size is it? Can I read it on the tube? On the toilet? How are images cropped and placed in relation to text? What is the sequence of stories and pictures? Which image made it into a spread and why?

All of this and more is how design acts as a lens through which we experience not only eroticism but every single emotion, on a page and beyond. For *The Boy Is Beautiful*, it's about how engaging, thought-provoking, and saucy text works with captivating imagery to provide an experience of escapism and immersion into the past, present, and future of queer lives. Meanwhile the materials, colors, and form of the magazine serve as a constant reminder of what this object you're holding between your palms is all about.

Matthias Straub

In the case of *THE OPÉRA*, the magazine design is both guidance and an outreaching gesture to lower unacceptance. Although the layout and design in *THE OPÉRA* always supports the art and the photographer's work, it's also a code of zeitgeist and offers another layer of approachability.

6
What emotional or intellectual journey do you hope readers undergo when engaging with your magazine? What questions or feelings should linger after the last page is turned?

Ghislain Pascal
My aim is to persuade people that it's fine to buy and hang beautiful queer artworks on your walls at home. There is still a huge stigma and barriers to overcome. However, by producing such a beautiful magazine filled with amazing images by queer and gay fine art photographers I hope we can normalize it and make it acceptable.

Lucy Roeber
I hope that readers feel that we are responding to a general curiosity and openness around desire. I would love to think that they might read or look at work with which they feel a real connection. We believe desire is an aspect of our common humanity, and we are not highlighting a particular gender, sexuality, or practice. More a feeling that we all long for sexual connection, it is just the object that changes.

Linda Zhengová
I can guide a certain mental space, shape the atmosphere of a publication, text, or body of work, but I can't predict people's reactions. That's not my job. What I hope to create is an open space–a place where readers can project parts of themselves onto what they see. If a page lingers in someone's mind or evokes a question they can't quite answer, then I've done my part.

The Dreamer aka Sotiris Trechas
The point of the magazine is to inspire and find ways to enjoy being sexual, regardless of gender or societal norms. Understanding our bodies, accepting them, and feeling safe to experiment–that's what I aim to achieve.

The purpose of *Fluffer Everyday* isn't to help you jerk off or reach orgasm. I want you to flip through the magazine, get inspired, grab your phone, and text your lover–or even your best friend–and start a conversation. I strive to spark excitement in people.

Moan
A journey of exploration, education, liberation, and curiosity. Through my illustrations, I aim to spark feelings of desire and intimacy in ways that feel authentic and inclusive. When it comes to the written features, they span emotionally led content as well as research-driven, educational articles. I strive to find a balance between the two because I believe passion and education go hand in hand–they complement and deepen our understanding of ourselves and our sexual experiences. I hope to inspire conversations and ideas for new, shared experiences. I want readers to walk away feeling less shame and more curiosity–excited to explore pleasure, embrace passions, and pursue meaningful connections.

After the last page is turned, I want questions and feelings to linger: What does intimacy mean to me? How can I connect more deeply with myself and others? By sparking this introspection, I hope *MOAN* becomes more than just a publication–it becomes a catalyst for liberation and meaningful exploration.

Greta Futura Langianni
I hope readers feel encouraged to explore sexuality from various perspectives, some of which may resonate with them and prompt deeper self-reflection. My hope is that by the time they reach the last page, they not only gain new insights but also find themselves asking questions they hadn't considered before.

Florian Boitin
Of course, our primary goal is to entertain our readers. It is not our intention to instruct or educate them. And yet, we ensure this entertainment never falls below a certain intellectual level. We want to inspire our readers, to stimulate them–even in areas that are clearly above the belt. However, I follow the principle of brain researcher Prof. Dr. Hans-Georg Häusel, who says, “Information which doesn't reach a person's emotional center is worthless to their brain.”

Kole Fulmine
I hope that our readers experience a sense of light knowing that our magazine exists! That queer and trans voices are rising up in a literary landscape that can, at times, feel overwhelmingly dominated by normativity.

When I read the magazine, I get a sense of collective joy from the community we have gathered in print–I hope our readers feel that too. I also hope we inspire curiosity and encourage readers to seek out more work from some of the writers, poets, and artists we feature.

Leonidas Liolios
I hope that when they see the magazine for the first time on a shelf, they'll experience a sense of déjà vu –like it's an object they've always owned but somehow misplaced and now want to reclaim.

When they catch the scent of the first few pages, I want them to feel a sense of excitement, like sitting in a class with a very passionate history teacher who doesn't read from a book, but animates her voice and body to convey a feeling. I want them to feel aroused by the way people describe one another and the emotions they've shared.

I hope they feel invigorated by the brilliant queer minds who infuse their lived experiences into beautiful architecture, photography, writing, and beyond. Nostalgic for what's come before and horny for what's to come.

Matthias Straub

THE OPÉRA does not have a purpose or an aim. It does not want to educate or teach. It's a manifesto for eternal beauty, that can easily be understood by any audience–with or without background knowledge of the culture of nude photography.

7

To what extent do you believe erotic magazines should challenge societal moral conventions, and where do you draw the line between provocation and alienation?

Ghislain Pascal

It's a question I always ask myself when editing and curating every issue of my magazine. My mantra to my photographers is always: "Less willy!" But then I also need to remind myself not to be prudish and that art is a form of self-expression and reflects our diverse community.

I often ask myself: What would I think if Robert Mapplethorpe submitted his artworks for publication today? As with everything, it is all about getting the balance right in each issue and every exhibition.

Lucy Roeber

Art has always been a provocation, it challenges convention at the edges. We aim to provoke but not salaciously shock. I don't want to alienate people; rather, I want them to reconsider societal conventions in different ways.

Linda Zhengová

Erotic magazines challenge societal conventions simply by existing. Their presence alone pushes against moral boundaries. I don't see the need to follow rules or trends when it comes to erotica–the power lies in its multiplicity and diversity of expression. There's no singular way to showcase or expose it.

As for provocation and alienation, those are reactions. They don't belong to the maker–they belong to the audience. My focus is on creating something authentic, not tailoring it to avoid or provoke a specific response.

The Dreamer aka Sotiris Trechas

Erotic magazines, like all magazines in general, are a medium that hold great power in inspiring conversations and bridging communities. By its nature, *Fluffer Everyday* presents everyday people in everyday scenarios, allowing the readers to expand the scope of their own imagination. I believe this approach allows the magazine to gently provoke and educate while never alienating.

Moan

Erotic magazines have always had a rebellious edge, and *MOAN* is no different. They exist to challenge societal moral conventions, provoke thought, and create space for conversations that have been silenced or repressed. Historically, banned erotic books were condemned not only for their content but for the ideas they represented: freedom, exploration, and liberation. That same spirit drives *MOAN.*

For me, provocation is essential to this process–it's what makes people uncomfortable enough to question their assumptions and consider new ideas. It sparks curiosity and challenges outdated norms, but it must feel intentional and empowering, not alienating. The line I draw is where the work risks isolating or excluding the very people it seeks to empower.

MOAN strives to challenge societal conventions while remaining deeply human, inclusive, and celebratory. Erotic magazines should feel radical and rebellious, but they should also feel like a space to connect, reflect, and celebrate sexuality without shame.

Greta Futura Langianni

When it comes to art, it's one of the few spaces where humans should feel free to dive deep into anything, especially those things they cannot explore through politics, society, or daily life. Creating is like entering another dimension where you are free to experience what you can't in life. When you exit that reality, it becomes your duty to understand. As we quote in our issue, from the Roman poet Ovid: "Venus ventus temerarius"–"Venus favors the bold."

Florian Boitin

I don't want to overestimate the role of erotic publications in society. On the other hand, we've noticed, reflected in our steadily growing subscriber numbers over the years, that more and more people see *Playboy* as a welcome counterpoint in an increasingly repressive present. In terms of content, we are not interested in breaking taboos or attracting attention with provocations. However, when we featured the model Giuliana Farfalla on the cover of the February 2018 issue–the first time in *Playboy's* history that a woman born as Pascal, i.e., assigned male at birth, was featured–there was a measurable amount of public outrage. In our perception, this reaction exposes those who are upset about the alleged taboo-breaking more than it reflects on us, the authors of the message.

Louis Shankar

There's definitely room for magazines to be provocative—but, if anything, I believe provocation has been watered down. Many things that claim to be provocative today are, in reality, rather mundane or ordinary. Provocation for the sake of provocation reeks of desperation.

I think what can—or should—be productively provocative has changed. Work that addresses institutionalized sexual abuse, for example, is far more provocative than work about sex in an erotic sense.

Leonidas Liolios

Unfortunately, we live in a world where owning a gun (looking at you, USA) or showing 100 people competing to the death on an international streaming platform (Squid Game) is more lawful than sex work, same-sex relationships, and, in many cases, porn. Erotic magazines challenge moral conventions, whether they intend to or not.

Sex is taboo in most contexts, professional and personal, if the people involved in those contexts are prudes and hypocrites who would rather watch people get gutted on film because it's "fiction" than two people fucking their brains out on paper.

As for "the line," it's drawn in the shape of the word "consent," which should apply to everything, really. As long as no one is forcing anyone to consume erotic material, alienation shouldn't be a problem.

Matthias Straub

First of all, *THE OPÉRA* is not an erotic magazine. It's important to differentiate between pornography on one side of the scale and erotic photography or nude photography on the other. Eroticism will always be a sublime aspect of nude photography, but it is never the focus of *THE OPÉRA*.

Generally speaking, photography can serve as a mirror of society, and it holds the power to change perspectives.

8

Sasha Grey once remarked: "What some may find degrading or repulsive, others see as empowering and beautiful." How do you navigate this tension in your work, and where do you personally fall on that spectrum?

Ghislain Pascal

I agree. Everything is personal taste. So *BOYS! BOYS! BOYS!* is always going to be my taste, my style, and my vision, as with any editor, curator, or creative director. The worst mistake is to try to second guess what people like or want. But I think that we can all agree what makes a good or bad photograph.

Lucy Roeber

Ha! This is really at the heart of the matter. We aim to open the dialog by publishing a range of work—some of it might be considered unusual, degrading, or even repulsive—but all of it is beautifully written and considered.

Through art, we see the world on many levels and can empathize, even if it doesn't work for us. For example, my 23-year-old niece, a mostly heterosexual musician, found the story by Cason Sharpe in Issue 1—about a bored young gay man cruising in a shopping mall in Toronto—very sexy. She connected with it, even though it's not something she would ever experience herself. This is where the tension becomes beautiful.

Linda Zhengová

The real resistance lies in staying true to oneself—that's the most radical and inspiring thing we can do today. What one person finds degrading, another might see as liberating, and that's the beauty of it.

Erotic work should never be afraid of its complexity. Beauty, desire, repulsion, power—these aren't opposites; they coexist. My task is to embrace that contradiction, not resolve it. Such tension is a space where we can question our discomfort and desires, and where conversations start. That's the power of art—it doesn't need to please or explain itself. It just needs to exist, unapologetically.

The Dreamer aka Sotiris Trechas

Everything is a matter of perspective. *Fluffer Everyday* has changed my life in so many ways, and I am truly thankful for that. Every issue of the magazine elaborates on a specific kink, so every time I get to research and find people to talk about these kinks.

I have met so many inspiring people because of the magazine, and heard so many stories that I wouldn't have otherwise, and all these stories stay with me. I have changed the way I understand my body, my sexuality, because I have been able to experience how differently others experience their own sexuality and the way they manifest their kinks.

I always keep an open mind and put myself in their shoes—why do they like what they like, and how can I help relay their stories? Accepting diversity is important, and that is why representation matters.

Moan

As long as it's consensual, safe, and built on choice and communication, I believe it's beautiful. For me, the diversity of desires and perspectives is what makes human sexuality so fascinating and worth exploring. Whether or not I share the same desires doesn't matter—what's important is creating a space where those desires can be expressed and respected without shame.

In my work, I navigate this tension by focusing on authenticity. Each issue of *MOAN* features stories, poems, and articles from people all over the world. I admire how many different desires exist within this world and aim to depict sexuality in ways that feel free from judgment. Not everything will resonate with everyone, and that's okay—what's empowering for one person may not be for another. What matters is honoring that diversity and challenging the idea that there's a "right" way to experience or express desire.

Ultimately, *MOAN* is about celebrating the complexities of intimacy and pleasure, holding space for different interpretations, and allowing readers to explore what empowerment and beauty mean to them.

Greta Futura Langianni

As I mentioned before, the key to sexual freedom shouldn't lie in what we like to do but rather in how we approach it, because everyone has different needs, kinks, and desires. These differences make it nearly impossible to define a "right way" to experience sexuality.

I completely agree with the perspective statet by Sashy Grey. Personally, I've realized that a significant point for me within this spectrum are power dynamics. During a period of my life that I consider deeply empowering in terms of my sexuality, I worked through this issue and came to understand that much of how I engaged in sex, and the partners I chose, was rooted in the power dynamics I was creating and shifting within those relationships. The theme of power, in all its forms, has become central to this exploration and ultimately became the focus of the issue we printed. It served almost as a form of therapy—a journey of personal discovery that merged with collective experiences.

Florian Boitin

I believe that sexuality and eroticism are fundamentally very personal areas that people perceive and feel very differently. And yet, it's that subtle difference that is important to us: *Playboy* erotica must never be perceived as degrading—neither by women nor by men.

Playboy erotica can, of course, be titillating and provocative. But it is always an expression of self-determined sexuality.

Louis Shankar

Taste is never universal. Throughout our magazine, we've aspired to embrace diversity and eclecticism—approaching it from an editorial rather than an authorial perspective. We've published work that explores sex from a variety of perspectives, including those that are provocative or potentially upsetting.

We're committed to exploring sex and sexuality from explicitly queer positions, especially where this might confronts and challenges cis- or hetero-normativity.

Leonidas Liolios

I can totally relate to that. At *The Boy Is Beautiful*, we choose not to navigate that tension but instead to surrender to it and celebrate what we—and all of our contributors—find empowering and beautiful, confident that like-minded people out there will feel the same.

Matthias Straub

My personal view and taste as a curator are always reflected in the magazine—but they're only part of the final display. There is, of course, the artist's perspective and the interpretation by the designers. In the end, it's a collaborative process that leads to the final issue.

9

Former adult actress and writer Stoya, known for challenging beauty standards in erotic content said: "If you think pubic hair on women is unnatural or weird, you're not mature enough to touch vaginas." How does embracing or rejecting natural aesthetics influence your editorial stance on body representation?

Ghislain Pascal

It is very important to embrace all natural aesthetics. Beauty is in the eye of the beholder.

Lucy Roeber

Our editorial stance is about exploring the erotic culture of the world we live in today. The aesthetics of the body are fundamental to that conversation.

I want to hear different sides of that debate. It's not necessarily what is right or wrong, more a matter of the effect that such extreme expectations have on the idea of body representation.

Linda Zhengová

From an editorial perspective, I'm open to any interpretation of bodies that leaves an impact on me as a viewer. Whether it's a deeply personal story or AI-generated content, I don't care. What matters is avoiding the tokenization of our bodies to fit trends or turning ourselves into sensations for the sake of spectacle.

In my personal photographic work, I collaborate with real people, and their bodies often become reflections of the times we're living in. My encounters are rooted in chance and connection, not defined by what someone has between their legs or the labels they carry.

Stoya's quote reminds me of a recent photoshoot where a model shared that a photographer had asked her to stick artificial pubic hair on her body. I find it ironic and absurd in this context. Today, what even qualifies as "natural aesthetics"?

The Dreamer aka Sotiris Trechas

Fluffer Everyday is all about everyday people in everyday moments. Real people living their lives. No models, no overly stylized sets. Natural aesthetics are key to this project. When researching for a new issue, I try to find the best people who fit the topic. When the time comes to do the pictures, I never control how they look or how they pose–it's all about them. The only thing I keep in mind when casting is diversity. *Fluffer Everyday* is a pansexual publication, so when you flip through the pages, you'll come across every type of human.

Moan

The idea that something as natural as pubic hair could be seen as "weird" or "unnatural" isn't just about maturity, I don't think–it's also about a lack of real, meaningful experiences and connections. It stems from relying on screens and narrow, mainstream narratives of sex to teach us about bodies and intimacy. This brings me back to the problem with mainstream sex narratives and the lack of education around them. These depictions strip away individuality, reducing sexuality to a sanitized ideal, often dehumanizes woman. The fear of pubic hair–or anything outside that "ideal"–comes from this overreliance on limited representations that fail to reflect real life.

I hope to challenge these narrow standards by celebrating the diversity, beauty, and individuality of all bodies. Pubic hair, stretch marks, scars, and every unique characteristic deserve to be seen and embraced. These are not flaws; they're part of what makes us human, and they hold beauty and power.

Greta Futura Langianni

This statement makes me laugh because the first time I shaved my vagina when I was around 17 (because I thought guys would like it more) I felt this overwhelming sense of wrongness when I looked at my hairless genitals. It mostly came from the fact that it looked like a child's vagina and I could not help but feel extremely infantilized in that kind of body, which made me feel gross.

Eventually it should be your choice when it comes to your body and how it looks, I think it becomes toxic when you do it compelled to change it based on what others want you to look like.

We try in our magazine to represent all kinds of bodies–different shapes, abilities, ethnicities, aesthetics, we try to point out how not only in sex but also with bodies there isn't one thing that's good for everyone there's a spectrum of beauty that deserves to exist and be represented in all its shades.

Florian Boitin

Ideals of beauty change over time. The hairstyle trends of the 1970s, for example, might seem strange to many younger people today. Similarly, pubic hair in erotic images is now often perceived as exotic. That said, what I mentioned in response to the previous question still applies: sexuality is deeply personal and highly individual. For *Playboy*, this means valuing diversity and naturalness. This is why, throughout all these decades, we've never completely banned pubic hair from our magazine.

Louis Shankar

This quote speaks directly to the cover of our second issue, a photograph from the series *Amor Entre Cucas* (2019) by Bárbara Sánchez-Kane, in collaboration with Dorian Ulises Lopez: a woman's pubic hair dyed orange and styled into spikes. It traces an alternative line between the natural and the artificial. While this is clearly no longer "natural" in the untouched, neutral sense, it nonetheless challenges beauty standards from an alternate perspective. We were initially worried that such an image on the cover might alienate or concern booksellers, but we only received positive feedback. Its status as an artwork seemed to temper reactions, along with the wry humor inherent in the piece.

Leonidas Liolios

Personally, I take an "anything goes" approach to beauty standards, and coincidentally, so does everyone else involved in the magazine. That's why you'll find anything and everything in *The Boy Is Beautiful* across all of our issues. Six-packs or bellies, hairy assholes or clean-shaven, we love them all. I find representation to be a tricky one, because the last thing we want is for it to be used in a tokenistic way. Ultimately, we strive to feature the work of people who feel important and who align with the themes of our project, without trying to tick any boxes.

Matthias Straub

Art is interpretation. So of course bodies or body parts are being put in scene in many different ways, using many different techniques. Any kind of interpretation is welcome, as long as it's conducted in a respectful, and possibly meaningful way. *THE OPÉRA* aims to tell stories about humans and their bodies–and since they differ quite a lot from each other diversity is a key factor for choosing and publishing nude photography.

10

The naked body has historically occupied a space between art and taboo. Do you see this tension as its greatest strength or a limitation that needs to be overcome? How does your work embrace or transcend that duality?

Ghislain Pascal

There is a great difference between the naked female body and the naked male body. The naked female body is totally acceptable in today's society, while the naked male body remains a taboo. These are the issues all my photographers face on a daily basis.

Lucy Roeber

I think it is the female naked body that has occupied the space between art and taboo in western culture—and this is very culturally dependent. The male body, particularly the aroused male body, was less explored in art until 20th century. Over the last 20 years, Internet porn has shifted the tension between nakedness and art and taboo, but we're still far from fully understanding its cultural impact.

At the *Erotic Review,* we want to look at all aspects of what is taboo and why. My feeling is that nakedness in particular is culturally dependent. I was just in Berlin and was invited to a spa and the attitude there to nakedness was so very different to the UK. You'd NEVER have a mixed spa where nakedness is normalized in the UK.

Linda Zhengová

Historically, this genre has carried so many problematic layers: racism, sexism, classism—you name it. And despite progress, many of these issues still persist. Today, the conversation often shifts toward distinguishing between art and porn.

But the real question is: why are bodies taboo in the first place? In which contexts? Why are certain bodies more taboo than others? Is taboo merely the result of repression? And more importantly, who gets to decide what is taboo and what is not?

To be honest, I don't think about taboos, because I'm not the one defining them. I am just making art out of the urgency to create. Taboos are constructs, and my focus is on dismantling those constructs rather than engaging with them on their terms. I'm interested in exploring what lies beyond them—in the raw, unfiltered expressions that don't ask for permission or seek validation. If my work confronts taboos, it's not intentional; it's a byproduct of pursuing truth and vulnerability. What drives me isn't what's forbidden but what's real.

The Dreamer aka Sotiris Trechas

I truly believe that the naked body is such a powerful weapon. It's a symbol for acceptance, independence, and personal expression, things that many could claim frightening. But how can something so natural be so restrictive or polarizing?

In today's world, exposure to naked bodies and pornography has never been easier. I believe that the lens through which *Fluffer Everyday* operates allows this tension to thrive, creating a space for conversation and acceptance.

Moan

The tension between art and taboo is what makes the naked body so fascinating—it's both its greatest strength and a limitation to be challenged. This duality creates space for powerful conversations, but it also reflects society's discomfort with bodies and sexuality—a discomfort we're still working to overcome. I think this tension—art vs. taboo—is, at its core, a conversation about art vs. pornography: art being something that demands respect, while pornography is seen as something that requires censorship.

MOAN is often described by readers and viewers as art, as it embraces qualities associated with art—provoking thought, evoking emotion, and capturing beauty. Yet, I frequently face censorship, raising questions about where *MOAN* is positioned. Does censorship automatically place it within the realm of taboo? And who decides what belongs to which category? I intentionally sit in that in-between space, embracing duality. My work is about celebrating sexuality and the human body. I don't shy away from intimacy or desire, but I refuse to reduce these subjects to something purely performative. For me, the goal isn't to avoid taboo but to use art to challenge why certain depictions are considered taboo in the first place.

Greta Futura Langianni

Strengths can sometimes be limitations as well, one does not exclude the other. In my view, this duality is at the core of many of our creative endeavors, particularly when navigating the boundaries between art and societal norms. As artists, we often find ourselves walking on a thin line, unsure of the direction we're headed, yet constantly aware of the constraints we're working within. This uncertainty is both a challenge and a driving force, pushing us to examine not just the art itself but the context in which it is presented.

There is a contrast between two forms of representation that speaks to the underlying tension society has with the naked body: it's either overly censored or exploited, but rarely celebrated for its artistic and human significance. This contradiction reveals that the naked body's position between art and taboo is not a challenge to be overcome, but rather a powerful space to harness.

The naked body is not just a physical object, but a symbol—one that can provoke thought, and challenge our most deeply ingrained beliefs about gender, identity, and freedom. By embracing this duality, we have the opportunity to use the naked body not merely as a subject of controversy but as a tool for deeper reflection and exploration.

Florian Boitin

Nudity hasn't always been taboo. In antiquity, for example, there was a cult of the body that celebrated, rather than demonized, the naked form. Even in churches decorated by Renaissance artists, physicality was represented as vitality and sensuality. It's clear that art has always been strongly driven and influenced by human sexuality—while simultaneously being taboo. Whether it's Auguste Rodin's *The Kiss,* which once caused a major scandal, or later, the kitsch artist Jeff Koons, who transformed his partner, the well-known porn star Cicciolina, into a work of art—there is little black and white in art. The line between art and porn has always been thin—and it still is.

Louis Shankar

It's all about context, isn't it? It's the difference between "naked" and "nude"—between a body in the changing room and one in the bedroom. The erotic invariably comes up against censorship, but both forces are constantly changing and evolving. Art has always had the potential to challenge our assumptions and expectations, but its impact depends on where it appears–a gallery, public space, social media, print, etc.

Leonidas Liolios

If we look at ancient Greece, the naked body was present in art in a casual way—often in sexual play. I use art here in the post-neoclassical sense of the word, because for the ancient Greeks, these were often just everyday objects like wine cups and amphoras used for storing grain.

In the Renaissance, rich men in power, whose male gaze ruled supreme, commissioned myriads of paintings that borrowed themes from Greek mythology to disguise their nudity as "pure," which was only necessary because those same people had vilified nudity through religion over the course of 16 centuries. It's quite absurd.

Almost 400 years later, the same people who experience awe and wonder when looking at a Botticelli painting feel shame or disgust when looking at someone else's—or even their own—naked body. It's a shame, really, but it's theirs to bear. In *The Boy Is Beautiful,* there is no space for shame or taboos—only terracotta-colored pages filled with beautiful people, words, and ideas, in the way of my ancestors. Casually.

Matthias Straub

Everyone has a body and can relate to nudity. Still there is a tension between what we are accustomed to seeing and what we desire to look at. This space is filled by artists and explored with different media and techniques. *THE OPÉRA* is investigating more of multi-dimensional universe in which the human body is a play and stage at the same time.

– essays (…)”

Dan Rhatigan
Dermot Mac Cormack
Larissa Brochella
Karina Panko
Ian Lynam
Pia Kristin Lobodzinski
Rebekka Seubert
Hubert Kretschmer

Hot Type: It's not about the pictures.

Dan Rhatigan

Dan Rhatigan is a typographer living in Portland, Oregon, with over three decades of eclectic experience as a typesetter, graphic designer, typeface designer, and educator. He runs a small type foundry called Bijou Type, and since 2009 has published Pink Mince, a zine devoted to queer culture and typography. He also maintains two web sites documenting his research into dry transfer type → *letraslut.com* and the history of gay magazines → *hottype.club* (Image 1)

During the second half of the twentieth century, the United States and many European countries developed more accepting attitudes towards? LGBT people, due to the cumulative efforts of numerous groups engaged in social and political activism. Along the way, one of the many challenges facing gay publishers and audiences was the difficulty of producing and distributing any books or periodicals with overtly gay content, which was under threat of various methods of censorship. However, even as legal hurdles fell away, social censure remained an ongoing challenge to gay communities and the publications targeted to them.

During that same period, the graphic arts industry experienced its own rapid evolution, as the development of ever faster and cheaper means of typesetting and printing made more typographic choices available with fewer barriers to their use and reproduction. Typewriters, phototypesetting systems, dry transfer type, and eventually desktop publishing software provided an increasing number of ways to easily prepare text for layout and reproduction, with less and less formal training required to do so.

Suffice to say, there was both the will and the ways to publish for gay audiences, whether the message was intended to lift up or turn on. A comprehensive discussion of that complex intersection of social and graphic history would be a meaty text, but for now, this is about how I started to find some unexpected design flair in a space where publishers weren't concerned with what the mainstream thought of them. A few years ago, I published an issue of my own queer zine, *Pink Mince,* in which I stripped away the pornography from the pornography, carefully recreating just the typography from a number of vintage gay porn magazines.

In doing so, I discovered how much lively typography had been hiding in plain sight. (Image 2 & 3) This journey started when I stumbled across a beautiful old magazine cover, and that led to that little *Pink Mince* project, which then led to research, and then many more questions. The magazine in question was the beefcake-focused premiere issue of *Bold!* (1978), but what really caught my eye was its use of the typeface *Stilla* by François Boltana. I have always struggled to find examples of *Stilla* in use, no doubt because its zesty letterforms can be awfully difficult to compose. The letters have to be arranged with care, and it almost never sets all that easily by default. Trying to reset the cover type, I realized that this particularly helpful form of "L" didn't exist in the digital font. The answer was in my reference material—a Letraset specimen book. The original design published by Letraset in 1973 included a number of alternate characters for many letters, including that form of the "L" that I was looking for. (Image 4 & 5) At that time, it was typical to use dry transfer type for the titling graphics, and it certainly made sense for a typeface like *Stilla* that works at its best when set down one letter at a time, consciously controlling the combination of the forms. This small epiphany led me to look more closely at how other magazines of the era handled their typefaces. (Image 6)

Later, I encountered an image of the cover from *Drummer* magazine, a title better known for its S & M content than its novel typography. *Drummer* was a very adult magazine specializing in very adult themes, but this particular cover avoided photography in lieu of a really lively typographic approach—practically a specimen poster for dry transfer designs from Letraset. It startled me once again to see a magazine like this taking such a fresh approach to its design.

Image 1

Image 2

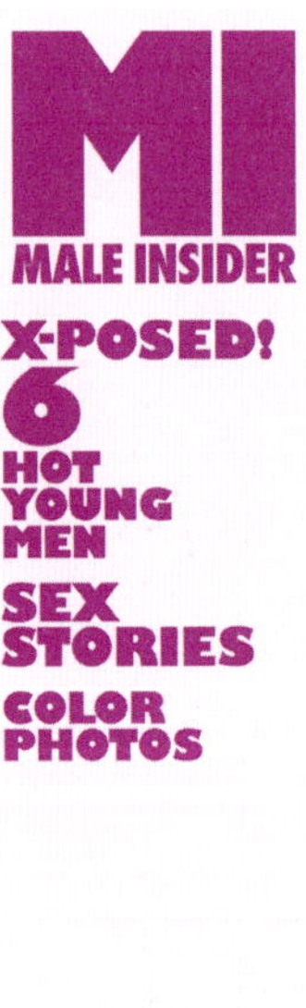

Image 3

These initial surprises felt more significant as I thought about the means of production available to these publications. I identified some typefaces that I liked, and I loved how they were used. My curiosity was further piqued, and I started gathering up more reference material: not for the pictures or the articles, but for the expressive typography. I found more magazines with unconventional type choices and sensitive type compositions, and wondered if these didn't face the same kind of commercial pressures to be as tasteful as the mainstream titles found on newsstands. (Image 7)

It's easy to focus on the campy humor of dirty old magazines with funny titles. For instance, a magazine called *Hot Dog! (Hold the Buns)* from the mid-1980s isn't shy about puns, but the title inspires an extra smile if you know that the typeface used is *Letraset Frankfurter*. In-jokes aside, *Hot Dog!'s* cover is set pretty well. The composition might not be the freshest but it responds to the main focus of the photograph. Considering how a magazine before the age of desktop publishing had to be produced by assembling analog materials, it is not amateur work.

Practicing everyday graphic production in this era required a number of refined visual and manual skills. Notation like Letraset's Spacematic system provided some help with rub-down type, but you still needed to be able to space type relatively well, and to be able to make optical adjustments when aligning letters or words. You had to know how to apply type carefully and firmly onto a layout board, how to scale artwork using a stat camera, and how to prepare layered mechanical paste-ups for color separation and printing. The work seen in these magazines may not reflect the most sophisticated graphic design, but it was still work that required some degree of training and familiarity with graphic art materials and production for print. If you wanted to publish a magazine, you had to rely on someone who had a basic understanding of the methods of production and probably some understanding of composition or at least some opinions about layout and typography.

I am pretty sure this explains a lot of the choices I discovered. Retail products like Letraset were very accessible and inexpensive compared to commercial typesetting services, so they were easy ways to provide variety in a crowded market segment in which titles needed to distinguish themselves from one another with minimal investment, since the cover photography was the primary selling point. There probably weren't a lot of staff meetings and market research about the cover typography for these magazines. I think people were given a stack of photos and told to "slap together a cover so this can go to the printer," and those people with a bit of experience and a lot of latitude took the opportunity to have what fun they could. (Image 8 & 9)

There are many, many examples of this, particularly during the 70s and the early 80s—before the age of digital typography, in the era when retail lettering products like Letraset, Chartpak, Zip-a-Tone, Mecanorma, and others were challenging the dominance of phototypesetting. The accessibility of dry transfer type was a catalyst for much of what we see in the publications from this era. (Image 10)

Despite the prominence of rub-down type in many cover layouts, phototypesetting was still the primary method of setting headlines and text type until PostScript fonts and desktop publishing software supplanted it in the late 1980s. In many cases, the publishers did not seem to pay for the highest quality composing services. But would professional type shops have taken on obscene jobs like these? A factor

Image 4: The typography of Bold!, issue 1. Above is what the digital version of François Boltana's Stilla looks like with its default spacing. Image 5: Sample of the typeface Stilla from a 1987 Letraset catalog, showing multiple versions of some capital letters like A, E, L, M, N, and T. Image 6: Drummer no. 6, May/June 1976. Image 6: Drummer no. 6, May/June 1976.

Image 10: In 1975, Rough Trade mixed a handful of Letraset faces for its cover: Marvin and Futura Display, with some smaller lines in Eurostile and Helvetica. Image 11: Letraset brochure, 1984. Image 12: One reports on its 1957 victory in court.

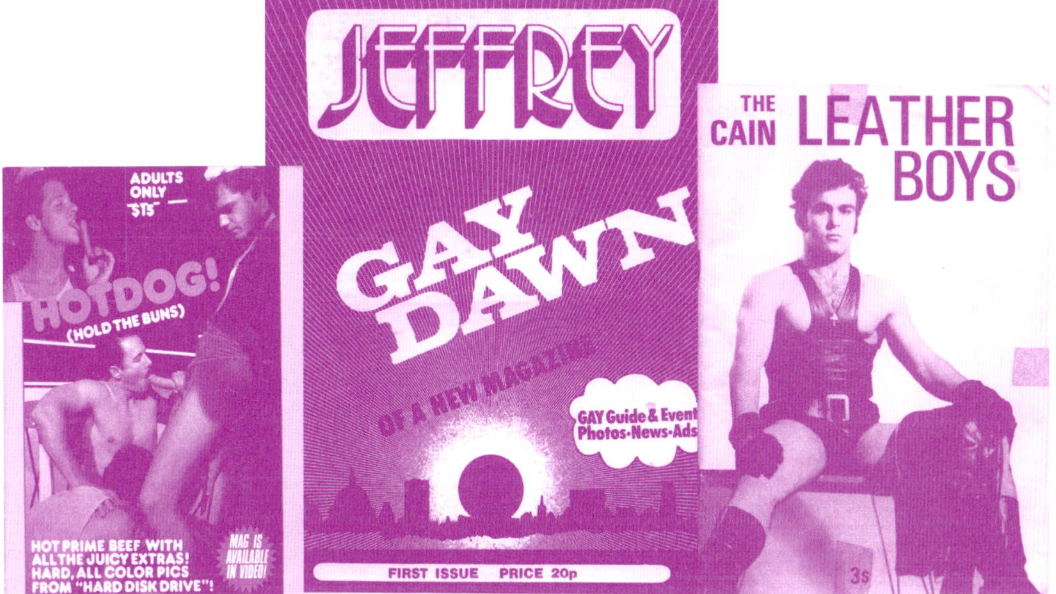

Image 7. Image 8: Jeffrey's first issue from 1972 used faces from French dry transfer brand Mecanorma, such as First Ombre and Volta Bold, plus more commonly available faces like Futura Extra Bold Condensed and Helvetica Bold. The radiant pattern in the background would have been done with an adhesive film, another graphic product from Mecanorma. Image 9: The cover for photographer Cain of London's self-published was made by rubbing Letraset transfer type right onto the photo print, which was then re-shot for offset reproduction.

Image 13: Mattachine Review, 1956, with a cover made with a mix of typewriter text and photoset headlines. Image 14 & 15: In 1959, MANual launched as a typical physique magazine claiming to promote health and fitness, even though its photographers focused more on scantily clad bodybuilders than on their workout routines. By 1965, its erotic intentions were allowed to flourish more openly.

in the use of Letraset and other kinds of rub-down type for these magazines was likely that it bypassed the middleman: one less service bureau that may not want to handle gay porn (A typesetter working in New York during the 1970s and 1980s told me that customers would regularly sneak headlines and captions for adult material within the middle of more mundane jobs. The typesetters would encounter specs for random bits of copy that didn't quite make sense, their meaning obscured by the overall context). (Image 11)

Letraset dry transfer type was invented in 1961 to be a professional graphic arts tool. The company rapidly discovered that it made typography very accessible in ways that were more significant than they anticipated. It democratized typesetting by making it possible for someone to go into an art or design supply store and buy their type easily and inexpensively. When it was possible to buy a sheet of rub-down type and throw a layout together, professionals and amateurs alike could try their hand at a bit of publishing and set a little text. That was very powerful. There was an explosion of graphic ephemera from the late 20th century because of that accessibility, that chance for someone without a graphic arts background, someone with neither the experience or other resources, to make something on their own that could at the very least include well-crafted typefaces.

Letraset and other brands of rub-down type rose to the forefront of the marketplace during the 60s, a time of incredible of social upheaval in the west. Just as there was an explosion of underground press supporting civil rights, women's liberation, and anti-war sentiments, there was also the dawn of a gay press. For gay publishers and readers, barriers were falling down that made it possible for the first time to produce and distribute material with overtly homosexual content. Social acceptance is a slow process, however: it was still very handy for publishers of gay material to have access to democratized means of production. (Image 12 & 13)

The earliest gay publications in the United States struggled against adversity both legal and practical because of the nature of their content. Digest-sized, single-color magazines such as *One* (launched in January 1953) and *Mattachine Review* (launched in January 1955) featured news, politics, and literary articles rather than anything sexual in nature, yet were harassed by law enforcement and the U.S. Postal Service alike. The Postal Service refused to mail *One* on grounds of obscenity, a decision which was eventually overturned by the Supreme Court in 1957. *Mattachine Review* tread more carefully with the authorities, but the reluctance of printers to take on a job that might be subject to prosecution led the Review's publisher to set up his own typesetting, design, and printing service–the Pan-Graphic Press.

Similarly, publisher Herbert Lynn Womack started his own printing business in order to produce a series of magazines under the imprint of MANual Enterprises (later known as the Guild Press). MANual Enterprises titles featured overtly homoerotic collections of photography without explicitly declaring homosexual intent. However, this was still enough to raise suspicion. Parcels containing three of Womack's titles–*Grecian Guild Pictorial, MANual,* and *Trim*–were seized by the Postal Service in 1960, which eventually led to a 1962 Supreme Court decision that ruled that nude or near-nude models did not necessarily qualify as obscenity.

These first few court rulings paved the way for a small explosion in modestly produced publications for a gay market, a customer base that sought out these titles furtively in the years before the legal triumphs and Stonewall and increasing social

Image 16

Image 17

Image 18

acceptance. This was the era of the physique magazine, such as those published by Womack and MANual Enterprises. Physique magazines kept a very straight face, as it were, in talking about the subject matter.

They promoted themselves as champions of physical culture, exercise, improving your muscle tone, watching your weight through healthy diet, and posing for the edification of artists and photographers in need of models. This was a conscious attempt to co-opt the aesthetics of typical magazines about sport, shifting the visual and editorial direction just enough to resonate with a gay audience. (Image 14 & 15) As Womack's efforts were emboldened by his victory in the Supreme Court and his control of his own press, the photographs in *MANual* spoke less to classical ideas of form, and started to become more suggestive and prurient. As the veil of pure athleticism was dropped, many physique magazines also reduced the amount of cover copy devoted to articles on health and sport, and relied more on attention-grabbing mastheads and bold photography. While Letraset and its plethora of display typography hadn't fully saturated the publishing market yet, the change in tone was happening that was ready to embrace it. (Image 16, Image 17)

The increasing acceptance and visibility of gay publications encouraged the growth of numerous gay lifestyle magazines, which often mixed culture and politics with a dash of nudity. More newsstand-friendly, yet still wanting to reach gay readerships in urban areas, these titles often relied on typefaces popular in more mainstream media. *Dilettante* launched in 1974 with a lot of photography that might raise an eyebrow, but featured articles on books and plays and movies, all set with a trendy mix of Letraset's version of A. M. Cassandre's *Peignot* (already well-known thanks to the popular *Mary Tyler Moore Show),* Herb Lubalin and Tom Carnese's *ITC Avant Garde,* and trusty *Helvetica.* In 1975, *Dilettante* quickly folded but was reborn as *Mandate,* keeping the same typographic formula for many more years. (Image 18, 19 & 20)

Drummer, launched in 1975, bridged a gap between the increasingly explicit descendants of the physique magazines, and the eclectic contents of the urbane lifestyle magazines. *Drummer* focused on the gay male S & M community, calling its readership the "Leather Fraternity." It grew out of a newsletter and then a political newspaper of the same name–that of the Homophile Effort for Legal Protection, based Los Angeles in the early 70s. H.E.L.P.'s *Drummer* paper already featured the incredible mix of type that made the magazine stand out later. Initially, this graphic effort helped to make a newsletter about legal issues more appealing and friendlier to the community. When the newspaper folded, and the "Drummer" name was repurposed for a magazine "dedicated to the leather lifestyle for guys," it became clear that the typography reflected the graphic sensibilities of publisher John Embry, whose apparent love of Letraset's typefaces provided a visual thread that connected the newsletter and the first 98 issues of *Drummer,* despite a frequently changing roster of art directors and designers. When *Drummer* changed hands after its 98th issue and Embry moved on to publish other titles, his love of *Compacta, Avant Garde,* and Walter H. McKay's *Egyptienne* went with him.

Other titles of the day, gay or otherwise, worked with the same materials and methods. Letraset, phototype, and paste-up art were widespread, after all. The characteristic eclecticism of *Drummer's* typography certainly helped it stand out from both the stroke magazines of the day–flashy title treatments but little cover text–as well as the mainstream gay lifestyle magazines–more verbose yet more typographically

Image 19

Image 20

Image 21 & 22: Drummer #115 and #118, 1988, bear the signs of the switch to desktop publishing software and the limited font vchoices of the day. Instead of a mix of typefaces, we see just a few typefaces slanted, scaled, layered, and outlined instead.

Image 23 *Image 24* *Image 25*

Image 23-28: The introduction of desktop publishing software such as PageMaker or QuarkXPress—and the use of digital fonts—did not often lead to more sophisticated typography in the world of fetish publishing.

predictable. Most magazines relied heavily on photography (and from all accounts, were able to do so because they paid more generously and more reliably than Embry would), and the results were often less memorable. The typographic playfulness of *Drummer's* covers provided contrast to the sexually graphic content within, and gave it a clear identity that contributed to its success as it connected S & M enthusiasts scattered around the country.

Even with more straightforward magazine covers and layouts, typographic variety was typical of working with a material like transfer type, where a designer may have a pile of different sheets available, forced to switch to a different typeface if only to set text at a different size, or because a sheet of a given design may have run out of the glyphs need. This practical eclecticism went away as these publications moved into the digital space, where it's much easier to scale the text and there were no limits to the use of any characters found in a font. That's when you see magazines following the more modernist approach of using just a couple of typefaces (somewhat) tastefully throughout the cover. (Image 21 & 22)

Drummer's look settled down in the years after Embry's departure in 1986, which coincided with a steady shift toward desktop software as a means of production. It was an uncomfortable evolution, as the typography became more formulaic and a little bit less sensitive to how things were handled. The overall composition of image and text became less considered, and playful choices from the Letraset library were replaced with formulaic use of the early digital versions of *Avant Garde, Helvetica,* and *Futura,* distorted and outlined and colored in ways made possible by the new software. As those means of production evolved, they showed the changing nature of the skills needed to practice graphic design. The judgement and perceptual skills needed to work with Letraset and pasted-up strips of phototype gave way to the technical skills needed to assemble documents in PageMaker and QuarkXPress. (Image 23-28)

Once desktop publishing became the working method of choice, the type choices were typically blander, and even the compositions are a lot more straightforward. Instead of careful arrangement of elements, there were more boxes or overlapping of type and graphic elements, much easier to do with software than it had been with multi-layered mechanicals and the analog reproduction methods. Often however, layouts could be even less considered than that. As the means of laying out a cover or an interior page became easier and more accessible, the tasks quickly fell to those who knew the software, but not much about design. While this was a triumph for access to the means of production, the results were not always as appealing.

There is a social history to the means of production for all things, even the tawdry genre of adult magazines. I can barely scratch the surface of this particular intersection of culture, civil rights, sexual expression, and opportunism in a limited space like this, but the research possibilities are vast. Investigating the publications and related ephemera of a specific community still gives some insight into an era of rapid change in the graphic arts, and how successfully technological advances democratized design and publishing, for highbrow and lowbrow subjects alike.

Lotus Feet, a Molted Cicada's Shell, and Cross-Dressing: Gendered Writing Systems

Dermot Mac Cormack

Dermot Mac Cormack is a designer, educator, and writer with a passion for typography and design education. He is Chair of the Design & Illustration Department at Tyler School of Art & Architecture, Temple University, and a partner at the award-winning design firm 21xdesign, which he co-founded with Patricia McElroy. His commitment to design and education stems from a deep curiosity–both to inspire and learn from the next generation of designers. In addition to writing about design for Slanted and Design 360, Dermot received the Hennessy Writer of the Year Award, and his work appears in The New Hennessy Book of Irish Fiction. As an avid typographer, he has presented his research and design work at leading conferences, including Typecon and ATypI. → *IG @fimfin, @21xdesign*

Imagine not being allowed to use the writing system you are reading right now or being denied access to it simply because of your gender. To gain access to this writing system, you more than likely had to be a man, someone in authority, or both. Well, this was precisely the case for segments of various societies around the world. If you were a woman living in a specific patriarchal society at a particular time, these were the hurdles you had to overcome and work around. As you know, writing systems are powerful and essential tools for communication. You have access right now to all the knowledge and information contained within the pages of this book that you hold in your hands.

Without writing systems, we would not be who we are today. Societies are built around communication. These systems serve critical functions within our society: they help preserve our cultural heritage and the formation (and development) of our cultural identities. Throughout history, while most writing systems are essentially available to everyone within specific cultures, there are some notable exceptions where the writing systems have been associated with a particular gender, particularly women. In other words, these are gendered writing systems. Imagine that for a moment. These remarkable systems offer a lens through which to examine the interplay between societal power dynamics, gender roles, and literacy. Whether it's the Nüshu system in China, Hiragana in Japan, or the Cuneiform script in Sumaria–they all highlight the restrictions and opportunities once presented to women in diverse cultural contexts and times.

NÜSHU

It is the 19th-century, rural China. A villager has just passed away, and friends and family surround her graveside. Alongside the deceased is a cloth-bound book with unusual, slender calligraphy. Whatever the "book" contains–poems, advice, or perhaps an autobiography–is soon to be buried, along with its owner. Undoubtedly, she is also a woman from Hunan Province. The deceased woman and her close female friends and family were primarily confined to the domestic sphere, engaging in household duties and child-rearing. Societal norms at that time dictated obedience to fathers, husbands, and sons, restricting their autonomy and access to education. This confinement often led to social isolation, as women had limited opportunities to interact outside their immediate family circles. Foot binding was also a prevalent practice during this period, typically initiated around the age of seven. This painful tradition aimed to achieve the "Golden Lotus" ideal of approximately three-inch-long feet, considered a status symbol and a prerequisite for marriage. The practice significantly limited women's mobility, further reinforcing their domestic confinement.[1] Yet, out of this culture of patriarchal oppression, there evolved a remarkable form of "secret" communication, a writing system called Nüshu. This unique writing system was developed for and used exclusively by women is Nüshu, generally meaning "women's script," from Jiangyong County, Hunan Province, China. This syllabic script emerged as a secret means of communication for women mostly excluded from formal education in a structured patriarchal society.[2] While the precise origins of Nüshu are still debated, it likely began as early as the Song Dynasty (960-1279) and gained prominence during the Qing Dynasty (1644-1912). Nüshu is, of course, derived from Chinese characters, but as you can see in the illustration, it has a more cursive, linear, and condensed style, sometimes described as "mosquito-leg script" due to its delicate, spindly appearance. It was used primarily by women during these time periods to communicate personal thoughts, poems, and stories with one another. This secret script allowed women to express their emotions and shared experiences, creating a space for solidarity and resistance against a system that often silenced or simply ignored them. Nüshu was commonly used among what were called "sworn sisters" or "laotong," who formed lifelong bonds and used the script to communicate their thoughts and feelings, especially in the form of what were called "third-day missives," or *sanzhaoshu*–which is a cloth-bound book written and delivered to brides the third day after their weddings.[3] These cloth-bound booklets, written in Nüshu, were presented to brides to offer support and solidarity. These "third-day missives" were an important tradition that provided emotional support for women facing challenges in marriage, for example, and further cement the role of Nüshu as a tool for female bonding and empowerment.

In 2004, at age 98, Yang Huanyi, passed away.[4] She is possibly the script's last proficient user and played a vital role in preserving this writing system. Her willingness to share her knowledge of Nüshu with researchers helped guarantee that this unique script would not be lost to history. If you want to hear how Nüshu sounds, check out the Chinese composer Tan Dun's *Nu Shu: The Secret Songs of Women.*[5] It's fascinating to listen to.

HIRAGANA

In Japan, the development of Hiragana offers another example of gendered writing practices. During the Heian Period (794-1185), women primarily used a system called Hiragana, while men used Kanji for formal documents, academia, and governance, all of which were the exclusive purview of men at that time. Hiragana (a simplified phonetic system derived from Chinese characters) was considered "softer" and more suited for poetry and personal expression, domains that were culturally assigned to women.[6]

Murasaki Shikibu (circa 973-1014 CE) was a Japanese noblewoman renowned for writing *The Tale of Genji.*[7] While *The Tale of Genji* is perhaps not the "first novel" in a global, absolute sense, it is often considered the world's first psychological or modern novel due to its innovative narrative style, emotional depth, and literary sophistication. And all of it was initially written in Hiragana, a gendered writing system at that time. Living during the Heian Period, Murasaki served as a lady-in-waiting at the imperial court, where she was able to observe and write about the intricate lives of

Tale of Genji. The „Butterflies" Chapter of the Tale of Genji Attributed to Tosa Mitsuyoshi. Minneapolis Institute of Art.

the aristocracy. Her daily life involved literary pursuits, the many court ceremonies, and interactions with other court ladies and nobles. Despite the court's dynamic environment, Murasaki often felt isolated. She expressed feelings of loneliness in her diary, especially after her husband's death in 1001. *The Tale of Genji* explores the complexities of love, politics, and human nature in the context of the Heian court. While the book does not explicitly describe sex (as we are used to seeing it portrayed in contemporary literature), it is hinted at in oblique ways. In chapter three, "Utsusemi" Genji is caught spying on a lady while peeping through a gap in a screen. This *kaimami* (a man spying on women through a gap in a screen) would later become a favorite painting device illustrated by Genji artists. After having spied on her, Genji, sneaks into her chamber, but *Utsusemi* manages to escape from Genji's embrace by discarding her outer robe like a cicada discards its shell (hence the chapter's title, *Utsusemi*). The lady also abandons her sleeping stepdaughter, who then becomes Genji's unwitting prey. Rather than sleep alone for the night, Genji ends up sleeping with Nokiba no ogi, who does not even imagine she has been the victim of mistaken identity.[8] In many ways, it is not too far a cry from our contemporary world, and yet, it is nonetheless remarkable that a woman of this time would even contemplate writing about such matters, albeit in gendered writing, exclusively for women.

Murasaki Shikibu, of course, lived in a strictly patriarchal society that restricted women's opportunities for formal education and freedom of expression. However, women were encouraged to develop skills in poetry and storytelling. While men wrote in Kanji, women used Hiragana, which gave them a unique and separate sphere of expression. Murasaki likely taught herself Chinese in secret, giving her access to a broader literary canon, and her mastery of both Hiragana and Kanji set her apart. Through her psychologically insightful narratives, Murasaki challenged the constraints of her time, creating a work that has endured for over a millennium. Her work, along with *The Pillow Book* by Sei Shōnagon, demonstrated the high level of literary achievement of women in the Heian court. Murasaki Shikibu's detailed depiction of court life provides historians with valuable insights into Heian Japan's culture, gender roles, and aesthetics. Several years ago, I had the good fortune to see some of the original writing in person in Japan. These manuscripts are exquisite objects, and the delicacy of the writing, coupled with millennia-old patina, only adds to their ethereal quality, helped in large part by the delicacy of the calligraphy.

Hiragana is no longer gender-exclusive today, but its historical association with women remains crucial in the history of Japanese literature. Once again, women's development and use of Hiragana highlight how marginalized groups can adapt an existing writing system and create a unique sphere of expression and creativity. The script's calligraphic elegance is often compared to the beauty of natural phenomena, such as the flow of water or the gracefulness of brushstrokes. This enhanced its role as a medium for emotional and aesthetic expression. This legacy continues today, where the beauty of early Hiragana is celebrated in Japanese art and calligraphy.

CUNEIFORM

Enheduanna, who was a high priestess in ancient Sumer (circa 2285-2250 BCE), is often celebrated as the world's first-known named author.[9] Once again, here is another woman living in a profoundly patriarchal society, but she was able to use her position as a priestess to compose hymns, such as "*The Exaltation of Inanna*," which not only praised the gods but also reflected her personal struggles and political challenges. Her role as a high priestess (appointed as an en, or high-priestess of Nanna (also known as Sin), a deity of Ur) gave her access to education and influence, usually denied to women in her society. However, she also faced challenges, such as being exiled during political turmoil. Interestingly, in this very poem (lines 115-131), Enheduanna praises the god Inanna for her gifts of desirability and arousal and notes how she has the power to "turn a man into a woman and a woman into a man" (line 121). This is a possible reference to the androgyny of Inanna's clergy and cult followers. According to Joshua J. Mark's excellent post on Enheduanna's work, "Inanna's temples and attendant rituals were administered by clergy of both sexes, and her devotees were noted for their habit of cross-dressing, blending, blurring, or eliminating the distinction between male and female in pursuit of transcendence through Inanna."[10]

Though technically not a gender-specific writing system, Sumerian Cuneiform provides a valuable case study of gendered access to literacy via its writing systems. It should be noted that Cuneiform was not tied to a single language. It was used to write Sumerian, Akkadian, Babylonian, Assyrian, Hittite, and other ancient languages, and its use lasted for thousands of years. As you can see in the accompanying image, it is quite a beautiful and grided writing system. While most scribes at this time and place were men, some women in religious roles, such as priestesses, were also literate. Social status affected access to education and literacy, and women like

Sumerian Cuneiform Stone Tablet, Ancient Near East Gallery, Louvre Museum, Paris, France. Complete indexed photo collection at WorldHistoryPics.com. Photographer: Gary Todd

Enheduanna, used the cuneiform writing system to compose hymns and literature, exploring the interplay between gender, power, and literacy in ancient Sumerian society. Cuneiform, which originated around 3100 BCE in Mesopotamia, is one of the earliest known writing systems, and its use by women in specific contexts reveals the complex nature of gender and literacy access in early civilizations. The case of Sumerian Cuneiform shows that while access to literacy could be restricted, some women still had opportunities to overcome such restrictions and create works of lasting significance. Women could leverage their positions to wield considerable influence and produce enduring literary works. Enheduanna's legacy as the world's first named author is a testament to her ability to gain access to hitherto forbidden writing practice, which enabled her to communicate to the world from a distinctly female perspective.

Gendered writing systems and practices reveal the intricate ways in which literacy, communication, and cultural roles can intersect. How remarkable is it that these writing systems were developed independently, across geographic locations and time, but all with the same purpose and intent? The above examples underscore how writing can be both a reflection of and a tool against societal power structures. Even Sumerian Cuneiform, which was not strictly gender specific, provides a study of how social status also influenced women's access to literacy. The literary achievements of Enheduanna and Murasaki Shikibu demonstrate the impact of their intellectual and creative contributions despite the limitations of their times. Collectively, they indicate that throughout history, writing has served as a place of restriction and empowerment, with women often finding innovative ways to make their voices heard. Whether through secret scripts, gendered writing systems, or subverting access restrictions, the adaptability of women throughout history to make their voices heard through written expression always shines through.

1 Wikimedia Foundation, *Foot Binding*, Wikipedia, accessed 10.01.2025, en.wikipedia.org/wiki/Foot_binding
2 Tim Brookes, *An Atlas of Endangered Alphabets: Writing Systems on the Verge of Vanishing.* (Quercus Editions Ltd, A Hachette UK Company, 2024), 68.
3 Hannah Sparks, "Nüshu: The 400-Year-Old Chinese Script Only Women Can Write," *Atlas Obscura,* 26.02.2020, accessed 08.01.2025, atlasobscura.com/articles/nushu-chinese-script-women
4 Ibid.
5 Elizabeth Hainen, "Nu-Shu: Secret Songs of Women, composed by Tan Dun & performed by Elizabeth Hainen," 2013, accessed 08.01.2025, youtube.com/watch?v=g-1t-lnJ3Yg
6 Lexis Japan, Hiragana and the 2000-Year Journey from Then to Now, *Lexis Japan,* accessed 06.01.2025, lexisjapan.com/hiragana-and-the-2000-year-journey-from-then-to-now
7 The Tokugawa Art Museum, "National Treasures and Important Cultural Properties: Paintings," *The Tokugawa Art Museum,* accessed 06.01.2025, tokugawa-art-museum.jp/about/treasures/painting
8 Melissa McCormick, *The Tale of Genji: A Visual Companion.* (Princeton University Press, 2018), JSTOR, accessed 11.01.2025, doi: 10.2307/j.ctvc7754r
9 John A. Wilson, et al., "Mesopotamian Hymns." *The Ancient Near East: An Anthology of Texts and Pictures,* edited by James B. Pritchard. (Princeton University Press, 2011), 330–42. JSTOR, doi: 10.2307/j.ctv21r3qow.20
10 Joshua J. Mark, "Enheduanna." *World History Encyclopedia.* (07.02.2011), accessed 08.01.2025, worldhistory.org/Enheduanna

Queer voices: The inequality of words

Larissa Brochella

Larissa Brochella is a queer visual artist and graphic designer based in Basel, Switzerland. In her work she is interested in exploring social issues and the way they interact with the mundanity of everyday life. In her master project at the Academy for Art and Design in Basel she explored two topics close to her heart–language and queerness–through a multimedia installation.

Language as a means of expression and storytelling first conquered my heart in my childhood, when I discovered that through books I could disappear into more exciting worlds and live more adventurous stories than my own. Although this is still true today, my interest in language has since shifted beyond the way words are spun to transform even the most mundane experience into poetic prose. And it has gained a social layer, that I would summarize quite broadly as: what language can do.

The interaction between our social reality and language frequently remains invisible. But there is a materiality to language. It's hidden in the way we speak–the air released from our lungs, the vibrations of our vocal cords, and the movement of the tongue as it shapes sounds, wrapping itself around vowels. It's in how our lips form syllables, creating the final boundary between thought and speech. There is materiality in the way we write–with color on paper, wood, concrete, and in the typing paragraphs into documents on a keyboard, letter by letter. And there is a material quality to language beyond the physiology of its use in speech and writing. Language can be understood as material in the sense that it constitutes the real–the institutions, structures, and bodies it encompasses.[1]

Language plays an important role in the mediation between these institutions and structures of power and the individual person.[2] It mediates, what Michel Foucault called discourse, so simply put: the way societies talk about things, people, groups. Discourse, and at its foundation the words used, often appear as a natural representation of reality. But for the latter half of a century post-structuralist theorists and social linguists have argued the importance of discourse, not only in representing reality, but also in its production.[3] Discourse analysis challenges notions of language as a stable and transparent medium for communication. Instead, discourse and language are perceived as being impacted by power structures and, additionally, playing a part in their production and reproduction. Ultimately, though the way we talk about social groups and issues–so through discourse–unequal relationships are produced and reproduced between larger social groups, classes, or communities.[4]

THE MATERIAL INJUSTICE OF WORDS

Language works to uphold social inequality, because it shapes a supposedly subjective perception of the world through the collective lens of a shared vocabulary and narratives about people, structures, and things–about how the world "works." This happens in many ways. One example of how discourse and language perpetuate inequality is stereotypical characterizations and prejudices.

Historically, marginalized groups of people (women, people of color, working-class, etc.) have been afforded with less power. This is reinforced by stereotyping that tends to "involve association with some attribute inversely related to competence or sincerity or both".[5] These negative qualities of the prejudices affecting marginalized people limit their capacity to gain social and economic power. This includes, on one hand, the power to shape discourse more generally speaking, and on the other hand, the narratives about their own group and the words available to describe the experiences commonly had within this group.[6] This phenomenon is what Miranda Fricker coins hermeneutical injustice. According to Fricker, the experiences and knowledge of marginalized people are typically not included in the general production of knowledge and therefore also significantly underrepresented in our shared conceptions and vocabulary. This not only reinforces inequality in the sense of reproducing false and hurtful conceptions of certain identities, but also in limiting marginalized people in achieving self-knowledge, going so far as in impacting their self-identity negatively.[7]

MOLDED TO FIT THE WORD

In my master thesis, I was especially interested in exploring this personal impact of language on the queer experience. One participant in the installation that resulted from my practice formulated their experience with the term gay as follows:

"Since elementary school, the word gay was a bad word. Being gay was something you really didn't want to be, but also something that was far removed from myself. Something there was no question of me being, and the same goes for my social circle. There were people that were different and there was us, and those two were clearly separable."[8]

Even a single word can be molded to hold meaning that oppresses and goes far beyond the simple act of naming. This is the case for many words queer people use to describe their gender and sexual identity. Words that are being weighed down by their history and sometimes also by their present use to degrade or pathologize. A weight that strongly impacts the path of self-discovery for queer people. In her lecture *Queer Use,* Sarah Ahmed elaborates on the word "queer,"[9] which was, and still sometimes is, used as a weapon. Ahmed argues that the reuse of the word "queer" can disrupt the insult of the word. To reuse a word, it can't be separated from its history and used "jokingly" as an insult. If "we reuse the word queer, we hold onto the weight, the baggage".[10] Although the term gay ("schwul" in German), similarly to the term "queer," has been reappropriated in the 70s to fight against the discrimination of gay men, the negative implications attached to this term persist—at least in part—to this day. This linguistic baggage not only impacts the relationship of queer people to these terms, but to the whole process of identity formation. Our understanding of ourselves in the world determines how we can move through it, if we can find community and move into collective action and resistance. The ability to recognize oneself, and for this recognition to be good, is crucial.

TO TAKE UP SPACE

We make sense of the world through language. We use words to communicate our experiences, and the words available to us shape our experiences in turn. And still, debates about "words" oftentimes ridicule and trivialize demands for the introduction of new words and the leaving behind of old ones.[11] Especially so, when these demands come from marginalized groups of people.[12] This was the case recently in Switzerland when the debate about the inclusion of a third gender in the civil registry was reignited with renewed fervor after Swiss non-binary artist Nemo won the Eurovision Song Contest 2023.[13] There is nothing trivial about the pursuit of space in language: It is about taking up space in reality—not merely at the margins of society,

In preparation for filming, wax was melted and then dyed to resemble skin. (Photo: Paulina Ojeda)

but in bold letters, in a collective vocabulary and understanding, and, in this case, on an official document. The backlash that frequently arises from debates about the inclusion of marginalized persons occurs because they pose a challenge to the status quo and, with it, existing power structures.[14] The admission of a third gender is a challenge to a world that is split into clear and distinct categories of two genders. Categories that appear natural and all-encompassing, with margins that are invisible to those who fit but restrict the space of those who do not. This restriction of space is an important aspect of marginalization as Ahmed defines it in her lecture on *Queer use:*

"You can stop others from using a space by how that space is being used (...). But it is not just that use is a restriction of possibility that is material. Restrictions can also become material through use. What is material to some, leaving you with no room, no room to breathe, to nest, to be, can be what does not matter to others because it does not get in the way of their occupation of space; it might even enable their occupation."[15]

THE CONSTRUCTION OF WORDS

The categories of sex, gender, and desire are organized and regulated by societal forces that they reinforce in turn–one of them being heteronormativity.[16] In *Gender Trouble,* Butler argues that heterosexuality has normative power on gender because it depends on the discursive construction of the binary of femininity and masculinity[17]. This is to say: Heterosexuality depends on the existence of two genders, that are constructed in opposition to each other. Heterosexuality itself serves a patriarchal system, by reproducing a binary logic of gender that allows for the dominance of one gender over the other. According to Butler, the categories of the biological sex are produced, similar to the way gender is, through practices, institutions, and discourses, and used politically[18] to restrict the formation of gender identities along the "axis of heterosexual desire".[19] During this process, Butler argues, neutral attributes of the body are artificially unified, reinterpreted, and imbued with social meaning.[20] The normative power of the linguistic categories of sex and gender are mirrored in the norms that regulate the use of the body through which gender is performed, and it is on the surface of the body, that cultural inscription takes place and social meaning becomes internalized. Language is the tool that casts "sheaves of reality upon the social body"[21].

TO FEEL THE POWER OF WORDS

A word is more than the sum of its letters and it can be affected by and reproduce inequality in several ways: In how linguistic categories limit identities to what is considered the biological norm, but also in the negative meanings that are still associated with many of the words used by queer people for their identity today. Words contain the power to injure, but what became apparent to me in my practical thesis work was that words also hold the power to offer identity, community, belonging, and connection.

I felt the power of words when the fear of being an undesirable word took hold of me at 13. There is terror and shame in the realization that you are different–and not in the cute and quirky way one desires to be different at that age, but in a way that feels like a threat, that tastes of loneliness. But there is also freedom. This, I would discover

Stills from the video installation: wax-covered bodies, linking the intangibility of language to the physical experience of inequality. (Photos: Larissa Brochella)

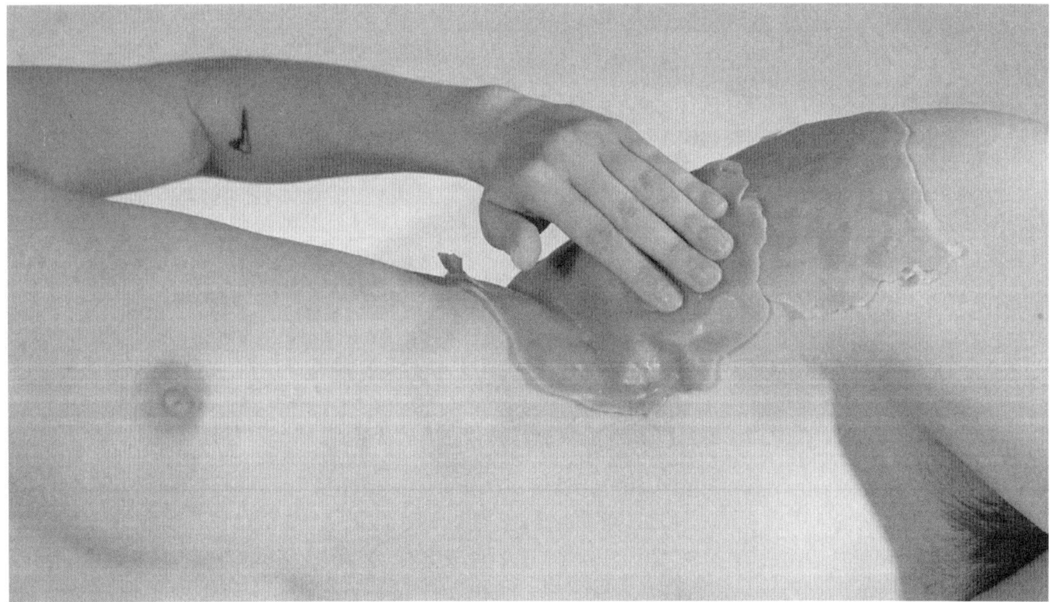

The melted wax was molded onto bodies, layer by layer, forming a second skin. (Photo: Larissa Brochella)

only years later, when being queer did not feel quite as threatening anymore. There are many stories I had the privilege of discovering during my research for my thesis project, of queer people and their relationships to these words: lesbian, bisexual, gay, trans, non-binary, and so on. And they are all as unique as they are similar: full of ambivalence. One person that took part in my thesis project phrased it as such: "The first time I spoke the word lesbian aloud it felt good, it fit with what I felt I knew and felt to be true. It felt like an arrival." At the same time, she recognized in herself, that "when I say the word lesbian, I often become a little bit quieter, just for this word, and only then I dare to say it."

1 Gerd Christensen, Three concepts of power: Foucault, Bourdieu, and Habermas. *Power and Education.* (2024), 16(2), 182-195. doi: 10.1177/17577438231187129
2 M. Bucholtz and K. Hall, Theorizing Identity in Language and Sexuality Research. *Language in Society.* (2004), 33(4), 492. escholarship.org/uc/item/8qw7d5s1
3 M. C. J. Stoddart, Ideology, Hegemony, Discourse: A Critical Review of Theories of Knowledge and Power. *Social Thought & Research.* (2007), 28, 191-225.
4 Ibid.
5 M. Fricker, Epistemische Ungerechtigkeit (2.). C.H.Beck. (2023), 38. chbeck.de/fricker-epistemische-ungerechtigkeit/product/34611587
6,7 Ibid.
8 Translated from Swiss German to English
9 Queer: odd, strange, unseemly, disturbed, disturbing. Queer: a feeling, a sick feeling; feeling queer as feeling nauseous. In older uses of queer–queer to describe anything that is noticeable because it is odd (Ahmed, 2018).
10 S. Ahmed, Queer Use. Feministkilljoys. (2018, November 8), feministkilljoys.com/2018/11/08/queer-use
11 J. Mansbridge and S.L. Shames, Toward a Theory of Backlash: Dynamic Resistance and the Central Role of Power. Politics & Gender. (2008), 4(04), 623. doi: 10.1017/S1743923X08000500
12 Ibid.
13 C. Neuhaus, Nemo kämpft um dritten Geschlechtseintrag–doch die Hürden sind hoch. *Neue Zürcher Zeitung* (2024), nzz.ch/schweiz/code-der-schweiz-ist-binaer-weshalb-ein-drittes-geschlecht-nur-in-einer-komplett-liberalisierten-welt-problemlos-eingefuehrt-werden-kann-ld.1830088
14 Mansbridge and Shames, Toward a Theory of Backlash: Dynamic Resistance and the Central Role of Power. *Politics & Gender.*
15 Ahmed, *Queer Use.* Feministkilljoys.
16 E. Levon and R. B. Mendes, *Language, Sexuality, and Power: Studies in Intersectional Sociolinguistics.* (Oxford University Press, 2016).
17 Bucholtz and Hall, Theorizing Identity in Language and Sexuality Research. *Language in Society.*
18 Wittig in Butler, *Gender trouble: Feminism and the subversion of identity,* Tenth Anniversary Edition, Routledge. (1999), 143.
19 Judith Butler, *Gender trouble: Feminism and the subversion of identity,* 33.
20 Ibid., 146.
21 Wittig in Butler, *Gender trouble: Feminism and the subversion of identity,* 147.

Other experimentations with wax became a part of the installation, adding a tactile element. (Photos: Larissa Brochella)

Feminist parameters in the computer-generated sex industry

Karina Panko

Karina Panko is an interdisciplinary designer from Würzburg, specializing in print and editorial design with a strong emphasis on typography. Thematically, she explores social transformation, feminism, gender identity, and empowerment. By integrating design with societal issues, she seeks to create visual concepts in her projects that combine aesthetic appeal with substantive depth.

FEMINISM AS A PREMISE

In the context of computer-generated pornography (cgP), feminist critique is essential not only when it comes to the objectification and sexualization of women in the pornographic medium or dominant male perspectives of the genre, but also to realize and integrate feminist principles. I feel it is a crucial step to look at women's self-empowerment and self-liberation as a motivator for the future, rather than exclusively engaging in discourses that repetitively name and perpetuate the problem of sexual violence against women by freezing women in powerless victim positions.[1]

Women discuss the empowering experience of participating in the porn industry, affirming the positive influence of sexually explicit images in reframing femininity, power, and sex. They also highlight the potential for sharing their own perspectives on lust, love, and intimacy.[2] The embedding of feminist approaches in heteronormative pornography is possible and can serve as a basis for feminist computer-generated pornography. Linda Williams examines the connection between female desire and power in pornographic film and outlines lustful utopias in various stages.[3] In *Behind the Green Door* (1972), the protagonist Gloria becomes the center of a forced erotic performance, but the film ends with her lust—despite the character's powerlessness. *The Resurrection of Eve* (1976) shows the development of the shy Eve into a self-confident woman who surpasses and leaves her dominant husband after she takes an increasing liking to his sexual experiments and emancipates herself. In *Insatiable* (1980), the main character Sandra is finally the ruler of her own desires, free from male control. Williams describes these characters, especially Eve and Sandra, as active subjects of desire who transcend patriarchal norms of representation.[4]

Radical feminist critics argue that pornography is not orientated towards the needs of women, as stereotypical, hyperfeminine representations dominate.[5] However, it is clear that pornography increasingly offers a variety of body types and representations that run counter to common stereotypes and cater to different preferences—often in deliberately feminist productions.[6] Feminist pornography aims to challenge traditional stereotypes and include women as subjects.

THE INFLUENCE OF PATRIARCHAL STRUCTURES ON TECHNOLOGY

The social structure of science and technology characterizes these as sexist and discriminatory fields of work that overly exclude women as actors. New information and communication technologies (ICT) have a certain social, political, economic, and cultural character, depending on the patriarchal and capitalist structures in which they are created. Accordingly, ICTs are characterized by heteropatriarchal prejudices and male supremacy. The strong persistence of these stereotypical patterns means that men are still predominantly involved in the development and design of cgP today. The fact that these men think and act for other men means that the spectrum of representations remains rather sparse. However, this characterization is neither substantial nor irreversible; a feminist perspective is able to expose the status quo of these fields as a male culture[7] and integrate femininity into the sociology of technology.[8]

THE EMANCIPATORY POTENTIAL OF TECHNOLOGY

Donna Haraway's Cyborg Manifesto sheds light on the emancipatory potential of technology and its ability to question existing power structures as a political tool. Haraway sees technology as a space for feminist intervention that makes it possible to break down traditional power relations and binary opposites.[9] However, this project harbors a "feminist paradox"[10]: In order to address gender inequalities, one must explicitly name them, which could entrench their existence. Adding a female perspective to the male perspective also reinforces the distinction between the two, which runs the risk of reproducing stereotypical gender roles. Nevertheless, it is necessary to include diverse voices in order to equalize power imbalances. Haraway criticizes the dichotomies in science, as they often reflect patriarchal power relations perpetuated by the dominant position of the white male in a military, late industrial, racialized, and male-dominated society.[11] Technology does not have to be developed exclusively by women or be driven by feminist intentions in order to have a feminist impact. If technologies, such as access to certain professions, have a lasting impact on women's lives and positively influence power structures, they can be considered feminist technologies that promote equality.[12] Janina Loh uses the example of the tampon to argue that even products that are created without feminist intentions can have a social impact that challenges patriarchal structures. However, there are different views within feminism: While essentialist feminism emphasizes biological differences and demands social adjustments, liberal feminism sees gender differences only in socialization, not in biology, and argues for equal conditions regardless of biological differences. Feminist philosophy of technology therefore analyzes when and how technologies can be interpreted as feminist.[13] Technologies and artifacts are not neutral; they reflect gender images and actively shape them. This emphasizes the importance of the context of use, which can influence and transform images, fantasies, and narratives.[14]

THE CYBORG AS A METAPHOR FOR HYBRID IDENTITIES

The initial question that arises is to what extent cgP is even claimed to look human-like. In relation to sex robots, Tanja Kubes suggests: "Why not free ourselves from the notion that our counterparts during sex have to look like a human? Maybe interacting with robots, we could delve into completely new spheres of sexual pleasure, of which we still have no idea today. Perhaps not only would the boundaries between men and women become obsolete, but also those between man and machine."[15] In the context of hybrid identities and the fusion of man and machine, Haraway is an important trailblazer who explores and reassesses the connection between technology, identity, and feminism.[16] The cyborg as "a creature of social reality as well as a creature of fiction"[17] shows that "the boundary between science fiction and social reality is an optical illusion".[18] She presents familiar dichotomies such as man and machine, nature and culture, reality and fiction, the physical and the metaphysical as historically evolved narratives made by (mostly male) people, but at the same time proclaims that alternatives are possible.[19] She questions these binary distinctions and essentialist notions of gender, emphasizing the fluidity of identity. From a feminist perspective rooted in Haraway's ideas, the representation of gender in cgP becomes a reflection of social power dynamics and a stage on which these norms can be scrutinized and reconstructed. A feminist analysis in the field of cgP aesthetics calls for a re-evaluation of these representations in order to create more inclusive, diverse, and empowering representations that challenge traditional gender roles and celebrate the diversity of identities.

Technological developments in the sex industry, such as vibrators, are already an integral part of women's lives.[20] The design of sex toys shows an interesting development: Initially, penis imitations were designed hyper-realistically with veins and folds, until designers realized that a lifelike replica was not necessary for functionality. Instead, factors such as size, shape, and feel are more important than a flesh-like appearance.[21] This decoupling from the realistic body image can also be applied to human-machine relationships and the depiction of synthetic pornography. When biological and socially constructed knowledge about man / masculinity and woman / femininity is no longer the central point of reference for the concept and visuality of designed products, the boundaries between biological and siliconized spheres are dissolved.[22]

CGP AS A PLATFORM FOR FEMINIST IDEALS

The fused entity of man and machine makes it possible to break through traditional gender boundaries and explore new forms of sexual representation, as well as to present alternative body images and sexual scenarios that reflect the diversity of human sexuality and identity. By moving away from normative notions of gender and sexuality, cgP could strengthen feminist ideals of emancipation, self-determination, and sexual freedom by creating a liberating aesthetic platform that gives space to the diversity of human experience.

1 Lena Gunnarsson, *Excuse Me, But Are You Raping Me Now? Discourse and Experience in (the Grey Areas of) Sexual Violence.* (2018), 2.
2 cf. Tristan Taormino et al., *The Feminist Porn Book: The Politics of Producing Pleasure.* (2013), 128-230.
3 Linda Williams, *Hard Core. Power, Pleasure and The "Frenzy of the Visible."* (1989), 218.
4 cf. Nicola Döring and Linda Williams' *Hard Core.* (2019), 44.
5 cf. Tobias Boll, *Pornografie.* (2022), 353.
6 cf. Ibid., 348.
7 cf. Cynthia Cockburn, *The Circuit of Technology: Gender, Identity and Power.* (1992).
8 cf. Donna Haraway, *Primate Visions: Gender, Race, and Nature in the World of Modern Science.* (1989).
9 cf. Lola Almendros, *The Private and the Public: Feminist Activisms in the Informational Turn.* (2023), 52.
10 Joan Scott, *Only paradoxes to offer.* (1996).
11 cf. Donna Haraway, *Situiertes Wissen. Die Wissenschaftsfrage im Feminismus und das Privileg einer partialen Perspektive.* In: Sabine Hark (Ed.): *Dis/Kontinuitäten: Feministische Theorie.* (Wiesbaden: VS Verlag, 2007), 305-322.
12 cf. Janina Loh, *What Is Feminist Philosophy of Technology? A Critical Overview and a Plea for a Feminist Technoscientific Utopia.* (2019), 4.
13 cf. Ibid., 7.
14 cf. Mark, Coeckelbergh, *Technology Games/Gender Games. From Wittgenstein's Toolbox and Language Games to Gendered Robots and Biased Artificial Intelligence.* (2019), 32f.
15 Tanja Kubes, *Bypassing the Uncanny Valley. Sex Robots and Robot Sex Beyond Mimicry.* (2019), 62.
16 cf. Donna Haraway, *A Cyborg Manifesto. Science, Technology, and Socialist-Feminism in the Late Twentieth Century.* (1985).
17 Ibid., 5.
18 Ibid., 6.
19 cf. Loh, *What Is Feminist Philosophy of Technology? A Critical Overview and a Plea for a Feminist Technoscientific Utopia.* (2019), 11.
20 cf. David Levy, *Love + Sex with Robots. The Evolution of Human-Robot Relationships.* (2007), 220.
21 cf. Kubes, *Bypassing the Uncanny Valley. Sex Robots and Robot Sex Beyond Mimicry.* (2019), 70.
22 cf. Ibid., 70f..

The Serpent, the Flower and the Human Furniture

Ian Lynam

Ian Lynam works at the intersection of graphic design, design education, and design research. He is Professor of Graphic Design at Temple University Japan. He operates the Tokyo design studio Ian Lynam Design and the retail shop Sailosaibin. His latest book is *Fracture: Japanese Graphic Design 1875-1975*. → *ianlynam.com*

Over a decade ago, I found myself in a mold- and dust-filled used book store in the wilds of rural Fukuoka Prefecture in Kyushu in the south of Japan. It is in that bookstore that I found a number of amazingly rare historic books and magazines that chronicled the development of commercial art and graphic design in Japan, but I also found a number of wildly unrelated things as well: a crumbling map of the Japanese empire from the interwar period, a poster advertising of Tsubame safety matches from the 1920s, flyers advertising local baseball games and community fairs in the city of Iizuka, and a worn copy of the magazine *Kitan Club* from 1952, nestled at the bottom of a plastic bin filled with curled and faded black-and-white photographs of naked young Japanese women bound in rope and suspended in the air.

Kitan Club (奇譚クラブ, literally "Strange Story Club") was a Japanese post-war monthly pulp magazine (or *kasutori zasshi* カストリ雑誌, named after the home-brewed moonshine-like spirit *kasutori shōchū* 粕取り焼酎) that was published in Osaka from 1947 to 1975. During the initial five years of the magazine's publication, *Kitan Club* was a magazine for non-heteronormative sexual enthusiasts that followed the preceding eroguronansensu (erotic, grotesque, nonsense) style of pulp writing that was popular in the 1920s and 1930s. *Kitan Club* was first published in 1947 by Yoshida Minoru 吉田稔, a former reporter for the *Senshu Nippo* 選手日報 newspaper. The following year, Suma Toshiyuki 須磨利之 joined the magazine's staff in order to publish his erotic illustrations, pushing the visual boundaries of the magazine.

Starting with the third issue, published in January of 1948, *Kitan Club* was censored by the American occupation Supreme Commander of Allied Powers (abbreviated as SCAP in English, but as GHQ, or General Head Quarters in Japanese), and from the fourth issue was forced to change its format to a regular pulp magazine containing no critique of allied occupation or black market activities–essentially watering down the publication to a very softcore literary pornography magazine. This continued until April 1952, when GHQ censorship ended.

From 1952 onward, the now censorship-free *Kitan Club* published articles, drawings, and photographs on hardcore sadomasochistic themes, including detailed illustrations and photographs of Japanese bondage, Western SM themes, and science fiction-driven imagery of sexual exploitation and dominance. The magazine's depiction of bondage was a factor in the popularization of Japanese bondage during the 1950s. Sales had declined drastically during the censorship years, but freed from occupation censorship, the magazine drastically changed its content to Suma's specialty:extreme sadomasochism, which led to an immense surge in popularity.

Aimed at readers interested in non-heteronormative sexual arousal and attraction, such as SM and fetishism, *Kitan Club* was not only a source of reading material, but also served as a place for anonymous readers to exchange letters and information. As a place for readers to communicate with each other, it also became one of the

Magazin Kitan Club 1952.11. Photos by Juvencio (Chi) Garza

few communities for SM enthusiasts in the immediate postwar period, prior to the subsequent increase in private SM circles in the 1960s. It is estimated that it sold around 50,000 to 80,000 copies at its peak in the early 1950s.

The magazine's explicit depiction of bondage was a factor in the popularization of Japanese bondage during the 1950s. Suma worked under a number of pseudonyms for *Kitan Club* including *Minomura Kou* 美濃村晃 and *Kita Reiko* 喜多玲子, taking on a variety of different roles as illustrator, writer, and editor for the reframing of the magazine as a fetish publication. The renowned fetish artist Harukawa Namio 春川ナミオ became a regular contributor to the magazine, which published some of his earliest work. The magazine also published the art of fetish artists from abroad, including the American artist John Willie (actual name: John Alexander Scott Coutts)–founder, editor, artist, and publisher of the American fetish magazine *Bizarre* and the Berlin-based German fetish illustrator Paul Kamm, who specialized in feminine domination works.

In many ways, *Kitan Club* was the descendent of prewar literature that emphasized the power of female sexuality–albeit as often cartoonish expressions of domination and subjugation and the fascination with the West, notably after Japan's loss in World War II. Perhaps *Kitan Club*'s most notable precedent was the 1924 novel *Naomi* (痴人の愛, *Chijin no Ai*, literally "A Fool's Love") by Japanese author Tanizaki Jun'ichirō 谷崎 潤一郎 (1886-1965), previously published in serialized chapter forms in a number of magazines. Narrated in the first person by the protagonist, a

Magazin Kitan Club 1953.9. Photos by Juvencio (Chi) Garza

Magazin Kitan Club 1954.0. Photos by Juvencio (Chi) Garza

Magazin Kitan Club 1954.1. Photos by Juvencio (Chi) Garza

salaryman named Jōji, the novel follows his attempt to groom a Eurasian-looking girl, the eponymous Naomi, to be a Westernized woman. *Naomi* is a significant work in its comic depiction of Japanese culture of the era and its fascination with the West. The clash between older and newer generations over the more progressive depictions of women, such as Naomi, has been viewed as a clash over Japan's transition into the modern period. Naomi's story is focused on a man's obsession for a moga もが (a "modern girl" in 1920s Japanese).

The narrator is a highly educated Japanese man, an electrical engineer living in the city, who hails from a prosperous farming family. Eager to distance himself from traditional Japanese culture, Jōji immerses himself in the burgeoning Western influences taking hold in Japan. His first encounter with Naomi takes place in a café, where he is immediately captivated by her striking "Eurasian" appearance, her Western-sounding name, and her sophisticated demeanor.

Much like the story of the young Murasaki no Ue in *The Tale of Genji*, Jōji decides to shape Naomi, a fifteen-year-old café hostess, into his ideal woman. His plan is to transform her into a glamorous, Western-style figure, much like Mary Pickford, the renowned Canadian actress of the silent film era, whom Jōji believes Naomi resembles. He invites Naomi to live with him and begins his efforts to mold her into the perfect Western wife. Naomi, for her part, proves to be a very willing and receptive student. Jōji pays for Naomi's English lessons, and while she struggles with grammar, her pronunciation is impeccable. He supports her Westernized interests, including her passion for movies, dancing, and fashion magazines. In the early part of the novel, Jōji refrains from making any sexual advances, choosing instead to focus on shaping Naomi according to his vision and observing her development from a distance. However, his attempt to instill Western ideals in her begins to unravel as she matures. At the start of the novel, Jōji presents himself as the dominant partner in their relationship, but this outward appearance proves to be misleading as the story progresses.

It quickly becomes clear, however, that Naomi possesses a much sharper social intelligence–and a certain cunning–that surpasses her shy and awkward benefactor. As Naomi matures into a strikingly beautiful young woman, she learns to harness the full power of her sexual allure. When Jōji eventually uncovers that she has been having affairs with several younger men, his initial fascination turns to jealousy and spirals into a frantic obsession. Seizing the moment, Naomi skillfully takes control, conditioning her repeatedly betrayed husband in Pavlovian fashion to obey her every selfish whim. She toys with him endlessly, engaging in "tease and denial" and other manipulative psychological games, keeping him under her influence. Overcome with frustration and teetering on the brink of a nervous breakdown, Jōji finally surrenders completely, vowing to fulfill whatever she desires, as long as she never leaves him. She agrees to his proposal, but only on the condition that he adhere to a set of non-negotiable, and decidedly harsh, terms:

1. He is to address her solely as "Miss Naomi" and refrain from any intimate contact with her, except for the rare platonic kiss as a reward for "good behavior."
2. He must sleep alone in a small, separate bedroom, while she is free to entertain a continuous stream of lovers in her more spacious adjoining boudoir.
3. He is required to give her half of his salary as a permanent allowance.

The humiliating treatment she regularly subjects him to, which he had once bitterly resented, now arouses him, and he finds himself eagerly anticipating it with a sense of giddy enthusiasm. His only request is that she stay with him forever, continuously feeding his obsessive addiction to her.

It is this preceding narrative of perverse power and subjugation that deeply inspired the later *Kitan Club* contributor Harukawa Namio's pen name "Namio" is itself a scrambled homage to the name "Naomi".

Post-censorship issues of *Kitan Club* immediately began featuring lavish illustrated features on bondage such as *Special Issue on War and Sexual Desire* and *Confessions of Perversion,* and offered related goods for sale. In the July 1952 issue, an advertisement was included for "Photographs of Beautiful Nude Bodies for Sale at Cost" and the August issue flaunted "Photographs of Dominated Women for Sale at Cost." The latter was an expression of kinbaku 緊縛—the Japanese art of consensual sexual bondage that began in the late Edo period of the 1600s to 1860s.

Long before curious Westerners discovered shibari 縛り rope binding ("shibari" itself is a term that was invented in the 1990s), the Japanese were enthralled by kinbaku-bi 縛り, "the beauty of tight binding." Painter Itō Seiu 伊藤晴雨 made kinbaku well-known in popular culture via his depictions of bondage in fine art in the early 1900s. In the mid-20th century, kinbaku came to the mainstream through *Kitan Club* and brought the erotica of restraining others to life in often-unsettling black and white photos. In a surprise twist of fate, Itō himself became a contributor to *Kitan Club*, offering up his first written contribution about kinbaku to the magazine he partially inspired.

Many of the photographic images within *Kitan Club* may be considered unsettling to some because instead of the exaggerated enjoyment or loathing we've come to expect in Western pornography, these images show women having a more abject and resigned response to being tied up and tortured—it is as if they'd resigned themselves to their captivity, or perhaps were just too tired to fight back.

It is not particularly surprising given that the magazine began publishing just two years after the end of World War II—there is a POW / Stockholm Syndrome aura to these images. Men returning from a war that flourished on taking prisoners and torturing them needed an outlet for their former battlefield proclivities, and the sexualized and historically encouraged act of kinbaku must have seemed as good a stand-in as any. Japan had created the hard-won Greater East Asia Co-Prosperity Sphere (the English name for the Japanese Empire) and having lost it all, many turned their penchant for sadism inward into the domestic scene.

Design-wise, *Kitan Club* was often a thoughtfully and competently designed publication that mixed illustration cuts, professional, considered hand-set letterpress typography with a clear typographic hierarchy, and ornamental rules and borders. Hand lettering was incorporated into much of the header illustration work, with all of the design elements separated by generous margins and considered negative space between ornamentation, illustration and text.

Occasionally, more daring editorial design moves such as images that crossed spreads were employed, and early issues featured French-fold tables of contents with often the most provocative images of each issue printed on the backside. Early issues bore full-color lithograph covers and inside covers, each bearing hand-set type and display lettering. In *Kitan Club*'s interiors, photographic imagery sat alongside monochrome illustrations—a mix of historic and modern aesthetics and photomechanical processes. *Kitan Club* was a study in dualities: images, essays and stories swapped male and female dominance, and fetishized death by ritual seppuku suicide was exoticized alongside a sense of loss, longing and sexual enthusiasm for the dead. The serialized novels that were published within *Kitan Club* became genre-defining for their novelty, innovation, cruelty, humor, and for their sheer imagination. The novel *Kachikujin Yapū* 家畜人ヤプー (or *Human Livestock Yapū*) is a near-future account of a wrecked spaceship in West Germany, that is later revealed as a lost vessel that has traveled in time from two thousand years in the future. The vessel hails from an era of Galactic Empire, named as the Empire of a Hundred Suns, and symbolized by its tricolor flag of black, white and yellow. In this far-future, eugenics-rampant scenario, white women are the dominant class, white men are effeminate and idle, while black men are a slave class and black women occupy nebulous liminal roles that hover between citizens and slaves. Alien races have been conquered, subjugated, and turned into pets, playthings, and tools. The worst fate, however, is reserved for the "livestock": Japanese men (called "Yapū" in this terrifying future), who have been transformed into genetically modified and physically mutilated heavily specialized slave-objects, including living human toilets, human furniture, and disfigured sex toys. Japanese women are willingly enslaved as surrogate birth mothers for Caucasian women. Intentionally grotesque and infinitely shocking, *Kachikujin Yapū* allegorizes pseudonymous author (or authors) Numa Shōzō's 沼正三 sense of overwhelming desolation following the end of World War II and the

Magazin Kitan Club 1954.2. Photos by Juvencio (Chi) Garza

subsequent dismantling of the Japanese imperial state by the Allied Occupation powers. The protagonists are an interracial couple—a submissive German woman and a dominant though genteel Japanese man—whose power dynamics are reversed over the course of the long novel, until the man "accepts his fate" as a subsequently castrated, genetically modified, and alien-implanted human-turned-forcibly-naked sex / furniture-object for use by his mistress when they travel into the future.

Other novels were serialized in *Kitan Club* such as Oniroku Dan's 団 鬼六 seminal *Hana to Hebi* 花と蛇 (*Flower and Snake*) series, an equally disturbing set of three novels revolving around race, rape, impotence, sex work, pornography, the Oedipal complex, and the fetishization of domestic laborers. The writing within *Kitan Club* was lionized in print by public figures such as famed author Mishima Yukio 三島由紀夫, who regarded these novels as some of Japan's greatest and most imaginative popular postwar literature.

Additionally, popular combined photo-illustrated essays such as Tsujimura Takashi's 辻村隆 series *Camera Hunt* カメラハント were published regularly in *Kitan Club* throughout the 1960s, highlighting real-time bondage experiences with a series of highlighted SM starlets as well as marginalized individuals such as a heavily tattooed young geisha and widow named Yamahara Kiyoko 山原清子.

Kitan Club ceased publication in 1975 after declining sales due to a series of censorship struggles, editorial mismanagement, and overextended budgets. However, the writing within, notably the *Hana to Hebi* series, has been used as the basis for an unrelenting series of SM-themed pornographic films up until the present day. *Kachikujin Yapū* has been reimagined a number of times in manga and anime forms as well. Perhaps the greatest spiritual and aesthetic successor to the legacy of the illustration work within *Kitan Club* is the lurid, often kinbaku-themed work of illustrator Saeki Toshio 佐伯俊男—his lifework (1945-2019) was in no doubt heavily influenced by the issues of *Kitan Club* published in his lifetime.

As for the "Kitan Club" brand name and trademark, they were handed down from copyright holder to copyright holder until they were sold in the early 2000s to the manufacturer of a line of precision model miniature toys that markets a line of cute animal mascot keychains under the "Kitan Club" name today, that have absolutely nothing to do with the name's origin, much less fetishism. It is a bizarre twist ending to an even more bizarre publication, and not at all the kind of finale that I expected when I first found that old magazine in the countryside so many years ago surrounded by evidence that bondage wasn't just a spectator sport there.

Love Bites. On the literal hunger to become one with the desired

Pia Kristin Lobodzinski

Pia Kristin Lobodzinski is a trained confectioner and chocolatier, editor-in-chief of *[kon] Paper* and a literary scholar. She is currently pursuing a PhD in Comparative Literature at the LMU Munich with a scholarship from the Hans-Böckler-Foundation. In 2014, Pia co-founded *[kon] Paper* with Berlin-based designer Julia Hell. *[kon]* is an independent magazine that combines feature articles, academic essays, and poetic texts. Each issue brings together different voices under one thematic keyword, such as "Sex" in the very first issue in 2015, fostering dialog between academic and creative perspectives. → *kon-paper.com*

"a kiss, a bite | The two should rhyme, for one who truly loves | With all her heart can easily mistake them"

Penthesilea, queen of the Amazons in Kleist's eponymous play from 1808, attempts to justify tearing apart her beloved, the hero Achilles, by drawing a parallel between tender kisses and hearty bites: "By Artemis, my tongue pronounced one word | For sheer unbridled haste to say another; | This, my beloved, just this, and nothing else [she kisses him.]."[1] After witnessing Penthesilea sinking her teeth–alongside her dogs–into her lover's alabaster chest, her argument of a mere slip of the tongue understandably fails to convince her fellow Amazons. However, on closer inspection, the link Penthesilea establishes between the three oral acts of kissing, biting, and speaking contains a certain, uncanny truth.

After all, there seems to be plenty of evidence to support Penthesilea's argument for a cannibalistic undercurrent haunting almost every (love-)language. First, there is the habit of addressing romantic partners with terms of endearment that associates them with sweet, edible delights: Just as sugar, cupcake, honey, and, following Penthesilea, perhaps even sweetheart—are common pet names in English, you can call your loved one "mon chou" in French (meaning my cabbage or cream puff), "Balım" in Turkish (meaning honey) or "corazón de melón" in Spanish (meaning melon heart). Second, there are also spicier, metaphoric connections: vegetables and fruits are often used as stand-in for genitals and expressions such as "you look good enough to eat" and "I could eat you up," as well as "eye candy" or "man-eater" indicate that on a linguistic level, kissing and biting are not only juxtaposed, but sometimes one is a proxy for the other. In this light, even innocent songs like Bruce Springsteen's *Hungry Heart* carry a hint of cannibalism

In *Spoiling the Cannibals' Fun* Helen Day even goes so far as to suggest that all (capitalist) societies, to some extent, are characterized by a cannibalistic impulse: "[a]s one of society's greatest taboos, cannibalism lies just below the surface of culture, a constant although barely conceptualized threat."[2] Although cases of real cannibals, such as Jeffrey Dahmer or Armin Meiwes, are unsettling indicators that Day's hypothesis is applicable in both a metaphorical and literal sense, this essay will only focus on examples that can be found in language, texts and (pop)culture where the constant threat Helen Day identifies is easiest to digest. After all, it's not only our love language that is full of cannibalistic moments: literature, from religious texts to classics to even children's books, is also teeming with a multitude of hungry hearts.

LONELY HEARTS AND EMPTY STOMACHS

But why does cannibalism, especially the idea of devouring a real or fictional beloved, even cause such a deep discomfort? On the one hand, mutual devouring is understandably considered as a fundamental threat to established social orders. On the other hand, the act of love-cannibalism—which in most cases requires death before consumption—seems counterintuitive at first. Yet, the idea and desire to incorporate the beloved is not limited to convicted criminals such as Dahmer or Meiwes. As with love-language, the very concept of love and devotion in Western cultures shows cannibalistic tendencies: For example, the tradition of the christian communion (along with the associated doctrine of transubstantiation), in which the body and blood of Jesus are consumed in the form of bread and wine, is a form of incorporating the beloved into one's own body. Plato, celebrated as one of the forefathers of Western philosophy, offers an explanation for the desire to incorporate the other by defining love as a state of constant lack: In his *Symposium*, one of the participants, the comic playwright Aristophanes, recounts an ancient myth in which humans originally existed as spherical beings "composed of both sexes and sharing equally in male and female".[3] If Eros is defined as "the desire and pursuit of wholeness",[4] then all erotic desire can be seen as the eternal attempt to restore this primordial unity through the absorption of the other into one's own body. The idea of love as a state of perpetual lack outlasted the ancient Greeks, and Aristophanes story is echoed by the first love story in the Bible: In Genesis, Eve is presented as a perfect match for Adam because she is literally a part of his body: "And Adam said, This is now [...] flesh of my flesh: she shall be called Woman, because she was taken out of Man." And as in the ancient myth, this initial separation between Adam and his former body-part is resolved through a (physical) reunion as "they shall be one flesh."[5]

That this narrative of love as lack still haunts contemporary Western concepts of love, is evidenced in popular culture by artists from the The Cure (1989) to the Atomic

Kittens (2000) who claim that only the object of their desire can make them "whole again." Even though the idea of "two become one"[6] means for most of the couples that they take their new partner into their hearts rather than their stomachs, the idea implies that there is a hole that needs to be filled in one way or another–it just seems to be a question of how far you are willing to go to become one. Correspondingly, the literal hunger and longing for the other makes Penthesilea's act of incorporating her lover seem less like an aberration and more like an extreme version of union-seeking.

FORBIDDEN FRUITS

The cannibalistic interpretation of the desire to become one with the object of love reveals the fundamentally destructive side of perceiving love as lack. But its revelatory potential does not stop there, for it confronts us with an existential unease about our own fleshly nature. After all, food and sex-arguably the most pleasurable of the primary needs–seem to unsettle Western societies not just when they are combined in a cannibalistic act. Even taken separately, these two urges are subject to the greatest number of regulations, taboos, and laws. In addition to the oral / linguistic overlap between kissing and biting mentioned by Penthesilea, the physical pleasure the two urges can provide, come from crossing physical boundaries, by absorbing something else (or the same thing) into one's body. In narratives, therefore, a bite is often not just a bite, but a marker of transition. In the Bible, for example, Eve's consumption of the forbidden fruit marks a turning point for humanity. Her bite draws the line between innocence and knowledge, establishing not only the naked body as sinful, but the pure enjoyment of food and sex in general as deadly sins. According to the Italian philosopher Giorgio Agamben, such an attempt to devalue physical needs as animalistic is paradigmatic of Western cultures: „in our culture man has always been the result of a simultaneous division and articulation of the animal and the human, in which one of the two terms of the operation was also what was at stake in it."[7]
Efforts to distinguish humans from animals–whether by Schiller, Locke, Descartes, Aquinas, Augustine, or Plato-reveal the 2,400-year long history of this deep-seated cultural discomfort with our physical side. Body and mind, nature and culture, civilization and savagery are presented as opposing forces in which the rational mind must master the animal urges. It is therefore not surprising that in Kleist's version of the drama, Penthesilea's cannibalistic loss of control, her violation of Amazonian law, leads to a comparison between her and her dogs–as one Amazon observes that the queen is "in a frenzy among her dogs," behaving "like a rabid dog".[8] But the cannibal as a symbol of animalistic, "uncivilized" behavior goes beyond German Romantic literature. It appears in Shakespeare's Caliban–whose name is an anagram of "cannibal"–as well as in the colonial travelogues of Cook and Columbus. In each version, the attribution of a cannibalistic nature is used as a form of othering, opposing a concept of (western / male) rational control. And traces of such a portrayal can even be found in modern series such as *Supernatural* (2010), where Valentines couple devouring each other, as well as in Bret Easton Ellis' *American Psycho* (1991).

IT'S A DOG-EAT-DOG WORLD: SEX, WEALTH, AND CANNIBALS

In modern literature, however, cannibals are portrayed in ways that do no longer fit this inherent belittling: Although the cannibalistic acts in *American Psycho* display an animalistic lack of self-control similar to Penthesilea's when Patrick Bateman leaps out at his former sexual partner, "jackal-like, literally foaming at the mouth" and kneels beside his victim, "eating that girl's brain, gobbling it down, spreading Grey Poupon over hunks of pink, fleshy meat",[9] Patrick Bateman is no racialized other. He is a cannibal in a suit who works on Wall Street. And contrary to Penthesilea, Bateman seems to remain an accepted member of New York society despite his total loss of control. Apart from Patrick Bateman, the most sexually active fictitious cannibal is probably Marquis de Sade's Minski who never goes to bed "without having ejaculated ten times." Unlike Bateman, however, Minski's cannibalism is fully thought through: since it is impossible for him to come without killing, his victims move from the bed to the kitchen as part of his sophisticated recycling system: "We fuck them, don't we? And is there anything better [...] you can do with a woman you have fucked than use her as you do your ox or a mule, as a beast of burden, or kill her for food?"[10] Besides those rational explanations it is Minski's wealth that allows him to live outside the conventions, fully embodying a "state of nature" in which his pleasure is the only guiding principle. What Bateman and Minski thus have in common—apart from their lack of moral codes—is an excess of wealth that allows them to circumvent legal boundaries that might limit their personal pleasure. They are no longer bloody romantics who consume the other to become "whole again;" instead, the killing and eating of former sexual partners is an act of exploitation and absolute power over the other's body. And while Bateman, as a Wall Street cannibal and a manifestation of Helen Day's "threat that haunts all capitalist societies," holds up a mirror to consumerist societies, Minski's lifestyle challenges Western culture's ingrained taboos and laws as well as customs: "it is absurd to turn up one's nose at anything, aversions are based on nothing better than the lack of habit; all viands are fit nourishment for man [...] and it is no more extraordinary, after all, to eat a human than to eat a chicken."[11] Or, in other words: Why is it okay to eat one animal and not another? And if we treat women like animals, why shouldn't we eat them? The cannibals of de Sade and Ellis give us a glimpse of a society that is based solely on the principle of eat or be eaten.

TAKING IN THE CANNIBAL

Sigmund Freud, the founder of psychoanalysis, goes even further by tracing the origins of all modern societies back to a communal act of cannibalism. Much like Eve's hearty bite, the transgression of bodily boundaries in *Totem and Taboo* (1913) results in a radical social transformation. Freud's band of brothers, however, do not eat a forbidden fruit but the admired, almighty father himself: "One day the expelled brothers joined forces, slew and ate the father, and thus put an end to the father horde."[12] What led to exclusion from paradise in the Bible marks a shift from patriarchal despotism to fraternal equality in *Totem and Taboo*. Freud's portrayal of the cannibal thus combines the two cannibalistic motifs we have seen so far, as the incorporation of the father is both an exercise of power and an expression of love, since the "cannibal has a devouring affection for his enemies and devours only people he likes."[13]

This version of the rebellious, ambivalent cannibal even found its way into Maurice Sendak's fantastical children's book *Where the Wild Things Are*, fifty years later. Sendrak, however, offers a bloodless solution to the cannibalistic dilemma of desire: Here, the unruly Max is sent to bed without supper after threatening his mother "to eat her up"—but instead of just going to bed hungry, he sails to a distant island and becomes "the king of all wild things." When Max finally decides to leave, the wild things repeat his cannibalistic threat: "Oh please don't go / we'll eat you up / we love you so!"[14] But Max breaks the cycle with a simple "no" and sails home to his room, where a hot supper awaits–proving that cannibalistic threats might be omnipresent, but kindness and a verbal negation as well as a hot meal may help to prevent the actual exercise. Another similarly positive solution is offered by the Italian writer Italo Calvino in 2012 when the cannibalistic urge to become one with the loved one is resolved at the level of language by the narrator of the short story *Under the Jaguar Sun:* "I concentrated on devouring, with every meatball, the whole fragrance of Olivia–through voluptuous mastication, a vampire extraction of vital juices. But I realized that in a relationship that should have been among three terms–me, meatball, Olivia–a fourth term had intruded, assuming a dominant role: the name of the meatballs. It was the name 'gorditas pellizcadas con manteca' [plump girls pinched with butter] that I was especially savoring and assimilating and possessing."[15] Here, language and the object of substitution become one in masticating. The devouring of the name-bearing meatball serves as a substitute for the other's body, and the couple transcend their impending cannibalistic intentions. In a reversal of Penthesilea, who blames language for her slip of teeth, Calvino interweaves all three oral acts of speaking, biting and kissing, opening a new way to act out the desire to become one. In addition to these two different ways of overcoming the cannibalistic urge, there is something that all three examples of modern-day cannibals have in common: All three reverse the tradition of shifting the cannibal threat–including the devaluation of any bodily pleasure–from the self to the other. Freud's, Sedak's, and Calvino's modern cannibals finally tear down the line drawn between "culture" and "nature," demonstrating that the "wild" can never be separated from the "civilized." Or, as Claude Lévi-Strauss states: "We are all cannibals."

In conclusion, cannibalism, in all its literary variations, forces humanity to confront its own fleshiness. When kisses become bites and love literally goes through the stomach, literature reminds us that humans are made of edible flesh and ruled by fleshly desires. Cannibalism like language itself exists in the liminal space between body and mind–and taking the other in just like speaking can bring pleasure as well as harm. This brief overview of the various forms of devouring desired or loved objects in literature shows that it is precisely in the ambivalent space of words that the cultural-critical potential of sexually active cannibals is revealed, which is why only in literature bites sometimes have to be (mis)taken for kisses.

1 Ibid.
2 Helen Day, "Modest Proposals and Love Supreme: Metaphorical, Literal and Virtual," in *Spoiling the Cannibals' Fun? Cannibalism and Cannibalisation in Culture and Elsewhere,* edited by Wojciech Kalaga Tadeusz Rachwal, Peter Lang. (2005), 27.
3 Plato, *Plato in Twelve Volumes,* Vol. 9, translated by Harold N. Fowler. (Cambridge: MA, Harvard University Press / William Heinemann Ltd., 1925), 190a.
4 Ibid., 193a
5 Gen 2:24
6 Spice Girls: *2 become 1.* (Virgin, 1996).
7 Giorgio Agamben, *The Open: Man and Animal,* translated by Kevin Attell. (Stanford UP, 2004), 92.
8 Heinrich Kleist, *Penthesilea,* translated by Joel Agee, Harper Collins. (1998), 123-24.
9 Bret Easton Ellis, *American Psycho.* (Picador, 2012), 315.
10 Marquis de Sade, *Juliette,* translated by Austryn Wainhouse. (Arrow Books, 2007). 580.
11 Ibid., 585.
12 Sigmund Freud, *Totem and Taboo,* translated by A. A. Brill. (Penguin 1940), 189.
13 Sigmund Freud, *Group Psychology and the Analysis of the Ego,* translated by James Strachey, Boni and Liveright. (1920), 62.
14 Maurice Sendak, *Where the Wild Things are.* (Red Fox, 1963), n.p..
15 Italo Calvino, *Under the Jaguar Sun,* translated by William Weaver. (Mariner Books Classics, 2012), 27.

The Power of Collective Simulation—From Utopian Bodies to an Embodied Utopia

Rebekka Seubert

Rebekka Seubert is a curator and Artistic Director of Dortmunder Kunstverein since 2020. Under her leadership, Dortmunder Kunstverein was honored with the ADKV / Art Cologne Prize in 2023, recognizing it for its innovative programming. Rebekka studied Cultural Studies at the universities of Regensburg and Clermont-Ferrand, as well as Fine Arts at erg in Brussels, and the HFBK Hamburg. → *dortmunder-kunstverein.de*

On the role of the body, the erotic, and the aesthetics of unity and immersion in the performative and environmental practices of the Slow Reading Club and Zoe Williams' Liquid Currency Bar, created in collaboration with (agf) HYDRA at Dortmunder Kunstverein.

The body as a carrier and performer of identity and history has been at the center of my curatorial practice. I work with artists to reflect on the body as space, archive, vessel or container, as an antenna, sender or network, as a shell and safe home for a person's life. The body is the projection screen on which all of life's joys and problems, both individual and social, manifest. In the arts, from the earliest moments of expression, the body has been an endless resource for artists themselves. Since the mid 20th century, audiences are increasingly included in public events, creating collective experiences and a sense of being here now. "What we call 'performance' might, from a certain perspective, be understood as a way of enlarging the frame around what was previously considered to be the work of art, as a material object, to include also the active presence of its maker and viewers."[1]

In the past couple of years, I have worked with artists to learn about the potential of shared experience in performative events, the opportunities and boundaries of immersion and collectivity and how they can further be explored through fiction. Part of this learning process arose from collaboration with the Slow Reading Club for recurring institutional interventions, a duo project by artists Henry Andersen and Bryana Fritz. Both artists consider reading not just a practice that can be performed but also a practice that can be choreographed in collective reading sessions through a set of specific scores: reading with numb tongues, mixing the own voice with the voices of others, sensing another person's voice through vibrations in their back or on the side of their neck, not hearing your own voice during white noise, becoming part of a reading choir, or challenging attention while reading, through spatial constellations of bodies or glance, through stroboscopic light, and through playing with the order of words aligned in a sentence, leaving out, jumping within the text, pointing at words, successiveness, simultaneity ...

Creating environments, immersion, or a specific atmosphere is a crucial element of these performative, participatory practices: "We cannot think of an organism without its environment, including ourselves."[2] What matters is the interplay of environment and body. But which body? The notion of the body and its properties is not just shaped through biological conditions but also through cultural and religious beliefs, and through a lived bodily practice. Examples are the Candomblé belief that a body can itself become the incarnation of a god.[3] Or the way in which dervishes get into a trance through turning movements in a floating robe. Or selfless experiences[4] in meditation, drugs, sex or near-death. Or, contrarily, the boundaries imposed onto bodies through sexist, racist, extractivist, and capitalist beliefs of domination and devaluation. Through body politics or necropolitics.[5] Through the othering of bodies. Through the limitations or lack of value attributed to workers' bodies, sick bodies, or bodies in trouble, to female, queer, or non-white bodies.

But our bodies are foremost social bodies: connected entities both on the macro and micro level. They can become part of a synchronized network of bodies, creating a shared environment—as has been observed in kinships between humans, in friendships, partnerships or families, or between humans and animals. And indeed, Michel Foucault describes the human body as a utopia[6]: A place that a person cannot know or only explore through the help of other people (or through technical tools such as mirrors, cameras, specula ...) to know what one's own back or eyes or the inside of our organs look like. If the body is a utopia, then the limits imposed on this body can also be expanded through new narratives, new cosmologies, using the body for collective excitement or for erotic experiences beyond the aim of reproduction. The body can become a place of storytelling, "Storytelling for earthly survival"[7] in the broader sense. For if the body is a utopia, a utopia is already being enacted through the body—as an embodiment of a cosmos and normative social structure that might as well be narrated differently: opening a door through simulation and bringing to reality an until then utopian cosmos.

From August 2022 to April 2025, Dortmunder Kunstverein hosts the *Liquid Currency Bar*, a temporary venue for performances and events by artist Zoe Williams with

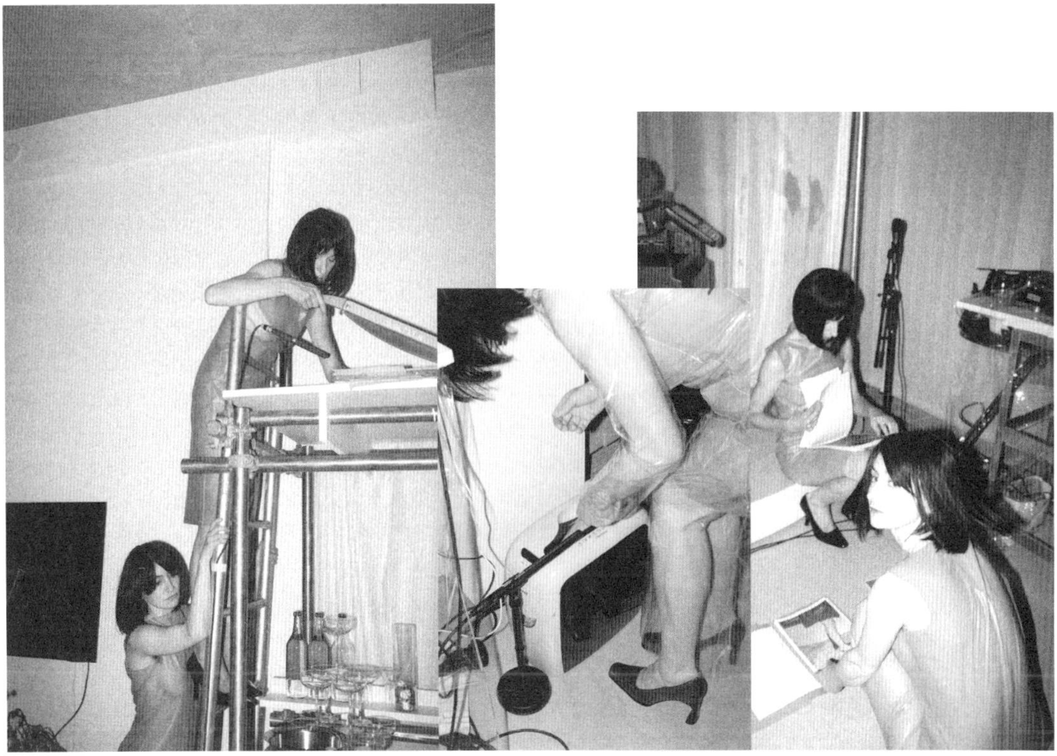

TLC23 at Liquid Currency Bar, Zoe Williams, Keira Fox, Katie Shannon, Dortmunder Kunstverein, 2024. Photo: Steven Natusch. Courtesy: the artists, Dortmunder Kunstverein

Liquid Currency: Last Orders, Zoe Williams, (agf) HYDRA, Dortmunder Kunstverein, 2024, still image. Camera: Nico Jarmuth. Courtesy: the artists, Ciaccia Levi Paris Milan, Dortmunder Kunstverein

latex spatial design by HYDRA (Anna Gloria Flores). The bar creates a parallel world with its own laws. Its means of payment, the Liquid Currency, is a golden coin with the image of a gorgon's head which also ornates the bar with its spinning, dropping, and melting emblem. The currency plays on the idea of a liquid to subvert monetary value chains: Flowing consumption of urine-colored liquids, bought in liquid currency, as a promise for pleasure–only for the liquids to be returned to waste and water, the environment, and ultimately back into our bodies. The excessive mix of gold rush and golden shower operates on the threshold between natural and artificial materials, between bodily experience and digital aesthetics, forging a conspiratorial community.

Through objects and scenes, Zoe Williams explores hedonism, camp, consumption, non-verbal communication, and physical behaviors, revealing the unspoken seductive dynamics of human relationships. Her theatrical sensory experiences engage the viewers "who are cast as: witnesses, accomplices, voyeurs, and victims."[8] This interplay sparks an intimate dialog around sex, power, and desire. In this vibe, Zoe Williams collaborated with further artists to create three main performative interventions for the *Liquid Currency Bar.* One during which Katie Shannon, Susu Laroche, and Zoe Williams acted as dripping wet urine colored mermaids and barmaids, wearing HYDRA bespoke latex artefacts as narrative carriers for the scenes. For another intervention, Zoe Williams hosted Katie Shannon and Keira Fox's TLC23 collective for the live creation of a magazine, reenacting office scenes, with costumes by both artists and Xenab Lone Jamil. And lastly, Zoe Williams and (agf) HYDRA conceived a closing circle cleaning service ritual. The HYDRA conjoint gown functioned as a ritualistic ceremonial apparatus–an extension of the

Left: Jean Biche performing at Zoe Williams' Liquid Currency Bar, Dortmunder Kunstverein, 2024. Photo: Roland Baege. Courtesy: the artist, Dortmunder Kunstverein. Right: Liquid Currency Bar, Zoe Williams, HYDRA (Anna Gloria Flores), Dortmunder Kunstverein, 2022. Photo: Roland Baege. Courtesy: the artists, Ciaccia Levi Paris Milan, Dortmunder Kunstverein

augmented liquid body. HYDRA spatial design and wearable artefacts translucent membranes function as an organic interface connecting the separate elements of the collective body via breathing and touch, training empathy through intimacy and desire. All of these elements are considered to be part of the HYDRA Uniform, a shapeshifting-archetypal character and augmented identity that exists in multiple realms. The uniform "produces its own offspring, a little bit like a plant or a polyp"[9]—a mythological narrative HYDRA likes to engage with. "When wearing the HYDRA Uniform, you're hyper aware of the way you're breathing, the temperature of your body, and the space around you. Also, because it has such a liquid fit and because it's quite heavy, the material is present with every movement you make—it's almost like moving underwater. So, it helps me, and it helps whoever experiences it, to remind oneself of the experience of the body itself."[10]

During the performances, the experience of otherness of the self in a more-than-real utopia intensifies and turns even stronger through a clash with the outside world: The location of the *Liquid Currency Bar* at Dortmunder Kunstverein sides a 10-lane street with heavy night traffic of cruising cars and car races. Their rhythms and realities don't mix, but the hyper-real setting opens a new perspective. For those at the *Liquid Currency Bar* the enactment makes the somatic experience and the temporary characters just as real as the cars outside. Individual artistic fiction expressed through embodiment can not only expand perception but also be a soft expression of opposition and a catalyst of change. Simulation may allow for a shift in the understanding of a limiting reality and can bring about a lasting physical experience in the bodies of whoever is part of it.

1 Catherine Wood, *Performance in Contemporary Art.* (London: Tate Publishing, 2022).
2 Lynn Margulis, *The Symbiotic Planet: A New Look at Evolution.* (New York: Basic Books, 1999).
3 In the Brazilian religion Candomblé belief, the orixá god is incarnated within each person's body. See: exhibition text *Körper. Kult. Religion. Ausstellung des Exzellenzclusters "Religion und Politik,"* Archäologisches Museum / Bibelmuseum, Münster, 2024/25.
4 *Unselfing,* Dortmunder Kunstverein, 2024, curated by Rebekka Seubert. Exhibition with works by avaf, Yael Bartana, Cevdet Erek, Ja Jess, Jessy Razafimandimby, David Reiber Otálora, Lillian Schwartz, Yuri Yefanov.
5 Achille Mbembe's *Necropolitics* (Duke University Press, 2019) is a sociopolitical theory reflecting the use of power in politics and society to dictate how some people may live and others must die.
6 Michel Foucault, *the Utopian Body.* (Radio Broadcast, 1966).
7 Title of the documentary about the work of Donna Haraway, directed by Fabrizio Terranova. (2016)
8 Press release by Vincent Honoré for the exhibition *Fondant* at Friche de la Belle de Mai. (Marseille: 2023).
9 A shaded View on Fashion: *Latex, Personal Mythologies, and Other-ness with AGF HYDRA,* Interview by Rianna Murray. (13.06.2023), ashadedviewonfashion.com/2023/06/13/portrait-of-an-artist-on-latex-personal-mythologies-and-other-ness-with-agf-hydra/
10 Ibid.

Archive Artist Publication

Hubert Kretschmer

From 1969 to 1975, he studied in Munich and Heidelberg. He then worked as a lecturer at design universities until 1992. From 1978 to 2021, he taught at various institutions and began developing the AAP Archive in 1979. In 1980, he founded his own publishing house, now known as icon Verlag. He was also involved in new media and arts promotion. Since 1993, he has been active in Munich as a publisher, curator, and archivist.

→ *artistbooks.de*

At documenta 6 in 1977, so-called artists' books were shown to a wider public for the first time in Germany. On the second floor of the Neue Galerie, *The Metamorphoses of the Book* presented by Rolf Dittmar (Wiesbaden) and Peter Frank (New York), as well as concept books, as well as concept books, in case you were looking for them. .After all, a start had been made. Dittmar showed largely sculptural works in the book by 53 predominantly German artists (including six women) and Frank brought works by 12 conceptual artists from New York to Kassel. The fact that the two curators were already at loggerheads during the preparations–documented in *New York Art-Rite #14* from 1976–shows the enormous range of what was then and is now commonly understood as an artist's book.

My call a year later in *KUNSTmagazin #84* for an exhibition of artists' books at the Produzentengalerie Adelgundenstrasse in Munich was just as broadly defined as at documenta 6. The response was overwhelming. 320 international artists submitted over 500 works. About half of these were reproductions of conceptual works. I was allowed to keep almost all of these books, as they did not have to be sent back to the artists. An archive–the Archive for Artists' Books–was born without me even realizing it. In other words, an archive was created here, and not a collection. The artists themselves had decided what was to become part of the exhibition when they sent it in. There was no conscious curation, as the participating artists understood what was meant by an artist's book:

"The artist's book is not an art book.
The artist's book is not a book about art.
The artist's book is a work of art."
– Guy Schraenen

This unintentional archive continued to grow organically when I founded a publishing house and a distribution company for artistic publications. The opportunity to swap books at trade fairs and meet new international artists meant the archive eventually grew to over 80 banana boxes by the end of the nineties.

WHY ARE ARTISTS' BOOKS SO INTERESTING ?

Just as artists practice their art in unique ways, they approach the concept of books just as differently—especially in the post-avant-garde era. Since the late 1960s, art objects have emerged that "are not presented as works of written culture or the information sector, although their various designations are always formed in some way with the noun book."[1] This includes concept books, book objects, object books—in short: artists' books.

The artist's approach to the book depends on their artistic focus, whether it's painting, performance, photography, poetry, music, architecture, sculpture, comics, drawing, typography, fashion, film, theater, installation, or even pedagogy. Each artist engages with the medium of the book in their own unique way, questioning its role as a carrier of information, a container of ideas, a means of agitation, a form of documentation, a stimulus for behavior, an object of representation, or a subject of technical and economic experimentation.

As a result, both the form and content of books have experienced unprecedented diversity, challenging traditional ideas of what a book can be and expanding its artistic possibilities.

THE ARTIST'S BOOK AS A DEMOCRATIC MEDIUM

Printed or reproduced artists' books predominate in my archive. These publications are usually produced in larger editions with around 100 to 1,000 copies. This makes them inexpensive and, more importantly, accessible—unlike rare or costly works of art. Similar to the multiple or a graphic, a larger group of buyers can be addressed. The two quotes from Anne Moeglin-Delcroix and Judith A. Hoffberg make it clear why I prefer the printed form to book objects and object books, such as unique copies or bibliophile books and hand-pressed prints:

"Like any other medium, artists' books are a means of transporting art ideas from the artist to the viewer / reader. Unlike most other media, they are available to everyone at low cost. They don't need a special place to be seen. Their value lies in the ideas they contain. They contain the material in an order determined by the artist. [...] Art exhibitions come and go, but books remain for years. They are works themselves, not reproductions of works. Books are the best medium for many artists working today. [...] Artists want their ideas to be understood by as many people as possible. Books make it easier to achieve this. [...]"[2]
– Anne Moeglin-Delcroix

"[...] The Book as an alternative to gallery and museum offerings allows a democratization of art, a decentralization of the art system, since books can be distributed through the mail, through artist-run shops, through friendship; books take-up less room are portable, practical and democratic, and create a one-to-one relationship between consumer and artist, between owner and creator. The artist-produced book is not only an instrument of communication, but also an extension of the artists' vision achieved through mixed media. It is as permanent as the artist desires it to be, as ephemera as a cloud, involving the owner in a solitary act. [...]"[3]
– Judith A. Hoffberg

THE EARLY EXPANSIONS

From the 1960s to the 1980s, it was primarily artists themselves who designed and produced supplementary materials about their artistic work and their books. All of these printed materials related to artists' books were, and continue to be, important documents of artistic practice for the archive: postcards, flyers, posters, price lists, advertisements, buttons, stickers, as well as letters, invoices, offers, and written inquiries in all forms.

In addition to books and ephemera, the other major pillar of the archive is periodicals such as magazines, publication series, and zines created by artists. Artistic concerns, political interests, and social demands could be more effectively asserted and consolidated through repeated publication. Artists, as publishers and editors, are often more courageous, more radical, and therefore more creative than economically driven journalists. In mainstream media–consumer magazines, major newspapers, and large publications–artists have had, and still have, virtually no chance of presenting their ideas and aesthetic concepts.

Consequently, the responsibility falls to the individual artist, a group of artists, or an artist collective. Regardless of economic success, a magazine is launched, either alone or in collaboration with like-minded individuals. These aren't necessarily traditional magazines but instead serve a small circle of insiders, connoisseurs, and friends. This was all before the advent of the Internet. Contacts, especially international ones, were still made through analog means–at the few art fairs, at rare exhibitions, in unique spaces like Ulises Carrión's bookstore Other Books and So in Amsterdam, and through advertisements in small niche magazines. Mutual advertisement exchanges ensured cost-effective and targeted distribution.

In this pre-digital era, the category of artist's book didn't yet exist in libraries. In the early 1960s, Ed Ruscha famously advertised that the Library of Congress refused to include his small photobook, *Twentysix Gasoline Stations,* in its collection. Similarly, a major German library declined to acquire some of my earliest publications because they didn't contain a single word inside. When such acquisitions were made, the questionable items were categorized as illustrated books. Reversible books were even taken apart and rebound "correctly and neatly" by in-house binderies.

At that time, searching for artists' books in the large card catalogs of libraries was a futile effort. Even after collections became accessible online, finding works under the category of artist's books was often impossible. Without knowing the name of the artist or the title of the publication, research would hit a dead end.

Those days, however, are now behind us.

THE UPHEAVAL

In the 90s, social and technological changes were so significant that the nature of the archive shifted as well. Booksellers who were still somehow committed to the artist's book in the 80s instead began to focus on expensive art books, coffee table books, mass-market publications, and the elaborate catalogs produced by large art institutions under economic pressure. For presentation at art fairs, the artist's book was too inexpensive, i.e. too cheap, to assert itself against original works of art. Where else did one have a chance of finding an artist's book?

The artists' turn to the media, the courses offered at art academies, and finally the Internet have fundamentally changed the production and reception conditions for the artist's book. The work of visual artists and the work of designers, layout artists, and book makers are now beginning to merge. The artist's book of the 1960s and 1970s—when the artist was typically responsible for the entire production process and often the distribution, gave way to an artistic publication shaped by several people. As a result, the democratic artist book, which was affordable for everyone, became an unaffordable work of art. Booklets I could still purchase from Walther König in the late 1970s for just 5 DM were now priced in the two- to three-digit DM range.

The treasure in the banana boxes had to be unearthed. The prerequisite for this was the recording all titles in a database, which proved far more effective and flexible than the typical entries in an Excel spreadsheet. As I said, my early Internet searches for artists' books yielded few useful results. Therefore, in the early 2000s, I decided to publish my stationary database online and free of charge. This OPAC (Online Open Access Catalogue) had two major advantages: I could access my holdings directly when I traveled and the archive was now visible internationally.

THE LATER EXPANSIONS

In a different context and in a completely different dimension, what the appeal for the 1977 exhibition of artists' books had achieved is now being repeated: unexpected things have flowed into the archive, sent as donations. An enormous democratic process has taken shape, giving the AAP (Archive Artist Publications) its current diverse character. The approximately 7,000 artist books recorded at the end of the 1990s have now grown to over 90,000 different objects.

The term artist's book no longer plays the role in the AAP that it did until the 1990s. From the very beginning there were the ephemera sideshows, the smaller printed trappings around the artist's book, as mentioned above, but now the character of the archive is changing fundamentally.

In my teaching assignments on media theory and art history, comparison was an important pedagogical tool for me: newsstand magazines were presented next to artists' magazines, art books and art catalogs next to artists' books, common advertising materials next to artists' advertising materials. I realized that it would make sense to expand the archive of artists' books into an archive of artists' publications. It should include printed matter that was influential to the broader culture of its time, e.g. IKEA catalogs, mail order catalogs, consumer magazines. Over time, the AAP has evolved into a research library that is open to everyday culture: to fashion, music, literature, architecture, sociology, art education, comics, punk, and mail art.

Another important reason for this change in the character of the archive was that most of the submissions came from artists with a very broad spectrum of artistic interests and working methods. As a result, the archive's themes and genres have expanded considerably. What began as a Künstlerbuch archive has grown into a pluralistic and inclusive archive of printed materials that were considered important by the contributing artists and should be preserved.

These include, for example, all kinds of academic works related to the artist's book–bold and experimental graphic and typographic examples from graphic design, printed materials from protest culture, subcultures, the DIY movement, works by schoolchildren and students from museum education, relics from the street, articles in newspapers and magazines, advertising material from art institutions, printed matter from committed political and socio-critical work, entire artists' estates, as well as, for example, the extensive poster archive of a regional printing company.

The decision to create an archive instead of building up a collection therefore had enormous consequences for the selection of what was to be preserved. In other words, with the archive there is actually no more choice. Access is not curated by me. The donors check my online database beforehand to see whether their collection fits into the AAP, they contact me and clarify whether it makes sense to hand it over. The archive grows according to these other laws.

"... Archives that are useful for the scientific study of history must house open, heterogeneous, uncensored collections. ..."
– Gabriele Weitenauer in a letter to the AAP, Munich 2024.

A FEW EXAMPLES

Mail art is certainly the most democratic art form since the 1960s. There is no selection process. Every submission to a call is accepted as long as it corresponds to the theme. It doesn't matter who made the mail art object, whether they are an artist, student, graphic designer, or househusband. Each mail art project is its own archive. With over 15,000 mail art artifacts, there are a lot of archives within the archive. Klaus Groh alone has contributed over 12,700 pieces. The mail art archive thus spans 57 years and 47 countries, and represents a comprehensive document of international subculture and the political and social commitment of over 700 artists. An art critic and a photographer donated approximately 20,000 invitation cards and press releases. With the acquisition of Olli Nauertz's private punk collection, consisting of over 2,100 pieces, a unique and distinct culture found its way into the AAP. A younger generation of artists—represented by over 900 active contributors from 37 countries—use zines to address a wide range of social issues while showcasing a broad aesthetic spectrum tied to the Do It Yourself (DIY) movement. Over 900 printed delivery lists from bookstores and publishing brochures are important documents for more recent art studies research.

A LIVING ARCHIVE

As an archivist, my role is not only to preserve materials, but, more importantly, to make them accessible to the public and ensure they are known. Since the early 1980s, parts of the archive have been showcased in numerous German cultural institutions, as well as at the Goethe Institute in Paris and the Swiss National Library in Bern. From 1982-1989, I was able to organize a large joint stand at ART Basel. This project was then continued for another three years at ART Frankfurt.

Inside the AAP Archive with Hubert Kretschmer.

Inside the AAP Archive. Photos by Christian Topp.

In addition to numerous lectures, publications, and exhibitions, visits to the archive play a decisive role. Groups of art students, students of architecture, book design, art history, art studies, and students of design and layout have selected exhibits from the APP presented to them. It is important that all archive materials can be handled. Direct sensory contact with the publications provides a more meaningful and engaging experience than digital copies ever could.

Workshops for students from secondary schools, technical colleges and grammar schools offer participants access to unique opportunities and to engage with rare and historical materials, which would hardly or not at all be possible in this form in a public museum or library.

For many artists, the digital visibility of their publications is highly important. Every object in the database is assigned its own URL (permalink), enabling artists to clearly communicate about their work. In many cases, the entries in the AAP OPAC serve as the only references for these works on the Internet. Public libraries rarely include gray literature in their catalogs, and ephemera are even more infrequently represented online.

A separate script ensures that new database entries are sent to the Google index on a daily basis and can therefore be found in the search engine promptly. All these aspects make it interesting for young artists to be represented in the AAP, but older artists also appreciate being found online. The detailed description and linking of the recorded titles has a very positive effect on the placement in the search results. The listing in the AAP catalog increases the attractiveness of the publications.

The convenient location of the archive in Munich's Kunstareal facilitates uncomplicated access for students at the surrounding universities as well as for interested art lovers from Germany and abroad. Events as part of the Open Studio Days, the Archive Day, and various other events in the Karrée often attract hundreds of curious and art-interested people to the archive. The breadth of content and history of the archive holdings makes it easy to develop exciting events. It is possible to put together meaningful exhibits on almost every topic of art from the 1970s to the present day, e. g. on nutrition, protest and resistance, typography, layout and design, punk and subculture, forms of the book, reproduction techniques, zines, independent publishing, dealing with recent history, the use and impact of printed materials in urban spaces, youth culture. This also includes–as this publication makes particularly clear–the examination of the body, skin, queerness, nudity, pornography, and sexuality.

I hope you enjoy reading this issue of *Slanted*. I would be delighted if we could get to know each other at one of the AAP's events or exchange ideas about exciting print products at the Unterbau at Türkenstraße 60 in Munich.

Hubert Kretschmer, January 2025

With many thanks to Lars Harmsen, Samira Niedermayer and the team at *Slanted*.

1 Artur Brall, *Künstlerbücher, Artists' Books, Book as Art*, (Darmstadt: 1986), 3.
2 Anne Moeglin-Delcroix in *Art-Rite #14*. (1976), 10.
3 Judith A. Hoffberg in *Art-Rite #14* (1976), 9.

appen-dix @

1 boysboysboys.org/products/new-boys-boys-boys-the-magazine-volume-8
2 doyoureadme.de/products/boys-boys-boys-8-2024?variant=50071927521624
3 englischezeitschriften.de/boys-boys-boys-magazine-abo
4 en.wikipedia.org/wiki/I_want_a_president
5 gatonegro.ninja
6 leviarte.de/produkt/das-liebeslexikon-herausgeber-martin-conrads-fons-hickmann-franziska-morlok
7 slanted.de/story/liebeslexikon
8 rootsofcompassion.org/?a=8334&lang=eng
9 bundesamt-magische-wesen.de/shop/trans_homo-von-justin-time
10 neu.transfabel.de/index.php?main_page=product_info&products_id=418.
11 verlag-hubert-kretschmer.de/produkt/liebe-ist-da
12 merve.de/index.php/book/show/547
13 thalia.de/shop/home/artikeldetails/A1059368460?ProvID=15322705&gad_source=1&clid=CjwKCAiA34S7BhAtEiwACZzv4T8Ad6CobgJy013Ah0GORdDtMZB2JACtPrxPAIiw_RucAzxzEQ9XghoCouMQAvD_BwE
14 hebbel-am-ufer.de/en/programme/pdetail/glitch-feminism
15 goethe.de/prj/zei/en/art/23130522.html
16 theideaofthebook.com/pages/books/438/endre-tot/dirty-rains?soldItem=true
17 mathiasguentner.com/kuenstler_in/endre-tot/biografie
18 sfkb.at/books/various-small-dicks
19 artpapereditions.org/products/jurgen-maelfeyt-toy?srsltid=AfmBOoq6rjjlWc41wQaQGv8WDB4JMeK5frnRe8mIuPT9gGSxScG6wWjK
20 sose20.ohmschau.de/viktoriaH.html
21 simonemond.com/en/projets/reshaping-the-sky-book
22 queer-festival.de/simon-edmond/?utm_source=chatgpt.com
23 fabienne-pakleppa.de/schriftstellerin/autorin-lustopfer.htm
24 volker-derlath.de
25 blad.us/releases
26 miscelanea.info/a77/enrique-doza-romero?lang=en
27 printedmatter.org/catalog/48850
28 de.wikipedia.org/wiki/Bernhard_Cella
29 fjk3.com/printed-matter/bernd-cella
30 a271.de/guestartist/austin-kimberly
31 abebooks.de/Zungenkuss-Gedicht-Disler-Martin-Biel-Edition/30822310490/bd?srsltid=AfmBOorCi4xqwrLnLV2vs1e-YzUTkHyXnnPTWmJj4CMG7hoczRHKnG2I
32 jeannoelherlin.com/product/martin-disler-der-zungenkuss-ein-gedicht-biel-edition-galerie-seeverstadt-1980
33 zaehringer-zuerich.com/disler-ab.html
34 viceversaliteratur.ch/author/16774
35 stiftung-kunst-heute.ch/de/Die-Sammlung/10?&a=12
36 lespressesdureel.com/EN/editeur.php?id=187&menu=2
37 lespressesdureel.com/EN/ouvrage.php?id=5496&menu=0
38 lespressesdureel.com/EN/ouvrage.php?id=4802&menu=0
39 lespressesdureel.com/EN/ouvrage.php?id=7217&menu=0
40 lespressesdureel.com/EN/ouvrage.php?id=4294&menu=0
41 ermagazine.com
42 doyoureadme.de/products/erotic-review-issue-2?variant=53580198478168
43 printedmatter.org/catalog/52958
44 oooz.club
45 romina-abate.de/alles-gluck-dieser-erde.html
46 100for10.com/product/myla-dalbesio-studies-ecstasy
47 moanzine.com/SHOP
48 100for10.com/product/fabio-bacchinieroticism-on-the-line
49 guillaumekashima.com/about
50 100for10.com/product/guillaume-kashima-hi
51 100for10.com/what-is-100for10
52 zinewiki.com/wiki/Master_Flame
53 museenkoeln.de/artothek/seite.aspx?s=869
54 slanted.de/story/100for10-starke-frauen-teil-1-martina-wember-jean-valencia-esther-c-czaya
55 100for10.com/product/esther-czaya-nobody
56 mikedianacomix.com/about
57 lesleyann.com.au/shop/product/mike-diana-needler-screenprint
58 anagrambooks.com/publishers/resurgo
59 biblio.com/book/shvantz-webaumann-various-authors/d/1422895732?srsltid=AfmBOoquZzW8rI0AP-O9tJLmgie5jgUmeXFPjfNvBCZ2jzuAfOAs8aU
60 verlag-hubert-kretschmer.de/produkt/griechische-mythen-03
61 hugendubel.info/detail/ISBN-9783946803164/von-Rimscha-Hans/Griechische-Mythen-03
62 miralookbooks.org/participantes/olaf-ladousse
63 stripburger.org/en/olaf-ladousse-on-bureks-and-doorags
64 dasmagazin.de/magazin-historie
65 ddr-wissen.de/wiki/ddr.pl?Das_Magazin
66 planet-franken-online.de/magazin/magazin.html
67 de.wikipedia.org/wiki/Manfred_Gebhardt
68 artmatter.dk/profile/frodo-mikkelsen
69 ruaediciones.com
70 graffica.info/holograma-book-zine-rua-ediciones
71 springmagazin.de/index.php?/ausgaben/16-sex
72 printedmatter.org/catalog/60021
73 serrote.com/livro_nus_vestidos.htm
74 comics.org/series/108177/covers
75 prowrestling.fandom.com/wiki/Editorial_Ejea
76 comicvine.gamespot.com/editorial-ejea/4010-2672
77 almanacpress.xyz/ISSUE-2-Sexuality
78 search.lib.uiowa.edu/primo-explore/fulldisplay/01IOWA_ALMA21672762100002771/01IOWA
79 apolloniasaintclair.com/patreon
80 archive.org/details/quiereme-monstruo
81 instagram.com/ediciones_la_rural_/p/CZabMuyA-GK/?img_index=1
82 instagram.com/p/CvPzj2_o8V8/?img_index=1
83 100for10.com/product/monoperro-101-magical-mouvements
84 monoperro.com/101mouvements-libro
85 illu-freiburg.de/zine-haar
86 kon-paper.com/shop/p/kon-paper-no-1-sex
87 artforum.com/events/stu-mead-197134
88 extraextramagazine.com
89 abebooks.de/erstausgabe/Reigen-Bl%C3%A4tter-galante-Kunst-Januar-1920/589223860/bd?srsltid=AfmBOoqoLuwcGJBS4y9gmKaNHeDwoA6zQVfFttwdjSbavs2YZBPsmUb3
90 suppes.de/bares_fur_rares/neun-reigen-zeitschriften-1922-wilhelm-borngraeber-verlag-leipzig
91 de.wikipedia.org/wiki/Der_Junggeselle_(Zeitschrift)
92 zvab.com/erstausgabe/Junggeselle-Jahrgang-1921-Umschlag-Zeichnung-Max-Schievelkamp/30789603316/bd
93 sayosenoo.mystrikingly.com
94 placartphoto.com/book/5491/bodies_that_shed_tears_3_(signed_and_numbered__edt_of_100)-sayo_senoo
95 maison-contemporain.com/fr/artiste/senoo-sayo
96 bdanielsson.com/#&gid=1&pid=8
97 lespressesdureel.com/EN/auteur.php?id=2126&menu=0
98 lubok.de/de/shop/ulalume
99 theapproach.co.uk/exhibitions/ulalume/press-release
100 de.wikipedia.org/wiki/Tempo_(Zeitschrift)
101 altezeitschriften.de/219-tempo srsltid=AfmBOopLZozguqgumIdgEkrcheParAVSk_Vvfn8TQzwsTWsjPG3d6pjG
102 kulturpapier.de/de/lifestyle/tempo-magazin
103 thebittersweetreview.com
104 stackmagazines.com/product/the-bittersweet-review-issue-2
105 100for10.com/product/ramon-keimigalien-planet-erde
106 fg.thws.de/arbeiten/schund
107 fkv.de/ramon-keimig
108 mepaintsme.store/collections/ramon-keimig
109 packpeelpour.com/interview-tim-best
110 pinupsmag.com/product/pinups-no16
111 artecontemporanea.com/product/12974
112 terranova.com/product/food-sex-and-tv-fast-easy-and-fun
113 fawbooks.com/products/catalogue-food-sex-and-tv-robert-heinecken
114 kochgallery.com/artists/robert-heinecken
115 en.wikipedia.org/wiki/Robert_Heinecken
116 paperviewbooks.pt/journal/newds
117 konkret-magazin.de/ueber
118 konkret-magazin.de/37-leseproben/501-von-konkret-5

119 nitsch.org/aktionen
120 schuelke-finebooks.com/buch/12867/hermann-nitsch-neapel-1974-45-aktion
121 nitsch.org/biografie
122 nypl.org/research/research-catalog/bib/b16039445
123 artkonzett.com/de/kuenstler/rudolf-schwarzkogler
124 kunstforum.de/artikel/sex-crime
125 germangalleries.com/Sprengel_Museum/SexAndCrime.html
126 printedmatter.org/catalog/55562
127 beatbooks.com/private-details.php?record=37709&soldItem=true
128 collection.belkin.ubc.ca/Detail/objects/9661
129 tape-mag.com/Vile_Vol.3_No.1+VILE+PRESS_und_ORG_LITERATURE-1-1-4778-7.html
130 100for10.com/product/070-simon-lohmeyer
131 simonlohmeyer.com/contact
132 stern.de/kultur/buecher/medienmacherin-luca-feigs-warum-ein-magazin-ueber-geschlechtsteile--3106718.html
133 theberlinchameleon.com/info
134 sfkb.at/books/das-sofortbild-polaroid
135 de.wikipedia.org/wiki/Gerhard_Johann_Lischka
136 gjlischka.ch/das-sofortbild-polaroid-1977
137 artpapereditions.org/products/richard-kern-polaroids?srsltid=AfmBOorH_7tb4C11-1tBUUlTJpvqZnpfeap49Misv7oM2syRhfqyklOu
138 vimeo.com/user29491069
139 dikfagazine.com
140 instagram.com/p/BP3RrFZBP8a
141 dienacht-magazine.com/2021/08/02/brian-sergio-dios-mio
142 printedmatter.org/catalog/52020
143 ppowgallery.com/artists/betty-tompkins#tab:thumbnails
144 awarewomenartists.com/en/artiste/betty-tompkins
145 bensaundersart.co.uk/shop/strap-magazine
146 kickstarter.com/projects/strapmagazine/strap-queer-trans-masc-magazine?lang=de
147 wunderhorn.de/?buecher=eric-carstensen-testsieger
148 kerberverlag.com/en/2081/the-opera
149 instagram.com/concretemagazin
150 muenchen.mitvergnuegen.com/2016/concrete-kultur-magazin-muenchen
151 mucbook.de/bewusst-frei-von-trends-und-kommerziellen-zwaengen-concrete-magazin-im-interview
152 antonschwarzbach.wordpress.com
153 prolog-zeichnung-und-text.de/index.html
154 100for10.com/product/florian-brugger-want-candy
155 melvilledesign.de/florian-brugger
156 philippgufler.de
157 platform-muenchen.de/archiv
158 onb.ac.at/oe-literaturzeitschriften/Freibord/Freibord.htm
159 daton.de/pips
160 buchfreund.de/de/d/p/50339621/der-alltag-nr-1989-1-die-sensationen-des
161 kerberverlag.com/en/1997/the-opera
162 theboyisbeautiful.bigcartel.com/product/the-boy-is-beautiful-3
163 slanted.de/story/garage
164 meireundmeire.com/garage-magazine-no-1
165 garagemca.org/en/personalities/dasha-zhukova
166 shop.berlinbook.com/Design/Twen-Zeitschrift-fuer-Literatur-Politik-und-Fotografie-10-Jahrg-1968-10-Hefte-von-12-ohne-4-und-12-Leitung-der-Redaktion-und-verantwortlich-fuer-den-Inhalt-Willy-Fleckhaus-und-Axel-Springer-jun-und-Udo-Wuest-Artdirector-Willy-Fleckhaus::13454.html
167 readymag.com/designstories/willy-fleckhaus/twen
168 fluffereveryday.com
169 film.at/ohne_pause_fuer_erwin_puls
170 kunsthallewien.at/ausstellung/erwin-puls-die-phantome-des-begehrens
171 booklooker.de/B%C3%BCcher/Erwin-Puls+Puls-f%C3%BCr-den-Intimbereich-Roman-Nicht-vor-der-Jugend-oder-sonst-sittlich-unreifen/id/A02kBHFu01ZZm
172 lubok.de/en/shop/stellungen
173 amazon.de/-/en/Sex-Press-Revolution-Underground-1963-1979/dp/1419705555
174 mailartists.wordpress.com/2008/01/04/josef-klaffki-joki
175 thing.de/projekte/7:9%23/smile_index.html
176 zdb-katalog.de/title.xhtml?idn=011788577&view=brief
177 spiegel.de/kultur/gesellschaft/psychedelic-sex-book-bildband-ueber-erotikmagazine-der-hippie-aera-a-1016632.html
178 amazon.de/dp/3822825581/ref=nosim?tag=wwwspiegelde-21
179 juliakoschler.com/bi-all-means
180 booklooker.de/B%C3%BCcher/Franz-Aum%C3%BCller+Instant-Nr-39-69-Frankfurt-am-Main/id/A02s6LQs01ZZw
181 spiegel.de/politik/scharfer-wind-a-c1c31db1-0002-0001-0000-000043019807
182 wikipedia.org/wiki/St._Pauli-Nachrichten
183 hallo-muenchen.de/muenchen/landkreis-ost/kuenstler-michael-ried-stuecken-11765396.html
184 muenchner-literaturbuero.de/veranstaltung/2098-mlb-lesung-michael-ried-abend
185 sueddeutsche.de/muenchen/ausstellung-kunst-mit-pauspapier-1.5022080
186 atomgallery.co.uk/mister-edwards.html
187 etsy.com/de/listing/593749960/mr-edwards-pop-tarts?show_sold_out_detail=1&ref=nla_listing_details
188 nieves.ch/817/halli_galli
189 mailartists.wordpress.com/2008/01/04/pawel-petasz
190 primo.getty.edu/primo-explore/fulldisplay/GETTY_ALMA21117025820001551/GRI
191 jonathanahill.com/pages/books/10724/e-f-higgins-iii/common-press-18-august-1979-nudes-on-stamps-editor-e-f-higgins-iii
192 instagram.com/___artbooks___/p/DDuRejSOeQw
193 buchfreund.de/de/d/p/93693704/acid
194 brinkmann-wildgefleckt.de/ralf-rainer-rygulla-zur-entstehung-des-romans-keiner-weiss-mehr-von-rolf-dieter-brinkmann
195 perlentaucher.de/buch/acid-neue-amerikanische-szene.html
196 1000flights.blogspot.com/2015/04/mani-art-44-fanzine-mail-art-global.html
197 mailartists.wordpress.com/2008/10/23/pascal-lenoir
198 beatbooks.com/pages/books/40657/sex-performance-and-the-80-s
199 beatpresser.com/publication/coming-attractions
200 sfkb.at

SLANTED MAGAZINE
TYPOGRAPHY & DESIGN CULTURE
SPRING / SUMMER 2025
45 SEX

PUBLISHER

Slanted Publishers UG
(haftungsbeschränkt)
Nördliche Uferstraße 4–6
76189 Karlsruhe
Germany
T +49 (0) 721 85 14 82 68
magazine@slanted.de
slanted.de

TEAM

Editor in Chief (V.i.S.d.P.)
Lars Harmsen
Co-Editor
Samira Niedermayer
Managing Editor
Julia Kahl
Creative Direction
Lars Harmsen
Graphic Design
Juliane Lipp, Samira Niedermayer
Final Design
Julia Kahl, Juliane Lipp
Cover Artwork
Guillaume Kashima
guillaumekashima.com

SLANTED WEBLOG

Editor in Chief (V.i.S.d.P.)
Julia Kahl
Editors
slanted.de/editors

VIDEO

Video Interviews
slanted.de/videos

ISBN: 978-3-948440-83-1
ISSN 1867-6510

PRODUCTION

Printing
Stober Medien GmbH
Eggenstein / Germany
stober-medien.de

Bookbinding
Buchbinderei Spinner
Ottersweier / Germany
josef-spinner.de

Cardboard Cover
Bindakote Chromolux 300 g / sm
Paper Inside Visual Part
Extramatt Recycling 120 g / sm
Paper Inside Text Part
Rough Air, 100 g / sm
Distributed by
Metapaper
Stuttgart / Germany
metapaper.io

Spot Colors
HKS 43 K (Cover), HKS 33 N

Fonts
Calvino, 2021
Design: Andrea Tartarelli
Label: Zetafonts / zetafonts.com

Snapshot, 2022
Design: Selma Losch
Label: Kilotype / kilotype.de

Suisse Int'l, 2011
Design: Swiss Typefaces Design Team
Label: Swiss Typefaces / swisstypefaces.com

DISCLAIMER

All publications presented in this issue originate exclusively from the Archive Artist Publications (AAP) collection and have either been purchased by or donated to the archive.

The texts accompanying the publications in the first chapter, *COVERS,* have been carefully compiled from the information and metadata available in the AAP database and supplemented through extensive online research. Despite our best efforts to ensure accuracy, errors or omissions may still occur.

The publisher assumes no liability for the correctness, completeness, or up-to-dateness of the provided information. The publisher and editor assume that all materials made available for publication are free from third-party rights. If you believe that any content in this publication infringes upon your rights, please contact the publisher immediately.

Reproduction, distribution, or storage of any part of this publication requires the publisher's prior written permission. While we strive to properly acknowledge all sources, inadvertent errors may occur.

Submitted photos and texts are welcome; however, the publisher assumes no liability for unsolicited materials. The views expressed in signed contributions do not necessarily reflect those of the publisher or editor.

The German National Library lists this publication in the German National Bibliography; detailed bibliographic data is available on the Internet at dnb.de